THE ANATOMY OF EXPERIENTIAL IMPACT THROUGH ERICKSONIAN PSYCHOTHERAPY

The Evolution of Psychotherapy

2017 Anaheim December 13–17

2017 Evolution Conference special preview edition.

The Anatomy of Experiential Impact Through Ericksonian Psychotherapy

Seeing, Doing, Being

Jeffrey K. Zeig, Ph. D.

The Milton H. Erickson Foundation Press
Phoenix, AZ

Cover painting by Paul Bartholomew Walton
Layout by Cole Tucker-Walton

Please note that names and identifying characteristics have been changed throughout this book to protect the privacy of individuals. Any resemblance to a known person is purely coincidental.

Library of Congress Cataloging-in-Publication Data

The Anatomy of Experiential Impact Through Ericksonian Psychotherapy: Seeing, Doing, Being

/ Zeig, Jeffrey K.—1st edition

p.   cm.

Includes bibliographic references
ISBN 978-1-932248-86-9 (pbk : alk paper)

Published by

THE MILTON H. ERICKSON FOUNDATION PRESS
2632 East Thomas Rd., Suite 200
Phoenix, AZ 85016
www.zeigtucker.com

Manufactured in the United States of America

Cyn: Te adoro.

I am one of many who owe a debt to Milton H. Erickson, M.D., for the wisdom and learning he offered me. And, I have been blessed with esteemed Ericksonian colleagues from whom I have learned immensely, including Stephen Gilligan, Bill O'Hanlon, Jay Haley, Stephen Lankton, Camillo Loriedo, Cloé Madanes, Ernest Rossi, Bernhard Trenkle, Paul Watzlawick, and Michael Yapko. In this book, I interweave concepts that I have gleaned from Milton Erickson and from these colleagues with my own.

Deep, enduring thanks to my editors, Marnie McGann and Suzi Tucker. Marnie: Your careful and deft touch has made the concepts that I present in this and other books and articles more fluid and comprehensible. Suzi: You are the best developmental editor I have ever encountered. Your presence in my life is one of my greatest blessings.

The staff of the Erickson Foundation makes my professional life possible. Thanks to all staff members: Rachel Callahan, Chuck Lakin, Stacey Moore, Leigh McCormick, Marnie McGann, Joshua McLaughlin, Jess Repanshek, Nate Sorensen, and Kayleigh Vaccaro. Joshua: Thank for you for helping me compile the references. Chuck: Your brilliant marketing strategies and knowledge of book production have repeatedly proved invaluable.

PREFACE

Between 1974 and 1976, I was in graduate school to earn my PhD in clinical psychology. At that time, if one of the students or faculty had asked me about my professional aspirations, I would have replied that I wanted to travel the world and teach hypnosis and psychotherapy. However, I did not expect to do that so soon in life, in my 30s, which turned out to be the case. Since then, I have been afforded myriad opportunities to lecture to students in many wonderful places.

The impetus for these opportunities was primarily due to being mentored by Milton Erickson, whom I met when I was 26 years old. It is impossible to imagine the trajectory my life would have taken had I not had this encounter. I owe a great deal of my happiness, both personally and professionally, to Erickson. Even today, nearly 40 years after his death, he remains integral to my practice. He is also central to what I teach throughout the world.

In this book, I present my fundamental teaching model. It has taken me decades to consolidate my teaching material, which is fortunate, because it is only now that I feel confident enough in my experience and wisdom to share this model.

I hope you will enjoy the book and find it useful.

Jeffrey K. Zeig, Ph.D.
Phoenix, AZ

Erickson and His Methods

If you asked psychotherapists around the world to name the greatest therapists in history, the clear majority would include Milton Erickson. Between 1973 and 1980 (the year he died), I had the opportunity to study with Erickson, which was comparable to learning psychoanalysis from Freud, or physics from Einstein.

I first met Erickson in 1973, at a time when he was renowned for his use of hypnosis, but he was not yet widely known in the field of psychotherapy. In 1973, he was basically retired. However, books that illuminated his work began to be published that year, the first of which was *Uncommon Therapy*, by Jay Haley (1973). This book positioned Erickson as a pioneering practitioner of brief therapy. Subsequently, many professionals came to Phoenix, Arizona to study with him. My initial visits with Erickson were private, but soon after, other students joined, and the group instruction became known as Erickson's teaching seminars.

Although ailing, Erickson was lively and charismatic. His poor physical condition was due to contracting poliomyelitis (commonly known as polio) at age 17. Although he was athletic in his youth, polio had paralyzed him for a year. Later in life, he had a reoccurrence of the disease (now known as post-polio syndrome) and it took a toll on his overall health. He suffered from muscle deterioration, and subsequently, loss of coordination.

The right side of Erickson's body was more affected than his left. If he wanted to write, he would sometimes guide his right hand with his left. To eat, he would twist his torso to bring a utensil to his mouth. In the last decade of his life, Erickson was confined to a wheelchair. When I first met him, he would flop from his wheelchair into his office chair, supporting himself only momentarily on his weakened legs. Eventually however, he could no longer manage even that, and he remained in the wheelchair.

Erickson's vision was double, his hearing was impaired, and he had chronic pain. He had lost all his teeth, and could not comfortably wear a denture. This was a man who had had an actor's control of his voice, but he then had to relearn to talk—without teeth. Erickson was also colorblind (most likely afflicted with red-green colorblindness) and always wore something purple, because it was the color he most appreciated.

Although Erickson was genius in his professional contributions, he was even more genius in the way he negotiated his life. He was the most impressive, inspirational human being I had ever met. In his professional life, he was a master at technique, but as a person, he was exceptional. He was attentive and focused, and even though he endured pain, he was often laughing. He perfumed his surroundings with the sense of being glad to be alive. If you had pain—he had more pain. If you had limitations—he had more limitations; and he was happy.

I initially went to see him to improve my clinical methods, but within the first few minutes of meeting him, being a better therapist was not the only thing that mattered. He inspired me to be a better person. I wanted to be around him because I felt like I was with someone who had mastered life. Under the most difficult circumstances, he transcended his own pain to help others. And, he had an uncommon way of presenting ideas.

My first visit with Erickson ended on December 5, 1973 (Zeig, 1985). In our session the previous day, he situated himself in his office chair, looked at the floor, and in a slow, measured voice recounted a story that took place in New Orleans—a city famous for its seafood. He was at a restaurant there and when it came time to order, he requested two dozen raw oysters on the half shell. After finishing the two dozen, he ordered a third. When he finished the third dozen, he ordered 12 more! He ate 48 raw oysters! Now I had no idea why he was telling me this story and what it had to do psychotherapy, but I was fascinated. Moreover, I had never known anyone who had eaten four dozen oysters in one sitting. But, the story got even better. After he finished the 48 oysters, he ordered a dozen more!! Upon ordering the final dozen, Erickson asked the dumfounded waiter, "Why shouldn't I have 60 oysters on my 60th birthday?!" Suddenly, I understood what Erickson was saying to me.

Erickson used a unique way of relaying a simple fact: that December 5th was his birthday, and he did this by packaging it within a story. Why did he do this? Was he teaching me a way of offering ideas, or was he orienting me to his strategic, experiential methods? Perhaps there were personal reasons for Erickson taking me on his oyster-eating adventure. Could he have told the story for his own amusement? Did he do it for his own aesthetic appreciation and expressive joy? Perhaps it was deliberate practice—as if Erickson were exercising his anecdotal method of relaying concepts, a method for which he was renowned. Regardless of his intent, the effect on me was memorable. I never forgot the message and his presentation style, and from then on, I sent him oysters for his birthday.

There is a principle that Erickson exemplifies in his oyster eating story: Create experiences to foster memorable realizations. Other principles will be highlighted throughout the book. They are ideas that have stayed with me and continue to unfold in myriad ways.

In addition to principles, in this book you will encounter a model of brief therapy that can be applied independent of a practitioner's preferred model of therapy. I use the problem of depression extensively to illustrate principles and practices, but depression is only one example as therapists can use the templates for a wide variety of psychosocial issues that clients present.

In Chapter One, the essentials of an experiential approach to psychotherapy are outlined, which are based in orientations that underlie hypnosis. Change in therapy is best elicited by the experiences people live, not the information they receive. Hypnosis is fundamentally an experiential method, the imperative of which is, "By living this experience, you can reclaim your ability to change or cope adequately." This book promotes experiential methods that are derived from a hypnotic orientation. Subsequent chapters offer a stepwise plan for creating an experientially based brief therapy.

Chapter Two offers a metamodel of intervention, which is based on five Choice Points. It is the spine around which concepts are developed in subsequent chapters. Chapter Three offers a method of deconstructing states, beginning with hypnosis. Deconstruction can foster the therapeutic process by identifying achievable goals. In Chapter Four, the process of mapping is introduced to further understand problem states, solution states, and even therapist states.

Once therapy goals can be identified, effectiveness can be enhanced by tailoring, the topic developed in Chapter Five, which involves focusing the therapy though the client's lens and speaking the client's experiential language. Advanced mapmaking is covered in Chapter Six, which provides a more detailed, systemic perspective on goal-setting.

Once a clinician has a goal and understands how to tailor to the individual, he or she will need a method to present that goal. Methods of presenting the tailored goal are covered (Chapter Seven). Chapter Eight discusses the combination of tailoring and gift-wrapping.

Chapter Nine covers the dramatic process of change, and one of Erickson's most creative cases is presented in Chapter Ten. Therapist development is the subject of Chapter Eleven, and Chapter Twelve provides clinical transcripts that show applications.

This book is the second volume of a trilogy, but it can be read independently of the other books in the series. The first book is *The Induction of Hypnosis* (Zeig, 2014), which presents my model of hypnosis. Many of the examples in this book develop hypnotic methods and can advance the practice of those who use formal trance. The third book is *Psychoaerobics* (Zeig, 2015), which is an experiential method of therapist development.

Contents

CHAPTER ONE

A Therapy of Lived Experiences

At a relatively young age, Milton H. Erickson established himself as a master clinician. Over time, he added hundreds of unique cases to the clinical literature—more than anyone in history. Freud added only a handful.

Freud was interested in why people were the way they were; Erickson was interested in how people could change. Freud's orientation was in the past; Erickson's orientation was in the present—directed into the future. He individualized each treatment and invented a new approach for every situation. Erickson was a great professional model for me, and he was an uncommon communicator.

Erickson used a form of communication that could be called evocative, in contradistinction to communication that could be considered informative. Customarily, psychotherapists give people information. For example, "Smoking is bad for you. It can give you cancer." Or, they offer advice: "Here's what I think you should do in your relationship..." But, many human predicaments are not empowered by information or advice.

Erickson commonly offered experiences through stories, metaphors, games, puzzles, tasks, and hypnosis. He did this to make simple ideas come alive.

Here is another case example of Erickson's experiential approach (reported in Zeig, 1985a):

Smoking a Pipe

In 1976, when I was still in school as a graduate student, I visited Erickson. As part of my training, I taught introductory psychology and saw clients. At the time, I smoked a pipe. I considered it a hobby. I had many different pipes, a pipe rack, special tobacco, a silver lighter, and an array of pipe tools. I was the archetype of a young psychologist, whom I envisioned as smoking a pipe.

One day, as I was relaxing in Erickson's backyard waiting to have time with him, he passed by in his wheelchair and saw me smoking my pipe. I wasn't there to ask for help; I was there as a student. When it came time for my instruction, he began by telling me a seemingly lighthearted yet curious story about a friend of his who was a pipe smoker. Erickson said the friend was awkward because he didn't know where to put the pipe in his mouth. Should he put it in the center of his mouth? Should he put it one millimeter from the left corner of his mouth? Should he put it one centimeter from the right corner? Should he hold it in the middle of his mouth? He was awkward.

And the friend was awkward because he didn't know where or how to blow out the smoke. Should he blow it upward? Should he blow it downward? Should he blow it out diffused, or should he blow it in a focused stream? He was awkward.

And the friend was awkward because he didn't know how to hold the pipe. Should he use his thumb and index fingers? Should he use more fingers? Or, should he tightly grip the pipe's bowl with all five fingers? He was awkward.

As Erickson told this story, I was thinking, "Why is he telling me this? I've been smoking for a while and I'm not awkward."

Erickson continued: And the friend was awkward because he didn't know how to light the pipe. Should he use a paper match, a stick match, or a lighter? Should the flame be placed toward the back of the bowl or in the front? Should the flame touch the tobacco or hover over the tobacco? He was awkward.

And the friend was awkward because he didn't know where to put the pipe. Should he put it on the table? Should he put it on a chair? Should he put it on a shelf? Should he continue to hold it in his hand? He was awkward.

This monologue seemed to go on for an hour. Because I am now so familiar with Erickson's work, he must have ended the story when I subtly indicated that I "got" the message. (I may have nodded or changed my posture.)

Days later, I was driving home to the Bay Area in Northern California. About half way between Phoenix and San Francisco I stopped at a red light, and at that moment, I silently declared to myself, "I don't want to smoke a pipe anymore. I never want to smoke a pipe." There was no withdrawal; there was no discomfort. There was only a decision—and it was my decision. There was only an accomplishment, and it was my accomplishment.

Erickson had changed the emotional background of my smoking habit. I was in my late 20s, and as a young professional, the last thing I wanted was to appear awkward. My unconscious had picked up his words: "pipe—awkward; pipe—awkward."

In a sense, Erickson used my conscious mind against my unconscious mind, because after hearing his awkward friend story, whenever I thought about picking up my pipe, I didn't feel comfortable holding it, I wasn't sure where to put it in my mouth, how to light it, or how I should blow out the smoke. I became so self-conscious that smoking a pipe wasn't fun anymore.

Erickson did not address the problem of my pipe smoking per se, he altered the components. And this is an important and basic Ericksonian principle: Don't address the category, address the components. A related principle is: Create the dots, don't connect them. It is more compelling if clients "connect the dots" to their own delight. When Erickson intentionally offered a new emotional background ("awkward"), I connected the dots.

Perhaps you played "Connect the Dots" as a child. When I was a boy, I used to color in coloring books that had pages of enumerated dots, which when connected formed an image. But I could never determine the image on the page unless I connected the dots. When I did, and a gestalt suddenly emerged, that thrilled me.

So, if a client complains, "I'm procrastinating," and the clinician wants to help that client, it is best not to address the category. Procrastination is not one thing; it is comprised of components, which are, in fact, processes. And rather than interpreting the underlying meaning, a clinician may be able to subtly alter the emotional background.

Oftentimes, when clients talk about a problem, they believe their problem is a single entity. Treating a complex process as an entity may help people effectively communicate, but it could also impede change. If Erickson had believed that my smoking was an entity, and treated it as such, the outcome would have been different. Instead, he oriented me to become overly conscious of the components of smoking, the category seamlessly changed, and I became a non-smoker.

Also, Erickson never inquired about whether I continued to smoke. Instead, he offered me an opportunity to understand my behavior against a new emotional background. Because I was astute, I used the opportunity and was successful. I stopped smoking…and it was my choice.

I have a name for the method Erickson used to help me stop smoking. I call it "the Farrah Fawcett principle." Farrah Fawcett was a beautiful American actress who became a sex symbol in the 1970s. College boys would plaster their dorm room walls with a famous poster of her in a red bathing suit. Around that time, I was having lunch with colleagues at the hospital where I worked. On the table was a popular magazine with a revealing cover shot of this actress. One of the people at lunch looked at the picture and quipped, "Her ankles are too fat." Another colleague looked at the cover and said, "Her calves aren't the right shape." Another offered, "Her hips are too big for her waist." Another: "Her breasts are too small." Another: "Her eyes aren't right." By the time lunch was finished, I no longer thought Farrah Fawcett was attractive.

Components synergistically create the entity. Therefore, if you divide an entity into components, it can lose integrity—and it can destroy the gestalt, and that's what Erickson did with my pipe smoking. Over examination can destabilize a crystallized state. That's why I often ask patients who experience pain to describe details of their discomfort, after which they commonly report a reduction in suffering.

But, due to the John Travolta principle, the Farrah Fawcett principle is not infallible and here's an example:

Around the same time Farrah Fawcett rose to fame, so did the handsome American actor, John Travolta. One day, I was having lunch with my assistant and John Travolta happened to be eating in the same restaurant. My assistant was obviously enamored and was staring at him so much that I couldn't get any work done. Her neck was so twisted in his direction that she seemed to have developed torticollis. To disrupt her focus, I explained the Farrah Fawcett principle. After which she firmly announced, "That won't work for John Travolta." (Thus, the John Travolta principle: When over examined, some things are immune to losing integrity!)

Over examining the components of problem is a heuristic—a simplifying assumption that is often, but not always, effective. And, it is just one way to destabilize a problem. But, the clinician should first create a map of the problem and/or solution. Creating maps and using them to decide treatment goals will be discussed in succeeding chapters. Now, let's further examine common orientations to psychological problems.

An Orientation to Problems

When a client comes to therapy with a problem, one treatment possibility is to look for underlying or historical causes. Although such a search may not facilitate change with many psychosocial problems, people instinctively believe that finding the cause of a problem will help solve it.

In some fields, knowing the cause is necessary. In medicine, for example, if the complaint is an infection, the physician must know the cause—the specific pathogen—to prescribe proper treatment. The mechanical world is similar. If the output of a machine is inadequate, it is imperative to discover the cause to remedy the problem.

There is a compulsion in our society to find cause and assign blame. People often make others culpable; the problem is ascribed to someone or something else.

But to be effective in social and psychological worlds, searching for cause and attributing blame are often unnecessary. In fact, finding the cause of a social problem usually does not lead to a solution. When married couples come to therapy, they often blame each other. And even if one of them is right, a bromide I use is: "You can either be right, or you can be married."

Looking for a cause in psychotherapy is not always ineffective. Sometimes a historical understanding can have strategic value in eliciting change. For example, an adolescent could start smoking because his or her parents are vigilant about health, and smoking would therefore be an act of defiance and way to form a new identity. In this case, the therapist could help identify the "cause" and prompt the adolescent to discover positive pastimes that are quite different from the adolescent's parents, and which could also offer a new identity. For example, the therapist might see if the adolescent has an interest in joining a band, doing theater, creating art, caring for animals, cooking, etc.

Problems can be examined from multiple perspectives, and discovering the "real" cause of many psychosocial problems may not possible. A problem could be attributed to genetics, trauma, circumstances, faulty childrearing, a combination of these factors, or some other factors. And, a problem could be seen as existing solely within a client, or the problem could have a relational aspect. For example, the problem could exist in one member of a couple, between the two partners, between the client and the entire family, or in the way the family interacts with an organization, or the way the family interacts with the culture. So, a problem can be viewed as residing within, between, and among—and all these perspectives are, to some extent, relevant, and all can be used to facilitate change.

But rather than searching for a cause to remedy a problem, another choice is to address the components of that problem. As we encountered in Erickson's way of dealing with my smoking, a problem is made up of components. Using the components, a map of the problem and/or a solution can be created, and altering components of a problem can be systemically significant.

Therapists can look for solutions from many different perspectives. And the way in which a therapist views the problem determines the treatment approach.

The Experiential Approach

A fundamental orientation of this book is that clients suffer from being locked into maladaptive states and therapy works best when it is experiential. Experiences alter one's emotions and state in a way that information does not. If you want someone to enter a humorous state, create an evocative experience; perhaps tell a joke.

Consider another state: being responsible. Parents often want to help their child or adolescent to become responsible. They might tell their child to be more responsible, and sometimes they offer an explanation: "Responsible children get better grades. Better grades mean you get into a good college and have a great life. That's why you should be responsible." Now, does the adolescent act responsibly because he or she is offered information about better grades and good colleges? Most likely, no. But what do most parents do? They offer advice and information, and they repetitively do this, even though they are often disappointed with the outcome. Information and advice may be used when suggesting a simple task, but to elicit a state, one must create a transformative experience.

Most children already know that responsibility exists and that it is considered a virtue, a desirable trait. But, developmental and psychosocial factors can get in the way of acting responsible. Sometimes protest facilitates the formation of identity. Adolescents strive to create identity, and they often do this by protesting or rebelling against parental ideas and beliefs.

So, the therapist can help access the desired state, in this case responsibility. To do so, the therapist can consider five positions of growth and change.

Position No. 1 is the idea. Does the adolescent have the idea of responsibility? If not, this can be taught.

Position No. 2 is the conceptual realization: "I can be responsible," which is an internalization of ability. But how do adolescents transition from the idea to the conceptual realization? Well, there must be a Significant Evocative Experience (SEE) that elicits the concept. Maybe the adolescent takes care of a pet. Maybe he or she signs up for gymnastics class or develops a crush on someone and realizes that to foster the relationship it's best to be responsible.

There are ideas and there are concepts. Experiences propel the idea of responsibility into the concept of responsibility: "I can be responsible."

Position No. 3 is a decision—an orientation that represents another step in the internalization process: "I will be responsible." Once the adolescent gets the concept—"I can be responsible"—another evocative experience can lead to the realization: "I will be responsible."

And this can lead to Position No. 4: "Ah ha! I am being responsible," which is stimulated into play by another transformative SEE. That moment can be considered a reference experience, which represents a more consolidated state. One reference experience can be transformative, which is not to say that more than one will not be required.

Finally, Position No. 5 is an identity: "I am a responsible person." A new identity, of course, is the goal. Reference experiences coalesce to form an identity. For example, satisfying relationships and accomplishments can lead to the identity of: "I am smart," or "I am a good teacher," or "I am married." But, reference experiences can also create ineffective identities, i.e., "I am not good enough" or "I am not lovable." Maladaptive identities can be created by negative evocative experiences.

Because we assume identities that are not necessarily effective, therapists need to have ways of promoting constructive identities, and that should be done evocatively. Identity doesn't change by using logic; a change in identity requires an evocative moment.

Fostering an adaptive Identity can be a central goal in therapy. Some people may have to step from the idea, to the concept, to the decision, to the state, and finally, to the identity. But, sometimes an identity can materialize from one significant, evocative experience. Here's an example:

I was conducting a class for experienced therapists, and in it I offered a clinical demonstration. The psychologist who was the subject discussed a problem concerning his consumption of alcohol, and he waffled about his goal: "Maybe I should only have one glass of wine." "Or, maybe two would be right." "Maybe I shouldn't have any wine." "Maybe I shouldn't have any alcohol at all." We were not making progress due to his attack of "maybe-its." So, I used a guiding Ericksonian principle: Look for an interactional solution, a solution that involves others. In this case I used myself. I offered, "I will make an agreement with you. I will not have any dessert for one year. What will you commit to?" Recognizing that social accountability can have impact, I made that declaration to create accountability for both of us. We both committed to constructive action. I was the expert offering a demonstration. Someone had to change, and if it wasn't going to be the client, it was going to be the therapist. But, there is also a backstory:

The morning before the session while I was exercising, I was listening to a medical expert lecture on diet. He advised, "Don't eat sugar." And I thought, "Okay. Sure. Sure." But, I had no intention of changing my diet. I didn't "get" the idea.

However, unbeknownst to me, something was gelling into a transformative conceptual realization. The next morning something quite unexpectedly happened: my identity changed, and I became someone who didn't crave dessert. That was amazing. When I offered the intervention the day before, I thought I would just use willpower and follow through with my commitment. But instantly, I changed identity. So, for one year I didn't touch dessert. Even to this day, I don't have more than a bite or two of dessert. I didn't know my identity would change. I thought I could just accomplish not having dessert by being determined. But the experience of that moment in the demonstration seamlessly transported me into being a different person: someone who didn't want dessert. As I personally encountered, it is not necessary to sequentially take all five steps for a new identity to emerge, be it positive or negative. Sometimes, we can jump over steps, and a new identity will instantly form. But in all cases, identities are realized experientially; and they are not realized because of provided information.

Knowing and Realizing

Assimilating facts and realizing adaptive concepts require different processes. When a client comes for therapy, a therapist should assess what the client factually knows about his or her problem, and what the client conceptually realizes. People know to be kind in relationships; they know to develop healthy habits; and they know to act responsibly at work or school. If an employee is not motivated, or if a couple is not connected, they may know what to do to improve, but do they realize and put into practice what they know?

The answer to the following question is imperative in resolving many human predicaments: What is the bridge between knowing and realizing? Erickson's answer to this question was that lived experiences create the connection.

But, there is inherent ambiguity in an experiential approach. Experiences, like metaphors, can be ambiguous. A person who is experiencing something is using an interpretative process, whereas with given information, no interpretation is necessary because facts tend to be concrete.

Take the oyster-eating story. Erickson could have simply and directly told me that December 5th was his birthday. Instead, he prompted me to understand something basic about his approach: that he was predominantly experiential. Packaging a message in a story was a mainstay of Erickson's experiential approach. It had the effect of making the implied message more vivid and memorable. His approach evoked meaning because he did not directly inform. In the unexpected story about eating oysters, I had to activate to discover its meaning.

Another principle that was prominent in Erickson's therapy was that he oriented toward rather than informed or advised. For example, he did not say to me, "Stop smoking." Instead, he told the story about his friend who was a pipe smoker, which led to an experiential moment that oriented me toward a realization.

Being Experiential

Perhaps this is hyperbole, but I don't believe it is too far off to say that Erickson was 100 percent experiential in his therapy. It was also his way of being in the world—and of teaching. When I was his student, he was consistently experiential. And, his experiential orientation was derived from hypnosis.

Erickson was an expert in hypnosis, and hypnosis is, at its core, an experiential method. You don't use hypnosis to offer information. You don't use hypnosis to offer advice. You don't use hypnosis to comment on someone's history or processes. You use hypnosis for the client to have a realization of empowerment—of being able to transition into an adaptive state. If therapists are grounded in the experiential orientation central to hypnosis, it becomes natural for them to be experiential in therapy. They may offer a formal hypnotic induction, which is fundamentally experiential. But if they do not, they may still work experientially using a process Erickson called "naturalistic trance."

Currently, I am writing Erickson's biography. I have interviewed dozens of people for the project, including three of Erickson's sisters, all eight of his children, some of their spouses, and a few grandchildren who knew him. Talking with Erickson's family and the colleagues who knew him has cemented my understanding that Erickson was also consistently experiential in interpersonal situations—with family, friends, colleagues, and students (although he was didactic in his writing). When I started doing therapy I was not experiential in my approach to therapy, but as I mature as a clinician, I become more so.

There are ways to make therapy an experience for clients and a good start is the therapist's orientation to the clinical setting. The therapy office can be thought of as a stage on which a therapist can enact a drama of change. Therapists can have a strategic plan to communicate to clients that by living the offered therapeutic experience, the client can be more adaptive in life.

The experiential methods in this book are derived from a hypnotic orientation. Learning hypnosis can be valuable for all therapists, even if they never apply it in practice, because whenever the goal is conceptual realization, experiential methods can promote change. (Further reading, see *The Induction of Hypnosis*, Zeig, 2014.)

Studying hypnosis has had a positive effect on my ability as a communicator. It has taught me to strategically use more channels of communication. Prior to learning hypnosis, I was trained in traditional methods of therapy: "My mouth to your ears; your mouth to my ears." The therapist speaks to client and vice versa. Such methods of therapy could be applied by simply reading a transcript, as traditional techniques are housed in verbal communication. Erickson, however, explored the use of many channels of communication; he did not restrict himself to words.

Consider painting as a metaphor for therapy. The tools of a painter are brushes, a palette of colors, and a surface on which to apply the paint. Painters explore how these tools can be used to create something unique and inspirational.

Hypnotic training prompts therapists to use the possibilities of their medium—to use their "palette of colors"—for therapeutic advantage. The many colors therapists have at their disposal include gesture, posture, physical proximity, the tempo, tone, direction of voice, etc. A subtext in all of Erickson's writings is the strategic use of these elements.

Artists explore the possibilities of their medium, but their expression is confined within the limitations of that medium. Painters normally have paint and canvas, poets have words and paper, choreographers have dancers and a stage, and playwrights have stories and actors. Within such parameters, artists strive to take expressive realization into a new realm; their art is designed to elicit conceptual realizations.

Here is an example of Erickson's exploration of his "palette." In a neutral induction with a patient prone to motion sickness Erickson explored the locus of voice as a cue that could elicit a physiological response (Erickson, 1973). With the patient's eyes closed, Erickson mimicked the way someone on a boat would experience sound. He did this by moving about, changing the locus of his voice. To the patient's surprise, motion sickness was elicited. And, Erickson did this at a time when the concept of mind/body interaction was not yet popular.

Erickson taught how as therapists we can use our entire palette to help people empower themselves; to help them realize adaptive and more flexible states. Another Ericksonian principle: Understand the medium of communication and use its potential.

For review, these are the six principles discussed in this chapter:

1. Create experiences to create realizations.
2. Address the components, not the category.
3. Create the dots, don't connect them.
4. Look for an interactional solution.
5. When the goal is to elicit conceptual realizations, orient toward rather than inform.
6. Understand the medium of communication and use its potentials.

Chapter Two explores a meta-model of intervention that serves as the framework around which this book is organized.

A Meta-Model of Therapeutic Intervention

Many pioneers of psychotherapy began by creating models of personality. For Freud and his followers, an explicit theory of personality served as the starting point from which intervention would be derived.

Freud's interest in human psychology was foundational. He paved the way for the field of psychotherapy and fostered a new historical trend: people became interested in exploring and changing matters of the mind. Freud focused on why people are the way they are, and he did an admirable job in exploring this. But, no one can comprehensively ascertain why people behave in certain ways because the formative factors are too complex to be encapsulated by any theory.

In terms of scope, Freud's theory of personality was massive in comparison to his theory of intervention, which was based on free association, interpretation, and clarification. In contradistinction, Milton Erickson explored myriad methods to promote change without an explicit theory of personality. Erickson also did not have an explicit theory of intervention; he was atheoretical. He flexibly invented a new approach for each client.

In this chapter, I attempt to consolidate Erickson's practical approach into a structured model—a meta-model of intervention. This model is a framework that can prompt understanding of how to create brief therapy by applying aspects of Erickson's approach.

By way of introduction, the meta-model of intervention is based on five Choice Points. Each Choice Point pivots on a central question. The Choice Points are interactive in that they influence each other.

Setting Goals

The first Choice Point to consider is the goal, but it is not necessarily the starting point for psychotherapy. Setting goals will be outlined here and developed in detail in the next three chapters.

The pivotal question for this Choice Point is: "As a clinician, what should I communicate?" Therapists need to strategically understand what they want their client to realize. In each clinical session, there are multiple ways to formulate a goal. In other fields, goal formulation can be simpler. In medicine, for example, if the patient has a bacterial infection, the physician would prescribe an antibiotic. If the patient goes to other doctors, the doctor will most likely also prescribe an antibiotic. But, psychotherapy differs from the algorithmic nature of medicine and the decision trees that comprise medicine's standard of care.

In psychotherapy, if a client complains, "I'm not motivated," different clinicians can have different goals. One therapist might say, "Let's work on changing your thinking." Another could offer, "Let's begin by changing your behavior." A third could propose, "Let's start by examining your attitude." Another might suggest, "Let's explore your interpersonal relationships to see how this relates to your problem." Another could say, "Let's examine your history to see why you feel unmotivated." And still another, "Let's begin by having the part of you that is motivated dialogue with the part that is unmotivated."

Therapy is driven by heuristic processes, not universal goals. In therapy, the goal is sometimes defined by the therapist's existent model. Different schools of psychotherapy target different goals. In cognitive behavioral therapy, the goals differ from those in structural family therapy and those in gestalt therapy. Moreover, therapists do not have to accept the client's definition of the presenting problem. Instead, they can negotiate goals, which can be a valuable therapeutic process.

The following is a list of orientations that can inform goals in Ericksonian therapy:

- Promote experiential change
- Focus on phenomenological goals and sub-goals
- Be positive; focus on strengths and abilities that create constructive adaptation
- Understand that change happens in the client's life situation, not just in the office
- Strategically orient to outcomes
- Attend to structures that exist in the present
- Be systemic; look for interactional solutions
- Access associations that activate resources
- Choose goals that you know how to solve
- Create a video description of the outcome

In the following, I explain the philosophy behind each of these orientations:

Promote experiential change.

The experiences that people live create shifts in conceptual realization and lead to constructive alterations in state and identity. To review, in Chapter One, I discussed adolescent irresponsibility. An adolescent usually knows the importance of being responsible, so it is often futile to explain it in linear terms. But, there can an experiential moment: a significant evocative experience or "reference experience" that takes the adolescent into the conceptual realization of: "I can be responsible." And, it may take another significant experiential event to transition a reference experience into the identity of: "I am a responsible person."

Reference experiences can be defining moments that create new identities. Defining moments in life, such as getting married or divorced, or landing a professional job, can lead to the realization of a new identity. There can also be defining subconscious moments that facilitate important realizations. For example, "I am now a man," "I have become a woman," or "I can now call myself 'a therapist.'" However, reference experiences can also precipitate negative identities, such as, "I am stupid"; "I am not creative"; "I am not lovable."

Therapy can focus on creating positive defining moments, which are opportunities for experiential realization that elicits adaptive reorientation. As we will see, to elicit evocative experience, goals can be packaged by the use of storytelling, hypnosis, directives, games, paradoxical tasks, etc.

Focus on phenomenological goals and sub-goals.

Phenomenology, or the reflection on the subjective world, is the study of lived experience. It stands in contradistinction to science, which investigates the objective world. Goals in psychotherapy are most often phenomenological. Goals in medicine are understandably more grounded in science.

The study of love, for example, can be phenomenological or scientific. Love can be studied by reading romantic poetry because the reader can have a felt sense of love. But love can also be studied physiologically, i.e., examining the results of an fMRI of the brain of someone in love. However, no amount of science will stimulate people to experience love subjectively.

Using a scientific approach to elicit love is futile. Love must "just happen" and cannot be forced, just like conceptual realizations of change must "just happen." Love doesn't happen by saying to the object of your affection: "You should love me, and here are five logical reasons why: 1) I am intelligent, 2) I have a good sense of humor, 3) I am healthy, 4) I am a good communicator, and 5) I am financially independent."

Eliciting love requires a phenomenological orientation, the same way that eliciting changes in state and identity in a client often requires a phenomenological orientation. Love is a syndrome—a series of elements that are not orderly and that change over time. The dimensions of love are elicited by heuristics not algorithms. Heuristics are simplifying assumptions that may be implicit to the parties involved. Being kind, protective, and attentive may lead to love; but then again, those approaches may not. The process of loving must be experiential, not academic or scientific, and changing one's state or identity is similar.

Psychotherapy relies on a heuristic approach because most often there are no concrete solutions to problems. Psychological problems and love both contain dimensional components that can be addressed as sub-goals. For example, someone in love might offer the loved one a profusion of experiences that consist of sub-goals, such as shared interest, passion, kindness, humor, etc. Similarly, therapists can elicit sub-goals by creating a map of the client's problem or solutions to the problem. The problem is composed of components. For example, as we will see, rather than treating depression as an entity, the therapist can focus on components, such as being internally preoccupied, lacking goals, avoiding connection, negativity, etc.

Another important Ericksonian principle (the 7th principle): Create a map of the problem. Create a map of the solution. (This principle and the development of sub-goals are explored in subsequent chapters.)

Be positive; focus on strengths and abilities that create constructive adaptation.

Goals should be positive and oriented toward strengths. They should also be oriented toward the future. Life should be lived in the present, not the past, and life should be directed toward a future. Therapists should discover the client's resources and stimulate them into play. If the client is talented in music, develop that strength. If the client is athletic or introspective, use that.

Change happens in the client's life situation, not just in the office.

Therapeutic change should not be limited to the therapist's office because real change happens in a person's everyday life. Therefore, clinicians can gift-wrap the goal, perhaps offering therapeutic tasks, whereby change happens in the client's life. Erickson is renowned for his use of directives to promote reorientations. There are many examples of this in the literature, especially in *Uncommon Therapy* (Haley, 1973).

Strategically orient to outcomes.

Literature, music, and movies are based on strategic development. Sequential steps lead to the realization of a theme. Similarly, clinicians can create a process that leads stepwise to a targeted goal. (This strategic process is developed in Chapter Nine.)

Attend to structures that exist in the present.

Goals can focus on a client's perceptions, behavior, thoughts, and emotional and relational states. It is not imperative to address a client's history, unless there is strategic value in doing so.

Be systemic; look for interactional and contextual solutions.

The 8th Ericksonian principle is: Look for an interactional solution—a solution that involves other people. Even if the problem seems to only exist within an individual, an interactional directive can complement the treatment. For example, if the client complains about a smoking habit, a hypnotic procedure can be used. However, the client can also be given a directive that involves others. For instance, I might suggest that whenever the client has an urge to smoke, it can be used as a signal to offer someone a compliment. Alternatively, I might suggest that the client makes a game out of abstinence by not telling others about it, to thereby determine if the change is noticed.

Goals should involve systemic elements, e.g., family, school, work, and religious, cultural, and social affiliations. Also, problems in one context can be solutions in another context. For instance, assertiveness can be a problem in one situation and a resource in another. And, context can be used to promote realizations. If the therapeutic goal is to experience beauty, a visit to a national park can serve as a reference experience.

Clinicians are often unaware of the systemic nature of change because systemic reorientation does not necessarily follow linear logic. For example, I was involved in a consultation regarding a professional basketball player who was consistently failing in one area of his game. The coaches were thinking inside the box, saying: "We will teach him more skills. We will make him practice." They were wedded to an internal, algorithmic formula.

My thought was that the best person to teach this athlete and ultimately change his performance was his mother, not the experts. This young man did not grow up with a father or father figure. Therefore, his most important relationship was with his mother. His mother went to his games and he talked with her during breaks.

I wanted to involve the mother in the practice sessions with her son, to help him overcome the weakness in his performance. I believed that she was the best person to coach him because mothers often teach their children games.

I explained to the coaches and sports psychologist that this young man's mother was already a member of the team, but their thinking was linear, and they remained steadfast and oriented to finding the best trainer and the best technique. Ultimately, it was impossible to get them to see things from a systemic perspective. Sometimes the homeostasis of the bureaucracy proves more powerful than the forces of innovation.

Access associations that activate resources

Associations are preconscious and consist of memories, thoughts, perceptions, and sensations. Our behavior is guided by preconscious associations. In his inventive interspersal technique, Erickson (1966) would elicit associations to affect behavior, emotion, thought, and relationships, until those associations built up enough to "drive" adaptive reorientation. The field of social psychology examines the way in which implicit associations drive behavior.

Erickson once used his interspersal technique with a girl who had anorexia (Zeig, 1985a). As part of the treatment, he told her stories about his father's adventures as a cowboy. Each story contained some implicit reference about food, and included elements that elicited in the girl a wide range of feelings, in contradistinction to her limited affective range. Gradually, the girl began to eat and feel more emotion because Erickson elicited associations that prompted change.

A related principle in hypnosis is called the "ideodynamic effect." Associations can drive sensory experience (ideosensory experience) and physical behavior (ideomotor activity). For example, a detailed description of eating a lemon could trigger salivation. Or, if a front seat passenger in a car wants to stop quickly, he or she could forcefully step on imaginary brakes, causing the driver to stop.

Choose goals you know how to solve.

The 9th principle is: Choose goals you know how to solve. The dictum of choosing goals based on the therapist's ability to solve them might seem alien to traditionally trained therapists who are more algorithmic when it comes to clinical goals and procedures. Still, there are many roads to home. If the client's complaint is depression, traditional methods may focus on that issue. However, a therapist can focus on something else and still effect change. I once attended a workshop on depression by the leading behavioral therapist, Joseph Wolpe. His preferred method was desensitization. He found anxiety in depressives and he desensitized it to effectively treat depression.

Client goals are malleable, not written in stone. Often there are resistances to change that are inherent in the client's complaint. After all, their appearance in the consultation room is proof that their problems remain despite their efforts to the contrary. Goals can be negotiated and reshaped. Therefore, redefining a problem or solution can be an effective therapeutic step.

A 10th principle is: Redefine the problem early on. For example, it is strategically possible to indicate that a client does not have "depression" (the presenting problem), but has repressed anger—something the therapist knows how to treat. And, in doing so, relief can follow.

Create a video description of the outcome.

There is a line in Proverbs in the Bible: "Where there is no vision, the people perish." In brief therapy it is advisable to have concrete goals within a session and between them. One method that I learned from Bill O'Hanlon is to create a video description, for example, saying to a client: "Envision a television set without sound. See what it is that you want to accomplish. Tell me what it looks like, including the context."

Video descriptions can facilitate change when used by both the client and the therapist. Brief therapists need to be intentional; they need to think about the response they are targeting. I advise hypnosis students to delay launching into an induction or hypnotherapy until they can envision the target.

***

In summary, in different schools of therapy there are different core competencies for goal-setting—and there's nothing wrong with that. Keep in mind that goals in a social situation, such as therapy, are not the same as goals in medicine, because goals in therapy can be co-created by the interaction of the client and therapist.

Gift-wrapping

As important as it is to specify a goal, there is the equally important step of strategically planning the way to present it. The clinician can ask himself, "How do I present this goal?" I call the presentation process "gift-wrapping," and when done properly, it can empower the realization of a goal.

The idea of "gift-wrapping" came to me many years ago when I was interviewed by a reporter who thought that perhaps there was a relationship between hypnotic suggestions and New Year's resolutions. When asked to define hypnosis, I explained that it was a way of gift-wrapping realizations.

Any therapeutic suggestion can be empowered by offering it hypnotically. The success rate of the therapy increases when ideas are packaged and marketed within the gift-wrapping of hypnosis. Hence, one facet of hypnosis is its function as a gift-wrapping method.

Gift-wrapping is not limited to hypnosis. A story, poem, picture, joke, or metaphor can also be considered gift-wrapping. Gift-wrapping is inherently ambiguous, which allows the recipient to activate to discover the intended message.

In 1973, I naively went to see Erickson specifically to learn techniques, many of which were not covered in my training. At that time, methods such as reframing and using anecdotes were new to the field. I was not aware at that point that Erickson was not inclined to teach techniques; however, he did write about them.

In the late 1970s, when I began teaching professionals, I primarily taught gift-wrapping techniques because I believed that they were essential to successful therapy. Some clinicians develop extraordinary competence with a gift-wrapping method, and therefore apply it with every client. In fact, the technique may be decided upon even before the client enters the consulting room. Some hypnotherapists use hypnosis with every client; some practitioners use EMDR as a mainstay; and some Gestaltists use an empty chair in every session. If a therapist masters a method, the given method might be sufficient to prompt adaptive change. However, there are many methods to choose from, and to settle on one method is limiting.

The following table features gift-wrapping methods that are commonly used by Ericksonian practitioners. The methods are listed (roughly) in the order of increasing indirection. There is an underlying principle with indirection (No. 11): The amount of indirection is directly proportional to the perceived resistance. A therapist could start with a direct suggestion and become more indirect if resistance is encountered.

Table 2-1: Gift-wrapping

1. Direct Suggestion

2. Hypnosis

3. Indirect Suggestion

4. Directives/Tasks

5. Ambiguous Function Assignment

6. Symptom Prescription

7. Reframing/Positive Connotation

8. Ordeals

9. Displacement

10. Fantasy Rehearsal

11. Future Orientation

12. Change History

13. Confusion

14. Metaphors

15. Symbols

16. Anecdotes

17. Sculpting

18. Parallel Communication

19. Interspersal Technique

Each of the gift-wrapping methods has been extensively written about and championed in books and professional journals. While it is beyond the scope of this book to describe all the methods in detail, each is further developed in Chapter Seven.

Here is a way to think about the table: Take, for example, the goal of exercising and how it can be gift-wrapped. It can be offered as a direct suggestion by simply stating: "Exercise five days this week. It will help you feel better." The same goal can be proposed in other ways. The direct suggestion could be empowered by offering it within a hypnotic frame. After an induction, the therapist might say: "Your unconscious mind understands the importance of exercise and will prompt you to go to the gym five days this week."

An indirect suggestion could also be used for the same goal. For example: "I don't know which five days you will exercise this week." Or, reframing could be used with a paradoxical prescription: "You cannot exercise at all this week, because it will bring out your partner's insecurity about being inactive. Only when we can help your partner feel more secure will it be possible for you to attain your exercise goals." In this case, the goal of exercise is proscribed and concomitantly reframed as a way of protecting the partner from his or her vulnerability.

It would be ineffective for a therapist to repetitively suggest exercise as a goal or to aggressively demand: "Exercise! Exercise!! Exercise!!!" However, being recursive and using multiple gift-wrapping methods might make a difference.

This leads us to the 12th Ericksonian principle, one that is common to music composition: Be recursive, not repetitive. Recursion is the act of returning to a theme with alterations. Recursion can be more effective than repetition and there are multiple ways that a message can be recursively offered.

Beethoven was a master of using recursion. In the Fifth Symphony, he opens with two notes and four tones (one, two, three, down). His theme is then developed in a series of recursions: variations on the theme.

In a physical system, increasing the intensity of something may effect change: Exert more force and the response is increased. But a social system doesn't operate in the same way as a physical system. Being recursive can be more effective than being repetitive.

In summary, there is a 13th principle: Techniques are ways of gift-wrapping concepts and experiences; techniques do not cure. In medicine, techniques are meant to cure. However, it is an epistemological error to think that psychotherapy works in the same way.

Hypnosis does not cure anyone. Neither does EMDR, systematic desensitization, or cognitive behavioral therapy. Gift-wrapping is a way of stimulating into play adaptive concepts (double entendre intended). Gift-wrapping serves as a kind of container for useful concepts, allowing them to reach the receptors of human beings that are in the layers beneath and around cognitive understanding. It is a vital and important way of making simple ideas come alive.

Tailoring

Brief therapy cannot be accomplished solely by having a gift-wrapped goal. The effectiveness of a message is judged by the response it elicits, not the cleverness of the method. To increase responsiveness, we can tailor the method to fit the values of the clients.

Tailoring is a matter of understanding the position that the client takes and discerning how to use it. This process can be challenging for therapists. The underlying idea is for the therapist to be free of judgment and open to understanding how to find a way to utilize the position of the client. Tailoring is therapy focused through the client's lens. If the client has a characteristic style that is slow and ponderous, the therapist can find a use for this position. Perhaps this patient can be tabbed as "Zen," taking time to be mindfully aware.

Gift-wrapping can be modified to fit the values of the client. But, keep in mind that reframing for Person A is not reframing for Person B, and hypnosis for Person A is not hypnosis for Person B. Therapists should strive to speak the client's experiential language. Nelson Mandela quipped: "If you talk in a language someone will understand, that goes to his head. If you talk with him in his language, that goes to his heart."

Tailoring means individualizing each therapy, and it was of primary importance to Erickson. Erickson's friend and collaborator, the renowned anthropologist Margret Mead, wrote a 75th birthday tribute to Erickson in the *American Journal of Clinical Hypnosis* in which she stated that he invented a new method for each client (Mead, 1976).

When I began to organize the first Erickson Congress in 1978, Erickson was alive. However, he died eight months prior to the Congress, which was held in December 1980. My hope was that the Congress would coincide with his 79th birthday, and although that didn't come to pass, he was aware that 750 people had already registered for the event, and that many had never previously attended a hypnosis conference.

In 1978, I asked Erickson to provide a quote for the brochure for the Congress that exemplified his approach. He wrote: "Each person is a unique individual. Hence, psychotherapy should be formulated to meet the uniqueness of the individual's needs, rather than tailoring the person to fit the Procrustean bed of a hypothetical theory of human behavior."

When doing therapy, I often do not start with the goal. Instead, I begin with tailoring. When I understand the position that the client has taken, and recognize the mechanisms that perpetuate the problem, I can more easily formulate the goal and select the gift-wrapping method. Beginning in Chapter Five, tailoring is extensively developed.

Creating a Process

Once a goal is tailored and gift-wrapped, a clinician has another challenge: to create an empowering process. As I evolved as a therapist, processing became increasingly important. Prior to understanding strategic process, I studied gift-wrapping and only gradually realized that therapy was more than technique. In rereading Erickson, I recognized an aspect of his genius that I had not previously thought about, namely that strategic process is imperative. In tennis or golf, the intervention is to hit the ball, but the process in these games also involves the set-up and follow-through.

And it's not just in sports that we encounter strategic development. A three-step process is also used in television and film. It consists of: enter, offer, exit. A shot of an airplane in flight (enter) could establish a scene that will happen inside a plane (offer). The exit could be music or dialogue that transitions us into the next scene. Filmmakers know how to communicate using this tripartite process, which enhances evocative realization.

Restaurant menus are built on a similar three-step process of appetizer, main course, and dessert. In therapy, hypnosis could serve as the appetizer, main course, or dessert. It could be used to set up an intervention, as the main intervention, or as a benediction after the main intervention by suggesting how the resources elicited by the main intervention can be utilized in life.

Table 2-2: Processing an Intervention

This table displays common steps that are specific to the three components of strategic development.

Set Up	Intervene	Follow Through
Assessment	Direct Suggestion	Ratify
Pacing	Hypnosis	Amnesia
Seeding	Indirect Suggestion	Process Instructions
Address Resistance	Directives/Tasks	Fantasy Rehearsal
Build Responsiveness	Symptom Prescription	Test the Therapy
Hypnosis	Reframe	Tasks
Empathy	Ordeals	Letters/Emails/Calls
Redefine	Metaphors	Hypnosis
Destabilize	Anecdotes	Motivate
Motivate	Interspersal	Ego Building

Diagram 2-1: Timeline of Psychotherapy

Diagram 2-1 depicts a timeline of a therapy conducted by Erickson. The video is available for purchase at: https://catalog.erickson-foundation. org/item/therapy-marital-system-dvd

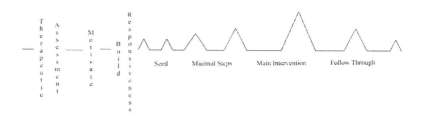

In this therapy, the main intervention was a five-minute story that Erickson told, but he built the drama for nearly a half hour before he told the story. Then, he took another half hour to follow through. Building in a series of strategic steps, Erickson set up the intervention, briefly offered the gift-wrapped goal, then followed through completing the process.

A scriptwriter thinks in terms of a strategic process. A central theme is gradually developed, events and circumstances are sometimes foreshadowed, and flashbacks may be used. But eventually, in most films, the elements are unified, producing a solid conclusion. Novelists and composers also use a dramatic process. Even architects may design an entry way with elements that seed a theme that is carried throughout the building.

A dramatic process could be thought of as a series of rhythmic steps:

Diagram 2-2: Intervention Sequence

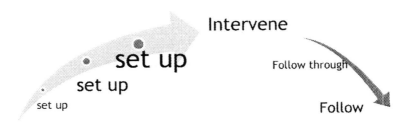

In my graduate training, I learned to communicate in simple sentences. Therefore, early in my career, I often used single sentences as interventions. Then I studied with Erickson, and I realized he often spoke in triplicates, using variations on the process: enter, offer, exit. I eventually came to understand the importance of this strategic development, and subsequently, it became a mainstay in my own approach to communication, both professionally and personally.

In my book *The Induction of Hypnosis* (Zeig, 2014), I describe the tripartite hypnotic form called "dissociation statements." Here's an example:

1. "Your conscious mind can attend to the sound of my voice, while...
2. ...your unconscious mind can explore sound changes inside, because...
3. ...it's nice to experience things comprehensively."

Number 1 paces immediate reality. Number 2 purposely contains the vague suggestion: "explore sound changes inside." Number 3 offers a motivation for realizing the effect. In its most fundamental form, the tripartite process is: pace, suggest, motivate. The vague suggestion "...explore sound changes inside" is designed to stimulate a client's realization.

If physicians adopted a tripartite process, patient compliance might increase. Let's look at how it might work. In this example, a professional musician goes to see his doctor. Here's what the physician could say: 1) "You've come to this appointment because there are important things to accomplish. And I know that consistency and diligence have been mainstays in developing your craft. 2) Here is your prescription (perhaps presented with para-verbal emphasis). Please take it as directed. 3) It will help you accomplish what you want in life. It's been a great help to others with a similar condition."

Again, the steps are: pace, suggest, motivate (enter, offer, exit).

Strategically presenting a tailored and gift-wrapped goal can help clinicians be more effective. Therapists who learn these steps and incorporate them into their clinical work can empower therapeutic directives.

Each of the four Choice Points previously offered center on a question specific to that Choice Point. But, taken together, they answer the meta-question: "How do I do therapy?" A therapist can learn the first four Choice Points by reading, or through traditional academic instruction. The fifth Choice Point, however, addresses a different question: "How will I be as a therapist?" This component is best learned through direct experience rather than didactic information—from a mentor or supervisor.

The Posture of the Therapist

The posture of the therapist is important to the success of therapy. Perhaps it is the determining factor. There are four categories to consider: lenses, muscles, heart, and hat. Personally, and professionally, we all have lenses: ways of viewing. We also have our muscles: ways of doing. And each of us has a heart: compassion; and a "hat," or social role. (In English, the idiom, "She wore many hats," means she had many social roles.)

Growing up in my family, I learned traditional ways of viewing and doing, and stereotypical things about compassion and social role. On the other hand, my professional training taught me something special about lenses, muscles, heart, and hat. For example, when I studied transactional analysis, I learned to look for "games" and "life scripts." The process often required me to be didactic, teaching patients structural analysis, which included assessing parent, child, and adult ego states. Because the therapy often happened in groups, compassion could be created among group members. My social role was to use my child ego state free-spirited), and I had fun in the process. In contrast, psychoanalysts would learn to look for transference and to use interpretation. They would have a more formal way of showing compassion, and their social role would be consistent throughout treatment.

Much of the effectiveness of therapy is determined by the posture/state of the therapist. And, the goal is determined by the interaction of the position of the client and the posture of the therapist. Developing therapist states is described in Chapter Eleven.

When I see clients, I often have a hallucination. I envision a diamond—more specifically, the Choice Point Diamond model (see diagram). My interventions are based in effecting five choices.

Diagram 2-3: The Ericksonian Diamond

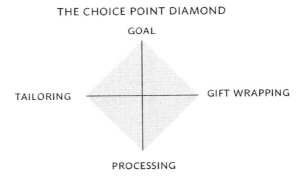

THE CHOICE POINT DIAMOND

GOAL

TAILORING   GIFT WRAPPING

PROCESSING

Position of the Therapist:
1. Personal
2. Professional Lenses, Muscles, Heart, and Hat

The Diamond is based on the five pivotal Choice Points: 1) the goal, 2) tailoring, 3) gift-wrapping, 4) processing, and 5) posture of the clinician. Again, the goal question for the therapist is: What do I want to communicate? A tailoring question is: How will I individualize or tailor the therapy? A gift-wrapping question: How do I communicate the goal? And for processing: What process should I create? Clinicians can also ask themselves: "As a therapist, who will I be and how will I be?

When psychotherapy began with psychoanalysis, there was only one position for therapists, and every therapist adopted the same stance. Having a rigid stance was important because the goal of the therapy was to elicit transference: the emergence of repressed memories that contaminate present functioning. In Freud's day, therapists were not trained to use all the "output" channels of communication to have an effect. They did not learn to use posture, gesture, prosody, etc. It was wrong if the therapist's behavior affected the transference of the client. The transference was only supposed to emerge against the "blank screen" of the therapist. If the therapist contaminated the transference, it was considered "countertransference." Countertransference is generally defined as a therapist's emotional entanglement with a client where the feelings toward the client are positive or negative feelings. They may be unconscious feelings that are stirred up during therapy that the therapist then redirects toward the patient.

In traditional psychoanalysis, social roles are formal. The patient has scheduled appointments, perhaps three to five times per week. The therapist shakes the patient's hand; the patient lies down on a couch and says whatever comes to mind. The therapist has three techniques: interpretation, clarification, and confrontation. The therapist is not especially active and will make interpretations, saying, for example, "I wonder if that reminds you of something from your past." Exactly 50 minutes later, the therapist announces, "It's time to end." The therapist and the patient shake hands again, and the patient leaves through a different door than the entrance so that the next patient doesn't run into the earlier one.

In Ericksonian therapy and other brief therapy models, the therapist is more flexible. Establishing a rigid frame for sessions has utility in some models, especially those in which personality change is the target. When the goal is circumscribed change, strategic approaches are used in which the intended goal takes precedence over a tightly determined frame.

A Hypothetical Example of Using Choice Points

The five Choice Points can promote therapist flexibility and effectiveness. If a clinician has a goal, it can be directly presented to the client, which may elicit change. If so, nothing else is needed. If not, the therapist could redefine the problem early and offer: "You have a problem with perception. The way that you see things affects your self-esteem and emotions."

If that intervention doesn't work, the clinician has other choices. One choice would be to do more of the same, only with increasing intensity. For example, "It's imperative that you change your perception of reality to feel better." And, "It's really, really imperative that you change your perception of reality to feel better." This follows a mechanical model. If an object resists movement, exert more force. Similarities can be found in some medical models. If the patient doesn't respond to a medication, the physician can increase the dosage, and there will most likely be a response.

In therapy, however, "titrating the dosage" often doesn't work. Therefore, the clinician has an option to change the intervention. The therapist could say (metaphorically), "Look at the flowers in life instead of the weeds." Or, "You're not using your past experiences to your best advantage." Or, "You're not relating to people in an adaptive way." Or, "You're not living life meaningfully. Or, "You don't have depression; you have ennui." Remember, goals are malleable.

As was previously stated, problems can be defined as existing within or among. They can exist inside a person, between two individuals, or among a group, such as a family or a work team. Problems can be defined by the way in which the group interacts with an organization or is influenced by a culture. Often therapists work with a patient's problem as if it were only within. However, that doesn't always work, and so therapists can try relational definitions. Look for solutions from many different perspectives, and remember, what works in one context may not work in another context.

The goal in some disciplines is universal. In medicine, for example, if someone has a broken bone, the physician often sets it. In a social situation like psychotherapy, however, goals are co-created by an interaction between the position of the client and the posture of the clinician. In social situations, goals are not fixed; they are malleable. This leads us to 14th principle for clinicians: Create goals that are easily achieved.

If a clinician does not want to change the goal, another choice is to find a new way to package the goal. If the goal is exercise, for example, the therapist could elicit hypnosis and then suggest, "Now you can exercise." The therapist could also use stories to embed the idea of exercise.

If that doesn't work, a clinician could use tailoring and work to speak the client's experiential language. Alternatively, change the process and use set up, intervene, and follow-through. If none of these things are effective with the client, there's a final choice: Change the therapist. This doesn't mean the therapist refers the client to a colleague, it means that the therapist needs to change, by becoming more playful, serious, didactic, experiential, flexible, etc.

I spent hundreds of hours with Erickson, individually and in groups, and half the time he was helping me to become more flexible. There's too much orthodoxy in psychotherapy. Therapy can begin with the flexibility of the therapist. After all, a common goal is eliciting client flexibility.

When a client has a problem, some therapists help the client look for a cause. In general, people like to find a cause because they think it's necessary. People often want to assign responsibility: "It's your fault; it's my fault." As I said earlier, in a relationship, a partner can either be right, or choose to give up this notion for the continuation of the relationship. We don't know the causes of many problems and everyone has an own idea, but we often are compelled to find a cause, or assign blame and responsibility—as if that will bring a solution. But, making it someone else's fault or someone else's responsibility just doesn't elicit solutions.

As we will see in the Chapters Three and Four, another approach is to discern components of the problem. Remember Erickson's story about his awkward friend who smoked a pipe? Using components, a therapist can create a map of the problem, and ideally a map of the solution. To better understand the importance of components, in the next chapter we will deconstruct hypnosis.

To review, here is a list of principles outlined in this chapter:

7. Create a map of the problem. Create a map of the solution.
8. Look for an interactional solution—a solution that involves other people.
9. Choose goals you know how to solve.
10. Redefine the problem early on.
11. The amount of indirection is directly proportional to the perceived resistance.
12. Be recursive, not repetitive.
13. Techniques are ways of gift-wrapping concepts and experiences; techniques do not cure.
14. Create goals that are easily achieved.

CHAPTER THREE

Lessons From Hypnosis—
Deconstructing Components

The following is a transcript of a group induction that I offered to an introductory class on clinical practices. This was not a class on hypnosis per se; only a few of the students had experience with hypnosis. My goal was to introduce the students to evocative communication and the way in which states can be redintegrated by orienting to components, a process that prompts the synergistic amalgamation of elicited elements. Moreover, I wanted the students to understand the process of establishing goals by deconstructing the patient's problem into components. The group induction was first introduced by didactic teaching, and then I gradually transitioned into a more hypnotic delivery by altering the tone, tempo, and direction of my speech:

Let's say that you are interested in hypnosis and you think that hypnosis is a good thing to practice; something to understand, to appreciate... and to realize. And you can understand hypnosis cognitively, but if you are really interested in realizing hypnosis, you could effortlessly take a moment...so that you could...seat yourself in a comfortable position... And that may mean your shoulders are relaxed and your hands are resting on your legs, and your thumbs are not touching in any way. And that can keep your feet steady. And that can keep your body steady. And that can allow your ears to be steady, and I am talking to your ears. And it can be interesting to...take a deep breath, and it can be delightful and valuable to...follow with another easy breath, noticing at what point you fully exhale...fully let go. And even with your eyes open, you can focus...really focus inside. And with your eyes open you can...focus on the realization of comfort. Or, you can...close your eyes. I don't know just how you can...realize comfort, but you may realize comfort as a sensation.

Suddenly, as you take an easy breath, as you fully exhale, you may feel comfort as a sensation of warmth. Will you experience that warmth in the center of your body? Or, will you discover that warmth in the back of your head? And it can be nice to...just rest effortlessly, and...realize effortlessly that your inner mind can help you to realize...realize a sensation of comfort. For some of you there can be an image of comfort. You might see comforting images, or there can be beautiful colors, interesting shapes, and a comforting movement. For others, there may be memories of comfort.

And for a moment, perhaps you're a little child. Perhaps you're in a place that's safe. Perhaps you're at home in your bed and you're listening to a relative tell you a story. And as you recognize your way of realizing comfort, you can gently...gently, with your eyes closed, look up. Take a deep breath, and as you fully exhale you can notice the way in which the comfort changes, and how the comfort can become more vivid.

Interestingly, you don't have to pay attention. Your feet are on the floor and you don't pay attention to that. You don't pay attention to the support...of the chair. All along it could seem as if you're a bodiless mind. It could seem as though you're just an intelligence, moving effortlessly in space and time. Suddenly, there can be images, sensations, and vivid memories that come to mind in your own way...in the way that's right for you. But you can always remember that any time you want to, with your eyes closed, you can take a moment to take a deep breath, look up, and fully exhale. And that point in which you fully exhale can be the most vivid physiological comfort.

And then there are changes, changes that occur as your body accommodates to the resting state. Your breathing rhythm has changed. Your swallowing reflex has altered. It may seem as though sounds are more vivid. It may seem as though somehow things are more stable. And you can have a reason for going into trance for a moment of relaxation, for the realization of a solution, for a moment in which you can explore the resources of your inner mind that can guide you.

I'm going to be quiet for just a few seconds. But that can be all the time in the world for you to subjectively explore a way in which you can use trance to strengthen your own realizations; strengthen your own conceptual realizations. Just a few seconds of real time could be all the time in the world...

Next, something that I'd like you to think about: What is most vivid for you right now? Is it the sensations, the images, the memories? And you can know what trance can be for you by reflecting on this question: What is most vivid for you right now?

Then, I invite you to bring yourself back. You can bring yourself back now... here now fully. Take one or two or three easy breaths, stretch and bring yourself back... fully alert.

After this induction, I queried the students about their experiences. One student said, "I went deep." Another said, "I saw blue skies, a white cloud, and a vast lake." Another reported, "I was with a man under a bridge," and someone else stated, "I felt hot and started sweating." One student revealed, "I felt empty," while another experienced resistance. Three other students described three different experiences: "I connected with my breath." "I was in a river and comfortable, but then felt like I was shocked and needed to get out of the river." "I experienced dissociation." The students had many different subjective experiences, and most of them were in the realm of hypnosis. My intent with the students was to establish a context for hypnosis to happen, and the students' different responses strongly indicated that hypnosis is a highly subjective experience.

I then explained: "The disadvantage of doing group hypnosis is that I can't individualize the induction. Another disadvantage is that hypnosis should be a conversation—and with a group, I can't make it into one. Essentially, a group induction is like a guided meditation."

I pointed out that the understructure of the hypnotic communication diverges from other forms of delivering messages. In the group induction, I was using evocative communication, not informative communication. I was not offering direct suggestions or advice, but rather experiences. My communication was mosaic, not linear. Informative communication is linear, whereas evocative communication is mosaic.

Earlier in the class, I used informative communication to teach. But as I segued into hypnosis and began offering experiences, I began using evocative communication. It was as if I were placing "toys" on the students' psychosocial stage, and inviting them to play with those toys. In the process, I established a context for hypnosis to happen. The induction that I offered the students was not read from a script; I improvised as I went along. Metaphorically speaking, I created poetry to reach the heart; I did not offer direct information to the left hemisphere.

Let's consider the strategic goals I used in the induction. My hope was to stimulate into play elements so that all the students would have an opportunity for trance. I did this because there is variation in the way people experience trance and I know that when people say they are hypnotized, they are basing the definition on their own criteria.

Pathways to Trance

The following are common pathways through which people experience trance:

1. When focusing internally, some people state, "I'm in a trance." If that is their criteria for trance, it should be accepted by the therapist.
2. Some people require an alteration in intensity to report trance. They are hypnotized when they are deeply relaxed and images and/or sounds become vivid. For others, things become less intense. Some people have a diminishing awareness of the position of their body, or the passage of time becomes vague. When things become less intense or vivid, these people often report that they are in a trance.
3. Some people need both a change in attention and intensity to report trance, while others need an experience of disas-

sociation. Disassociation be one, or a combination of any of three processes:

a) When things seem to "just happen." For example, images suddenly appear. Or, hypnotized people unexpectedly feel a sensation or unexpectedly have unusually vivid memories.

b) When a person has a sense of feeling disconnected. There is a sense of being "a part of and apart from." For example, the client involved in a scene of walking on a beach may say: "I know I'm *here*, but I'm also *there*."

c) When a person has a mild feeling of destabilization—a sense that something is somewhat out of balance.

To report trance, some people need a change in all three domains: attention, intensity, and an experience of disassociation.

4. There are those who need to implicitly experience a change in responsiveness. They respond without fully realizing the cue that led to their response. Sometimes they respond without realizing they responded. Hypnosis is centered on building implicit responsiveness. Here's a metaphor: The hypnotherapist knocks on the client's door, and when the client responds to the implied meaning, it's as if to say, "You are welcome into my home and you can help me redecorate." The study of response to innuendo is the purview of social psychology. It is also fundamental in all the arts. (To understand implicit suggestion, especially as it concerns hypnosis, see Zeig, 2015.)

5. Some people need a contextual marker—something in the situation that frames the experience as trance. In the demonstration with my students, I used a method that Erickson championed in which he would indirectly define the situation. For example, in a consultation, he might suddenly intone, "I'm going to remind you of something that happened a long time ago." When he changed the tone and

speed of his voice, and directed his voice away from the client (most often, toward the floor), he implied: "This is a time for trance." By defining the situation indirectly, Erickson accomplished two goals simultaneously: He garnered a response to implication, and he defined he situation as hypnosis. (See *The Induction of Hypnosis*, Zeig, 2014.)

To report the experience of trance, some people need to experience all five elements: 1) an internal focus; 2) an alteration in intensity; 3) disassociation; 4) a change in responsiveness; and 5) a contextual marker. I never know when a client is going to say, "I'm in a trance," or what he or she will need to come to that conclusion. Therefore, I commonly begin by placing all five elements (or toys) on the client's psychosocial "stage," and I eventually learn the client's criteria by making the trance into a conversation. To elicit hypnosis, a clinician can orient the client to constituent elements. To promote change, a therapist can do the same with the client's problem or its solution.

Now hypnosis is not one thing; it is a way in which things happen. It is a compilation of components that change over time. Hypnosis is a syndrome, in the same way that some diseases are syndromes. For example, although Meniere's disease is a physical disorder, which technically makes it a disease, it is a condition characterized by a set of symptoms, namely tinnitus, loss of hearing, and instability. A few years ago, Chronic Fatigue Syndrome was redefined as a disease. But because it is characterized by a set of symptoms, it is still widely known as a syndrome. Hypnosis is a syndrome because it is a psychosocial, contextual amalgamation. There are three intrapsychic elements in hypnosis: 1) an alteration in attention, 2) modifications in intensity, and 3) the elicitation of dissociation. The psychosocial element is the client's response to implication. The contextual element is the overt or implied definition of the situation.

I also never know what a client may need to report being responsible, motivated, happy, curious, or effective in relationships.

Hence, I look for components to elicit those states. I don't address these states as a single entity. Instead, I understand the components of each state and address the components. I "map" the components of the client's problem, and doing so inevitably creates a map of solution components.

It is an epistemological error to think of hypnosis or psychosocial problems solely as entities rather than synergistic amalgamations of components that change over time. And when a therapist understands the elements of hypnosis or the problem, it is easier to fashion a tailored induction. A similar process of deconstruction can be used when establishing goals in therapy, which is discussed in Chapter Four.

Lessons from Hypnosis— Establishing Goals in Therapy

The practice of hypnosis stimulates practitioners to understand states. Even a neutral induction can have a palliative effect. It demonstrates to the client that he or she can change states. In this chapter, we will build on our model of hypnosis to widen a clinician's understanding of establishing goals in therapy by understanding problems as states that can be divided into components.

Altering states can even serve as goals when teaching. Here's an example: When I visited Erickson in the 1970s, I stayed in his guesthouse. There was a box of old reel-to-reel tapes of his lectures on the floor of the closet, and I asked if I could listen to them and transfer them to cassettes. Subsequently, I commented that his lectures were more like hypnotic inductions than professional instruction. He explained, "I never listen to those lectures. I usually didn't teach content; I taught to motivate." (Zeig, 1985 p 6.)

At the time, I was a graduate student and the focus of my education was absorbing and regurgitating facts. It was hard to imagine that a goal for a lecture could be eliciting a state. It took considerable effort to digest that construct.

A fundamental principle (No. 15) of eliciting states, such as hypnosis, is to understand components and stimulate them into play. Let's think about peoples' problems from the perspective of a "states model." If the problem is that the client is in a maladaptive state—one that is ineffective for the client, as well as others—then it's the clinician's job to help the client access an adaptive state, which can be done by eliciting components. Hypnosis can be considered a construct of convenience; a way of labeling a gestalt. It can also be considered a state. Hypnosis and other states are best elicited by using heuristic processes. But, protocols are commonly used that turn hypnosis into an algorithm.

Heuristics and Algorithms

There's a difference between algorithms and heuristics. Algorithms are a set of rules for problem solving; an algorithm is meant to inform. Heuristics are strategies derived from previous experiences; they are simplifying assumptions, and therefore, they tend to be more experiential. (For information on heuristics in therapy, see Zeig, 2002.)

Computers work by algorithms. and with an algorithm there is always a concrete solution. Using an algorithm involves a linear process and logical steps that lead to the tangible outcome. In many situations, a computer performs better than a person. A computer can be taught to play chess with more skill than an individual because the computer has massive computational power to analyze the possibilities inherent in every move.

Algorithms can be elegant. There is an apocryphal story about the famous mathematician, Carl Friedrich Gauss. When he was in primary school, the teacher gave the students the task of summing the numbers from one to 100. Without using a chalk and slate for computation, Gauss simply wrote down 5,050. He did it all in his mind. Demonstrating his mathematical genius at an early age, when he was asked to describe his process, he replied, "1 plus 100 is 101. 2 plus 99 is 101. 3 plus 98 is 101. 50 multiplied by 101 is 5,050." Gauss demonstrated an elegant algorithm. But social behavior cannot be computed like this because there is no a concrete answer or solution. Happiness is a process, not a concrete outcome.

Most clinicians are trained algorithmically: Here's the formula; follow the formula. Here's a protocol; follow the protocol. The problem with this method is that a client rarely presents a problem that has a concrete solution. For example, if a client says, "I want to be happy," or "I want to be effective," or "I want to be motivated," or "I want to have good relationships," there are no definitive solutions. Clients are frequently stuck in maladaptive states and want to transition into adaptive states. Therefore, clinicians should eschew using algorithms in most therapy situations. Given that there are no concrete solutions to most therapy problems, clinicians should instead rely on effective heuristics. A common heuristic in my therapy is to create experiences that elicit states and sub-states.

Consider the common clinical problem of depression. With some clients, a therapist might ask, "How do you know that you're depressed?" The question would be an attempt to understand the map—to understand the components of this person's depressive experience. One client might respond, "I know that I'm depressed because I'm so lost inside myself." Another might respond, "Because I can't stop thinking about the past." Another might answer, "Because I'm not doing anything and I'm withdrawn," or perhaps, "Because I don't have any energy," or, "Because I'm a victim of life." So, there are many components that people experience to report being depressed.

Creating Maps

Table 4-1 (on the following page) is a generic map of depression. Of course, most valuable would be a map that represents how a *specific* client "does" depression.

If a client "does" some combination of the elements in the table, the client could tab his or her experience as "depression."

There are many lenses in the philosophical universe. A physician might consider depression a disease of insufficient neurotransmitters that needs to be treated with medication. In some cases, this is true. However, depression often involves other factors. Therefore, the therapist who intervenes socially should define the problem in a way that it can be treated socially. From the position of social construction, depression doesn't exist. Depression is just a category, like hypnosis is a category. Therefore, the clinician needs to understand the components by which depression is maintained, because doing so can facilitate the creation of effective strategies.

Table 4-1: Depression

DEPRESSION
Is too internally focused
Lives in the past
Is inactive
Is negative
Feels hopeless, has no goals
Is intropunitive
Is socially withdrawn
More of a tactile person
Is closed and jugmental
Discounts accomplishments
Absorbs social energy
Uses the phrase, "If only..."
Feels physiologically deadened
Existentially believes, "I am not okay"
Feels like a victim
Is limited in scope and depth

Once depression (or anxiety or any other problem) is mapped, solution components become obvious. When one "flips" the problem, a map of components of solution components emerges.

The next table (4-2) lists components of both depression and happiness. Those who do some combination of elements on the left side of the table will most likely be depressed. Those who do some combination of elements on the right side of the table will most likely report happiness.

Table 4-2: Depression and Happiness

DEPRESSION	HAPPINESS
Is too internally focused	Is externally focused
Lives in the past	Lives in the present
Is inactive	Is active
Is negative	Is positive
Feels hopeless, has no goals	Feels hopeful and goal-oriented
Is intropunitive	Is balanced
Is socially withdrawn	Is socially engaged
More of a tactile person	More of a visual person
Is closed and jugmental	Open to life, people, all possibilities
Discounts accomplishments	Acknowledges accomplishments
Absorbs social energy	Emits social energy
Uses the phrase, "If only..."	Uses the phrase, "Yes and..."
Feels physiologically deadened	Experiences adaptive arousal
Existentially believes, "I am not okay"	Existentially believes, "I am okay"
Feels like a victim	Feels like a victor
Is limited in scope and depth	Exhibits scope and depth

Once components of the problem state are identified, it is easy to "flip" them and see components of a solution state. Every "depressed" client has historical experience with solution components and they can be experientially awakened.

Clinicians should map components of solution states. One way of creating a map is to consider distinctions in human functioning, including behavior, cognition, affect, attitude, perception, somatic arousal, posture, linguistic patterns, perception of time, and relational patterns. Any problem or solution can be mapped using these elements.

To review: 1) Create a map of the problem. 2) Create a map of the solution.

A more complex mapping system will be offered in Chapter Six, but to continue developing the concept of states, let's take one more step. What if someone wakes up tomorrow morning and says, "It's a beautiful day. I think I will be a traditional psychologist." Or, alternatively, "It is a beautiful day. I think I will be a traditional hypnotist." Consider the sub-states that the person could enter:

Table 4-3: Therapist Sub-states

Traditional Therapist	Traditional Hypnotist
Empathic	Directive
Attentive	Authoritarian
Accepting	Commanding
Quiet	Suggestive
Educational	Imperative
Inquisitive	Dynamic
Composed	Calculating
Warm	Active
Present	Persuasive

A traditional therapist would be empathic, accepting, present, etc. If the traditional therapist were a type of music, he or she would be mildly thematic with dulcet tones. A traditional hypnotist would be direct, commanding, suggestive, and dynamic. And, if that person were music, he or she would be *Thus Spoke Zarathustra* by Strauss. If someone wakes up tomorrow morning and says, "It's a beautiful day. I think I'll be an Ericksonian therapist," well, this person will be experiential, metaphoric, flexible, and understand systems and orient toward. A musical metaphor for this person could be something with a rich, complex understructure. For me, that's Beethoven. And, any of those states could be desirable to prompt client change.

The following are components of an Ericksonian state:

Table 4-4: Ericksonian Sub-states

ERICKSONIAN THERAPIST
Experiential
Strategic
Active
"Tour Guide"
Flexible
Metaphoric (Orienting Toward)
Utilize
Systemic
Individualize, Tailor
Gift-Wrap

Being a therapist means accessing components to embody a global state. Therefore, at any given time, therapists should understand the state they desire and activate the appropriate components.

The states model can be used to examine and understand hypnosis, problems, solutions, and even the posture of the therapist. In the case of depression, for example, the therapist could establish an orientation that leads to happiness. One way of proceeding could be to address a component to precipitate systemic change, thereby creating a "snowball effect."

Erickson once had a female client who was a depressed, suicidal artist. His therapy was to orient her toward a component of happiness, and he did this by giving her the task of finding a "flash of color" during her day. He knew that she was the happiest when she was doing art and working with color. Therefore, a boy on a bicycle became a flash of color. A plane flying overhead became a flash of color. The leaves rippling in the wind became a flash of color. The woman enjoyed the game so much that she played it with her children. Erickson reported that this game was important in helping her recover from depression.

Depressed people are often preoccupied with their depression. But, every depressed person has historical experience with the components of happiness. However, it would not be effective if a clinician merely said to a depressed client, "Be happy because it's a beautiful world. And, there's a lot to live for, so you might as well be happy." Again, to affect human systems, one cannot use an algorithm to elicit states. Instead, one creates an experience whereby the person is awakened to something that is dormant. It's a process of eliciting experiences and resources, not a matter of logical, linear thinking and offering information. And that's the paradox of hypnosis: Hypnosis may seem like people are being put to sleep, but, the art is to awaken people to capabilities that are lying dormant.

The following table illustrates the states model and potential choices:

Table 4-5: The Phenomenological Perspective

Depression	Happiness
Internal	External
In the past	Present
Inactive	Active
etc.	etc.
Hypnosis	**Therapist**
Attention	Experiential
Intensity	Strategic
Dissociation	Systemic
Response	Active
Contextual definition	Utilize
etc.	etc.

A therapist has several choices in the states model: 1) Address the components of the problem, not the category. 2) Elicit components of a possible solution. 3) Use hypnosis.

Hypnosis can be a bridge between the land of the problem and the land of the solution. Think of a car that's in reverse. Similarly, clients are often "in reverse" and ineffective. The client is in reverse psychologically and socially, limited in scope. If the client is in reverse, to get into first gear, he or she must go through neutral. It is not necessary to spend a lot of time in neutral, but being in neutral represents a change in state. If someone who is tremendously tense or in pain moves into neutral, even momentarily, that is progress. Neutral can be a steppingstone to a more desirable state.

There is a fourth choice for clinicians: Change the therapist. But once again, this does not mean that the therapist should refer a client to a colleague, rather it's an invitation for the therapist to change, because like hypnosis, the therapist acts as a bridge between the problem and the solution. Great psychotherapists, such as Milton Erickson, Virginia Satir, and Victor Frankl, were powerful, present, and intense, and the impact they had on clients was tremendous. Their influence could be attributed to how they were with people, but their theories of change were decidedly different.

And while we're on the subject of the process of change, let's take a lighthearted look at the history of psychotherapy.

Psychotherapy began with hypnosis. Freud went to France to study hypnosis with Charcot because there were no social techniques to treat mental problems; hypnosis was all that existed. But later, Freud rejected hypnosis in favor of his psychoanalytic method of free association, which involved the patient lying on a couch while the analyst sat out of view.

Freud lived during the Victorian Era, so when he said to patients, "Come into my consultation room, lie down on the couch and say whatever comes to mind," it was totally bizarre and completely unheard of at the time. But, people got better quickly.

Freud made therapy into an "unusual conversation." This is an important principle (16th) to consider: Therapy can be an unusual conversation. The fact that clients pay a therapist to focus exclusively on them makes it an unusual conversation. Other examples of therapy as an unusual conversation include requesting that the client talk to an empty chair, or hypnotically suggesting to a client that his or her arm is lifting but the client will not experience it as voluntary.

Using the metaphor of a tree, Freud was interested in the roots. He implied that if you understand the roots of a tree, you change the tree. After World War II, psychotherapy flourished in the US and it gave birth to treatment based on behavioral conditioning. This school of thought maintained that if you want the tree to grow in a certain direction, shine a light, and the tree will grow that way. Soon after, the humanistic approach was developed. It focused on offering empathy, genuineness, and positive regard. Love the tree. Appreciate the tree. If you love and appreciate the tree, it will grow. Next, there was family therapy based on systemic principles, and it focused on changing the environment to change the tree. Currently in the US, the primary approach is cognitive behavioral therapy, which began as the application of behavioral methods to cognitions: Change the way in which the tree "thinks." Erickson represented a radically experiential focus: Evocative experiences promote and enrich conceptual realizations, adaptive states, and positive identities. The goal was to awaken the tree's dormant potential. In the past few years, affective neurobiology has taken center stage in psychotherapy, which has led to advances in the practice of mindfulness and meditation. Genetic and epigenetic understandings can make the tree flourish.

Some humorous snapshots of schools of therapy: The patient exclaims to the therapist, "It's really a beautiful day!" The therapist, a psychoanalyst and follower of Freud, replies, "I wonder why you're speaking so familiarly with me. Perhaps you're confusing me with a figure from your childhood. Perhaps you're confusing me with your father." Psychoanalysis focuses on interpreting how the past contaminates the present. The analyst knows that past experiences can distort the present. And if past experiences are analyzed, the patient may no longer be plagued by them.

Now, if the patient sees a humanistic therapist and says, "It's really a beautiful day," the therapist might reply, "It seems you're feeling good today." This clinician's goal is to bring emotions to the present so that the patient can understand his or her feelings and express them clearly.

If the patient sees a cognitive therapist and reports, "It's really a beautiful day!" the therapist might reply, "How do you come to that conclusion? What is the data?" The approach is to elicit cognitive schema and distortions that limit adaptability.

Now, if the patient announces to the Ericksonian therapist, "It's really a beautiful day!" the response is probably along the lines of, "That's right. It is now a really beautiful day. And you can take a deep breath and close your eyes and as you exhale fully, really experience, 'It's a beautiful day.' And I don't know if you can have images of, 'It's a beautiful day,' or if you can have sensations of, 'It's a beautiful day,' or if you can have memories, 'It's a beautiful day.' And as you take another deep breath, you can, in your own way, go inside and memorize, 'It's a beautiful day.' And just as you can think back, you can look forward. Because, when you enter your home, you have the key in your hand, and it's your key, and it's your ability to open the door and you feel the key click into place, suddenly…it really is a beautiful day." And the client may think, "Oh my god, how did he come up with all of this with my simple expression about a beautiful day?"

Now, if we want to reach a deeper area of the brain, such as the amygdala in our limbic system, we should use communication that is designed to impact that part of the brain. Experiential communication reaches the limbic system. Animals communicate experientially, not by using human language. Artists also communicate experientially. For example, music is a form of communication that influences our emotions in a way that language cannot. Dance, film, poetry, painting, and other forms of fine art are also designed to have a limbic resonance. To reach our clients on a deeper level, we need to become excellent experiential communicators. We need use evocative communication to create experiences. Creating maps will improve therapist choices. Also, to foster adaptive states, the therapist can tailor the message to the unique nature of the client.

The principles in this chapter are as follows:

15. Understand components and stimulate them into play.
16. Therapy should be an unusual conversation.

CHAPTER FIVE

Tailoring: Assessment

Preview

In medicine, the diagnosis dictates the treatment plan. For example, if a psychiatrist diagnoses a patient with schizophrenia, specific medications are prescribed. And, in medicine, the diagnostic entity is treated as a complete unit, in and of itself. For example, an infection is an entity; depression is an entity; cancer is an entity, etc. However, only a person's pathology can be diagnosed, not his or her assets, including strengths and potentials.

In psychotherapy, a diagnosis implies that the treatment to follow will primarily be formulaic and that an individual's differences are of secondary importance, which, of course, should not be the case. Social interventions, moreover, differ greatly from physical interventions because the psychotherapist can address components rather than entities.

In most psychological practice, determining a diagnosis is emphasized. I prefer instead to think in terms of assessment. Diagnosis evokes the negative connotation of pathology, i.e., a malfunction in one's system. Assessment, however, invites us to think of a person's assets, as well as their deficits. And, eliciting strengths can be more effective than addressing problems. The terms "assessment" and "evaluation" are more flexible and encompassing than "diagnosis."

The Ericksonian model emphasizes individualizing treatment. Hypnotherapy and psychotherapy can be effectively personalized if the clinician assesses the cognitive, perceptual, emotional, psychological, behavioral, contextual, and relational "position" of the patient, and then tailors the therapy according to that assessment.

This chapter examines assessment strategies that the therapist can employ to evaluate the patient's position. It also presents an

overview of how the therapist incorporates this information to tailor goals.

Introduction

People who seek therapy often portray themselves as "victims," and
feel wronged or deficient in some way. They frequently use phrases
that communicate powerlessness: "I can't stop smoking"; "I can't
think positively"; "I can't have good relationships"; "I can't forget
my past"; and "I can't stop anticipating future failures."

A wise therapist presupposes that the patient has dormant resources. Therefore, patients can have a good relationship; can stop
smoking; can think positively; and so on. The presupposition is that
at some point in the client's history, he or she has demonstrated
such abilities. The task of the therapist is to uncover the patient's
constructive history and elicit dormant resources. The therapist can
present this knowledge to the patient, gift-wrapped in such a way
that the patient can realize and subsequently assume ownership of
it.

Two tailoring questions should be paramount for the therapist:
1) What is position of the client? 2) How do I use this position to
individualize gift-wrapped goals? It is our job as therapists to cata-
lyze patient transformation. To do this, we must understand (to the
extent that we can) our patient, and our patient's problem.

The emphasis in this chapter is assessing structures that exist in
the present, which can be used to elicit adaptive realizations.

The assessment framework I present bears no resemblance to
ICD or DSM classifications, both of which classify psychiatric conditions. As an experiential therapist, I am more interested in eliciting change than classifying a disorder and offering a diagnosis. So
instead I create an assessment, which forms the basis for a constructive treatment plan. The schema outlined in this chapter incorporates observable characteristics that can be used to guide the therapy and hypnotic induction. Not only can these distinctions serve
as road signs to steer the therapist in a desirable direction, they can
also be harnessed as resources.

This chapter addresses the position that the patient assumes—his or her style of perceiving and relating—that can be "read" from close observation. Such assessment provides the therapist with valuable information for treatment. Chapter Eight explains how to assemble the clues revealed by the patient to design and tailor interventions to which the patient will be most responsive.

A structural assessment focuses on existent conditions rather than hypotheses about etiology. And, of course, the assessment is dependent upon the perspective of the therapist. Assessments and even diagnoses are influenced by the position of the clinician's entrenched ways of viewing, doing, and relating.

An assessment essentially offers the therapist insight into a patient's situation, and will help the therapist to individualize a meaningful and effective intervention.

The Position of the Patient

In this chapter, how a person processes information about his or her world can be examined within two systems: 1) assessment categories (perceptual and relational styles); and 2) "hooks" (values).

My attempt to summarize characteristics of human personality and behavior in a few pages is, by necessity, generalized. And, the distinctions that are addressed are not empirically validated. However, these are distinctions that have helped me in my clinical work.

Tailoring

Tailoring is an anthropological adventure for the therapist—a matter of understanding another culture. When we tailor in therapy it's as if we've travelled to a foreign country and we hope to make our visit as enriching as possible by learning something about the culture, language, history, and special attractions. Our clients inhabit different geographies, and it is our job to discover as much as possible about whatever makes them unique. You might consider this chapter a travel guide, offering handy phrases and insightful tips for exploring new territory. Successful travel is about adaptation: the ability to adjust to the surroundings, instead of trying to make the strange land into a replica of home. As much as possible, the Ericksonian therapist adapts to the "terrain" of the patient, rather than forcing the patient to conform to the therapist's subjective perspective or preferred theory of human behavior.

In this chapter, we'll look at the patient terrain. In subsequent chapters, we'll explore how the therapist adapts to the varying landscapes.

Assessment Categories

Assessment categories fall into two major groups: intrapsychic and interpersonal. The intrapsychic group includes both perceptual and processing operations. Both intrapsychic and interpersonal evaluations are primarily conducted according to where clients fall on a continuum, with the two descriptors at each end, identifying the extremes of the characteristic. For instance, "enhancer/reducer" represents the two opposite ends of a range of behaviors—a spectrum along which the patient's behavior lies.

I have identified 16 assessment categories for therapists to use with clients. However, not all distinctions are necessary or important for any given client. To determine which are most significant in a situation, consider the following:

- The assessment category that is most out of balance.
- Assessment categories that seem especially relevant to the client's problems. These might also be categories that are out of balance.
- The patient's flexibility in changing a category to successfully adapt. Assessment categories should vary with changing environmental circumstances, with individuals readily able to shift their positions as the tasks require. Troubles arise when someone is stifled by learned limitations—rigidities that prevent effective shifting.
- Differences in how clients appear to others (including the

therapist) and how they view themselves. Usually there is concordance, but when incongruities exist, I attempt to relate to patients from the perspective of their subjective image of themselves.

The following assessment categories are ones that I have found important in my work. I have distilled them from a variety of sources. Other practitioners will have different categories, based on their own perceptions and predilections. Erickson, however, did not postulate assessment categories and would, I suspect, find too limiting even those as general as the ones I've listed. Perhaps he had implicit categories, but none that were explicit. Erickson extolled flexibility. For example, if he recognized that a person was more internal than external, he would work to create a balance by eliciting a more external orientation, but he did not discuss this method.

Table 5-1: Assessment Categories

Intrapsychic:

I. PERCEPTUAL OPERATIONS
A. Attentional Styles
1. Internal <--> External
2. Focused <--> Diffused
B. Preferred Sensory System
1. Auditory
2. Visual
3. Tactile
II. PROCESSING OPERATIONS
1. Linear <--> Mosaic
2. Enhancer <--> Reducer
3. Specific <--> General
4. Create <--> Delete <--> Distort

Interpersonal:

```
III. Relationsal/Social Categories
1. Birth Order: Oldest or Only Child, Middle, Youngest
2. Formative Background: Urban/Suburban, Rural/Small Town
3. Extrapunitive <--> Intropunitive
4. Absorber <--> Emitter
5. Direct <--> Indirect
6. Pursuer <--> Distancer
7. One-Up <--> One-Down
```

Perceptual Operations

Perceptual operations refer to the normal, free-flowing, and primarily automatic processes of perception. Attentional style is a perceptual operation that has two salient polarities: internal/external and focused/diffused.

1. Internal/External

Does the client's attentiveness tend to be more external or internal? Obviously, specific conditions will alter this factor. For example, driving a car requires more external attention than looking at a sunset. However, outside of context-specific parameters, a client may prefer to be in one state or the other.

Erickson was externally oriented in his attentiveness. In fact, he was one of the most externally oriented individuals I have ever met. Perhaps years of enduring severe, chronic pain turned Erickson away from a concentrated internal focus, which would have only magnified awareness of his discomfort. By focusing on the nuances of the world outside his body, Erickson achieved an extraordinary level of external perceptiveness. His ability to observe minimal nuances of nonverbal behavior in others is legendary.

In contrast, I once studied with a Jungian therapist who was so preoccupied with his internal state that I doubt if he knew the color of his wife's eyes. Such information would have seemed unimportant to him, compared with exploring all the nooks and crannies of his own psyche.

Assessment categories can be used in guiding induction and therapy. Using the assessment information as a road sign, the practitioner could create an induction for an internally oriented person by concentrating on the patient's internal experience. (See *The Induction of Hypnosis*, Zeig, 2014 for information on induction.) Eventually, the induction could move toward more external perceptions with the intent of eliciting a perceptual change. As a result, the patient might report an experience that was "really different"—an outcome conducive to the experience of hypnosis, and the patient's acknowledgment of experiencing a different (hypnotic) mode of processing.

An induction for an internally oriented person might go like this:

You can close your eyes and go inside, recognizing some of the sensations of comfort that can be apparent in your body. And you really can't know how those sensations of comfort will develop. Will you find them more inside your chest or your stomach? And will they radiate up or down?

Then, directing externally:

Now, as you notice those sensations of comfort, it really isn't important to attend to the sound of the air-conditioner or traffic outside.

Note that the induction begins with a discussion of internal experiences that are physical, before moving to external experiences that are auditory. The induction could just as easily begin with internal visual experiences or internal auditory experiences, depending on the predilection of the client to be either more visual or auditory.

With someone who is externally oriented, the induction could start at that end of the spectrum and move toward a more internal orientation.

As you are sitting here, you may notice the color of the desk behind me, or the way I am seated in the chair, but you probably don't have to recognize the position of your feet on the floor, or the way that your hands are...resting...in your lap. But, you can notice your eyes blinking as your lids close. Because as you attend to the things that occur, you may also begin to recognize the drifting of your thoughts inside, so that you could remember a pleasant scene from your childhood, or soon be absorbed in an interesting daydream.

In this example, the induction starts externally with a visual orientation, and then moves toward a visual internal experience.

A task for an "internal" person could address that component: "Take a moment to close your eyes and get a feel for what benefits exercise can bring you." For an external person: "Exercising outdoors is a way that you can better enjoy the sights and sounds of nature."

As mentioned earlier, rigid assessment categories can be problematic for the client. If a person is primarily internal, that might, in and of itself, create difficulty. For example, an internal person could try to ameliorate pain by searching inside for solutions. If an individual is diagnosed as being depressed, the therapist will most likely find that the patient's orientation is overly internal. The goal of therapy might then be to help this patient develop a more external orientation. On the other hand, those diagnosed with impulse disorders tend to be external in their orientation. The goal in therapy for patients with this disorder could be to develop a more satisfactory and vivid internal life. Now, becoming more external is not a cure for depression. But, it might start a patient on a path of reorientation.

In psychotherapy there is no one specific tool for treatment of a condition. All psychological problems are composed of components. Redintegration is a process of building a state by orienting to partial cues that are components of a hypnotic or solution state.

Now, for some unintelligible reason, if you wake up tomorrow morning and say to yourself, "It's a beautiful day, but I think I will be depressed," a good start would be to do one of the components of depression, i. e., "being lost inside" or internally preoccupied.

2. Focused/Diffused

Most of us have a free-flowing attention style: sometimes we're sharply focused; other times, amorphous. Obsessive patients are often highly focused while paranoid patients and acting-out adolescents are often diffused in their attention. These individuals are vigilant about monitoring their surroundings and are often distracted; alive to nuances in their environment.

An eye-fixation hypnotic induction with a focused individual might initially consist of details about the fixation object. The same induction for a diffused patient would be more random, with the therapist guiding attention back and forth from different foci, sensations, feelings, behaviors, and so on. The therapist might then work to elicit a response in an opposing direction from the preferred orientation: diffused from a focused person; focused from a diffused person.

The following is a hypothetical example of an eye fixation induction with a person who tends to be highly focused:

There's a spot on the wall that might interest you to focus your visual attention. You might be curious about the shape of the spot. Perhaps you're fascinated by the color of the spot. It may seem as though the object of your attention has more than two dimensions.

Shifting to diffused:

But you don't need to attend to the sounds outside that may seem to be getting closer, and the sensations of comfort that may seem deeper as you rest in the chair.

Again, an induction should be designed to take the patient from a customary state to a different state. The therapist can start by pacing an individual's preferred style and move in a direction that creates this shift.

Here's a two-dimensional grid displaying attentional style:

Table 5-2 Attentional Style

Internal	External
Focused	Diffused

An individual's attentional style could be internal and focused, or internal and diffused; or external and focused, or external and diffused.

Preferred Sensory System

Bandler and Grinder (1979) discuss the use of representational systems in their Neuro-Linguistic Programming (NLP) model. In processing information, a person could unconsciously favor one of three sensory systems: visual, auditory, or tactile, and his or her language might reflect this predilection. Those who perceive their world visually might say: "What I see...," "The way I look at things...," "It appears to me that..." Those who primarily process information auditorily might use phrases such as, "What I hear...," "It sounds to me like...," and "That rings true for me." Tactile individuals may offer: "My gut reaction is...," "My feeling about the matter is...," or, "My heart tells me that...."

To illustrate how these sensory preferences can shape an individual's response to hypnosis, here's a story:

When I was a graduate student, I practiced an induction with an undergraduate who maintained that during the "trance" he was not hypnotized. However, when I asked him to open his eyes and see a rose, he reported that he saw the imaginary flower, and then described it in detail. Yet, he emphatically denied that the visualization was somehow "proof" that he was hypnotized. I was perplexed. After further conversation, I inquired as to his major field of study. He was a photography student. Visualization was such a common experience for him that he experienced it without any alteration of volition or subjective involvement. Therefore, he did not report the experience of trance. Trance is a subjective phenomenon that may exist to the degree that it is reported by the client.

When I worked with the photography student, I was a novice practitioner of hypnosis and my technique was mechanical. Now that I'm more experienced in Ericksonian methods, if I had it to do over, I would alter my technique to create a more subjective involvement with autonomous activity by suggesting tactile experiences (perhaps numbness of a limb) rather than visual ones. I believe this approach would have been more successful.

There are also behavioral concomitants of the preferred perceptual system. A therapist might recognize an individual's predominant sensory style through his or her physical behavior and demeanor. An auditory person, for instance, might turn his or her dominant ear toward the therapist, concentrating on every word; a visual person might have a conspicuous pattern of intensely observing the surroundings.

In an induction, the therapist can use sensory systems by beginning with the preferred mode, and then eventually move toward another sensory system. Again, the purpose is to establish a perceptual alteration.

In the mid-1970s at one of his teaching seminars, I observed Erickson using a student's preferred sensory system. Erickson knew the student was visually perceptive so he focused his questions on auditory modes, asking the student questions such as, "When you were here last, who seemed uncomfortable? How can you determine that from what was said?" My observation was that Erickson was striving to increase the student's flexibility in using his auditory sensory system. However, when Erickson was working with me, he noted my auditory preference and directed his attention toward developing my visual perception. For example, he once proposed this hypothetical to me: A man is walking toward you in street clothes. He's a policeman. What do you notice that indicates his occupation?

I eventually came to recognize Erickson's sensitivity to aspects of one's orientation that were out of balance. He would hone in on less well-developed aspects in people and use gift-wrapping methods to help them strengthen their latent/dormant abilities. Living effectively relies on developing the flexibility to use a processing mode appropriate to the situation. Having access to various processing modes promotes adaptation.

Processing Operations

Processing involves an individual perceiving the world, and then developing a framework for response. While most of us have an automatic and free-flowing attention style, processing is more conscious and volitional. The three major processing operations are: 1) linear/mosaic, 2) enhancer/reducer, and 3) specific/general.

1. Linear/Mosaic

Erickson once compared his thinking style to his wife's, describing Mrs. Erickson's as more of a direct, sequential process, and his as "a little bit here, a little bit there." (Zeig, 1980) Erickson noticed how his children reacted to the differences in his and Mrs. Erickson's processing. When his two oldest sons were young they had different strategies for finding hidden Easter eggs. Bert always found the Easter eggs his father hid, while Lance always found the eggs his mother hid. The reason for this was because Bert's thinking was more mosaic like his father's, whereas Lance's thinking was more linear, like Mrs. Erickson's. Dr. Erickson's strategy of hiding Easter eggs was more random, and Mrs. Erickson's strategy was likely more systematic. One Easter, Bert surprised everyone by finding the eggs hidden by Mrs. Erickson. Erickson asked Bert how he did it. Bert responded, "It was easy, Dad. I just thought, 'Where would Mom hide them?'"

A linear thinker, processing sequentially, might say, "Here are ten principles in the induction of hypnosis," and then list them. In contrast, a mosaic thinker might use anecdotes to illustrate the same principles. Again, according to the demands of existent conditions, individuals should be able to move fluidly from one type of processing to another. Writing a book, for example, usually involves a linear strategy. Perhaps that's why Erickson did not write books, but instead wrote articles, which may have fit more with his mosaic style of thinking.

There is a difference between attentional style and processing. A person can be focused in attention, but remain mosaic in processing. This, in fact, seemed to be Erickson's orientation. He could be extremely focused on a patient, but when processing the patient's information, he was still a mosaic thinker.

An induction for a linear person could begin with progressive relaxation, starting from the head and moving methodically down to the toes. For a mosaic person, the induction could randomly wander. In this example, we move from one to the other:

Now, as you relax your hand, you might want to notice the relaxation of your fingers. But it could also be interesting to notice how you relax your knees, because you don't have to think about the relaxing sound of my voice. But you can begin to notice the relaxed movement sensations in your fingers and how those movement sensations can progressively develop, and how that sensation starts at the tips of your fingers and continues to the palms of your hands and then to your forearms, up to your shoulders, and then finally to your neck and head.

In this example, the induction moves from a mosaic style of thinking to a linear one. Again, the direction of the induction can move from the dominant style to the non-dominant one.

For a therapy task a linear person can be given sequential steps, while a mosaic person can be given a number of untethered possibilities.

2. Enhancer/Reducer

An enhancer looks at a mouse and sees an elephant; a reducer looks at an elephant and sees a mouse. Likewise, an enhancer will notice-ably react to an unexpected sound or movement. A reducer might not acknowledge the same event. Enhancers often make a big deal out of something, and reducers make a lesser deal out of the same thing.

Gestures and the redundant phrases and words used can distin-guish enhancers from reducers. The enhancer's speech is often filled with superlatives and exaggerated descriptions, with words such as "incredible," "extremely," "fantastic" peppering his or her speech. Enhancers also display grand gestures. Reducers, in contrast, use minimizing qualifiers, such as, "somewhat" "just," and "a little," and they tend to constrain their gestures.

Reducers tend to be pragmatic and enhancers tend to be spon-taneous. Reducers are usually quiet and reserved; enhancers, so-cial and gregarious. Reducers are less emotional than enhancers. Reducers are more controlled and rigid, and enhancers are more free-spirited. Scientists are often reducers; artists are often en-hancers. Oddly enough, enhancers and reducers frequently marry each other. But although the match between an engineer and art-ist can be complementary on some levels, it can be problematic on others. Early in the relationship she might think, "It is completely amazing how he's so totally stable and balanced." He might think, "It is a bit curious and somewhat interesting that she seems rather enthusiastic at times." But a few years later, she might say to a friend, "He's incredibly boring!" and he might tell a coworker, "I'm getting a bit tired of her histrionics."

Consider therapy for an adolescent who is acting out. This per-son may be a reducer, and diffuse in her attentional style. She seeks stimulation by constantly scanning her environment. If you ask her to close her eyes and relax, she may fidget and inquire, "What are we going to do next?" This type of individual often lacks a solid in-ternal life. However, using hypnosis to help her develop the ability for reverie and expand the capacity for internal processing might be a step in helping her change her behavior.

In offering an induction for an enhancer one could appeal to this characteristic style:

This is going to be the most amazing, spectacular, fantastic experience that you've ever had. It can be so incredibly relaxing to take a deep breath and really let go so that you are deeply in trance.

The approach for a reducer is markedly different:

You may find hypnosis a bit interesting. There just might be a few small things that occasionally you can find somewhat curious. It seems they may just be of some value to you at some time in some place in the future.

Note that in these examples the categories are being used to motivate the client. They are not being used to guide the induction from one modality to another. Tailored motivations may increase therapeutic compliance.

Oftentimes, patients know what to do, but they do not act in accordance with that knowledge. Good communicators elicit motivation; they don't just offer directives. For example, a physician might say to an enhancer, "Here is your prescription. This is absolutely the best medicine for your condition. Many patients have had tremendous success taking it." For a therapist suggesting family therapy to a reducer: "You might consider bringing your family to at least the next session. It could possibly be somewhat of an opportunity to learn how they seem to acknowledge you for at least some of things that you've accomplished."

One of the most valuable things that I've learned from my decades-long devotion to studying hypnosis is the principle (No. 17) of suggest-->motivate. Every directive can be followed with a personalized reason for carrying it out.

Enhancer/Reducer may be the most important characteristic in this grouping. It is axiomatic that many who seek therapy have developed a rigid pattern of enhancing the negatives in life and reducing positives. An obvious strategy to be happy in life is to enhance the positives and reduce the negatives.

3. Specific/General

Some people are more holistic in their orientation and some tend to focus on the details. For example, if two people attended the same event, one might reflect on the overall experience, while the other talks about intricate details. Clients tend to speak in generalizations, for example: "I am always uncomfortable." "I never get to places on time." "I never do anything perfectly." In these cases, focusing on specifics may help. The therapist could say: "Wouldn't you say that you are only uncomfortable when seeing your family?" or, "From what you tell me, you are mostly late for work."

4. Create/Delete/Distort

People are adept at creating, deleting, and/or distorting experiences. Human experience is subjective. We act on our perceptions of the world rather than on objective, quantifiable determinations. Thus, human behavior is highly idiosyncratic. We sometimes become rigidly fixated on one style, which can precipitate psychosocial difficulties.

In the practice of hypnosis, Create/Delete/Distort has heuristic value. Hypnotherapists learn to elicit hypnotic phenomena, including auditory, visual, and tactile hallucinations that can be positive or negative. Time distortion is a hypnotic phenomenon; so is age regression. An axiom of hypnotic treatment is to apply to the problem the hypnotic phenomena that the patient exhibits with ease. For example, if the problem is pain and the patient can easily achieve time distortion, he or she can increase the amount of time when feeling comfortable and decrease the amount of time when in pain. Someone who is good at age regression could go back in time before there was problematic pain.

In early sessions of hypnotherapy, practitioners might explore which hypnotic phenomena the patient does best. Understanding if a person can easily create, delete, or distort perception can facilitate the process. Those who are adept at deleting experiences might easily experience amnesia and/or negative hallucination. Those who distort experiences might be good at time distortion. People who create experiences might do well with age regression and hypermnesia (vivid recall).

Earlier, I listed three different ways of using the assessment categories: 1) To understand the position the client takes; 2) to guide the direction of the therapy or hypnosis; and 3) as motivators. Now, we can consider two additional uses: 4) How the person does the problem, and 5) How anyone does the solution to that problem. For example, if you wake up tomorrow morning and say to yourself, "It's a perfect day to be depressed," you might use a series of perceptual categories: internal, tactile, and negative enhancement. But if you wake up tomorrow morning and decide that you want to be like Milton Erickson, you will be external, visual, and enhance the positive.

Human behavior is both intrapsychic and relational. The following is another series of categories that are interpersonal and social.

Interpersonal (Relational/Social)

Human behavior has interpersonal valence. Most therapeutic problems are relational. People develop certain techniques and tactics for interacting with others, and the way in which one interacts could have to do with the following classifications:

1. Birth Order
2. Urban/Rural Upbringing
3. Extrapunitive<-->Intropunitive
4. Absorb<-->Emit
5. Direct<-->Indirect Responsiveness
6. Pursuer<-->Distancer
7. One Up<-->One Down

1. Birth Order

Oldest/only children tend to be shy, intellectual, serious, conscientious, and conservative. It's probably no coincidence that a high percentage of psychotherapists are oldest/only children, since these individuals in their formative years often assumed the responsibilities of caregiver to siblings or even parents—an established role that is continued in their profession as a psychotherapist.

Middle children tend to be independent, rebellious, and gregarious. They often excel in the arts. Youngest children can possess the characteristics of their older siblings. They may be charming, immature, affectionate, and agreeable.

Of course, such statements about birth order characteristics are only broad generalizations. Nonetheless, these generalizations can be used therapeutically to enhance compliance. For example, oldest children can often be motivated with directives that entice them to take care of things. Those born in-between two siblings might be given paradoxical directives because of their rebellious nature. Youngest children can be motivated by making them the center of attention.

There is much written on birth order. Those interested in pursuing this line of research might enjoy *Born to Rebel: Birth Order, Family Dynamics, and Creative Lives* (1997), by Frank Sulloway.

When patients and students consulted with Erickson he did not spend much time taking a history. Instead, he commonly asked them to complete questionnaires that supplied him with detailed information regarding birth order and whether they had an urban or rural upbringing. (Zeig, 1980, p. 32) Birth order characteristics and the characteristics of those reared in either a rural or urban environment carried much significance for Erickson. Erickson firmly believed that birth order and where individuals spent their formative years came into play in the therapeutic process. (An explication of Erickson's perspective on the difference between an urban and rural orientation can be found in *A Teaching Seminar with Milton H. Erickson*, Zeig, 1980, pp.232.)

2. Urban/Rural Upbringing

Erickson believed that people who grew up in the country were oriented to the future, whereas those who were reared in the city were more oriented to the present (Zeig, 1980, p. 231). Erickson was raised on a farm and was future-oriented. He might have acquired this orientation from his father who in his 90s planted fruit saplings, despite the odds of ever seeing them mature into fruit-bearing trees. Both of Erickson's parents possessed the trait of future-orientation. Early in their marriage, Erickson's mother canned a special batch of preserves. She told her husband that they would share the preserves on their 50th wedding anniversary. When that day arrived, the couple forgot to open them. Later, they decided to have the preserves on their 75th wedding anniversary. Unfortunately, they only celebrated 73 years together, and the preserves were handed down to Dr. and Mrs. Erickson.

Milton Erickson spent his formative years on a small farm in rural Wisconsin. The farm existed primarily to feed the family. The frigid winters in Wisconsin were so daunting that the family often preserved food for the winter. With his parents as exemplary models of future orientation, it's no surprise that Erickson himself was so motivated. In the first year of his marriage, he gave his wife, Elizabeth, a gift that he asked her to open on their fifth wedding anniversary.

I personally encountered Erickson's trait of long-term thinking when I took a spontaneous family photo of Dr. and Mrs. Erickson, their daughter, Roxanna, and Roxanna's newborn, Laurel. Before taking the photo, Erickson insisted on having an ironwood sculpture of an owl in the photo. In the photo, seated in his wheelchair, Erickson is cradling his granddaughter in his left arm while in his left hand, below Laurel, he is cupping the small, hand-carved ironwood sculpture of an owl that he had gifted Laurel to celebrate her birth. Laurel was fondly nicknamed "Screech" by her mother because the baby's powerful cry would sometimes pitch to what sounded like a screech. Thus, Erickson's gift to Laurel was apropos. However, later in the day, he pointed out to me a less obvious significance of that gift and why the owl sculpture had to be in the photo:

The screech owl adds tremendous meaning to that picture. It gives you the sense of humanity and kindness and thoughtfulness, and tremendously so. And it is a very simple thing. And it is a screech owl and yet she was a big girl, relatively speaking. The screech owl was down here. She was up here…Now, at age 16, when she looks at that, she is going to see the smallness of the screech owl, and the bigness of the little girl. That will be reunited with all her own feelings of bigness in high school and the warm memories of being a little baby and that little screech owl. So, you see how all of those memories are put together, unnoticeably. (Zeig, 1980, pp. 312-313)

Erickson was crafting an intervention, planning for an effect 16 years into the future. Now that is a rural orientation! As a farm boy, Erickson understood that when you plant seeds, you should not expect to immediately harvest crops.

An assessment of rural and urban characteristics can be made from language styles. As someone who was raised in an urban environment, I would never say, "I hopped on that quicker than a chicken on a June bug." Another characteristic that may betray my urban New York City upbringing is my Jewish ethnicity, because there are more Jewish people living in urban environments than there are in rural ones. Also, my physique may indicate that I spent time reading books as a child and not working in the fields. Regional accent, language style, style of dress, temporal orientation, and physical characteristics may indicate either a rural or urban upbringing.

I remember a case in which Erickson used his understanding of the "seasons of life." A woman was referred to me by Mrs. Erickson after Dr. Erickson died. She had previously been a patient of Dr. Erickson's when she was about 18 years old. The problem that she faced at that time was that she was falling and there was no medical explanation. The patient, an artist, was married to a stern, controlling husband, who happened to be an engineer. The physical manifestation (and certainly a metaphor) of this woman's dysfunctional relationship was that she could literally not stand up under the pressure of her dominant husband. But Erickson did not make that interpretation; it was not his style. He suggested to the couple that they consider divorce, but they protested, saying that they wanted to stay married for religious reasons. Erickson involved them in family planning, and the woman stopped falling. At the end of treatment, Erickson said to her: "You don't need any more therapy now. Some time when you are in your 40s, you may need more therapy." It was when she was in her 40s that she sought more therapy and became my client. Again, she was falling.

It was Erickson's future orientation that allowed him to create his prognostication. When she entered her 40s, the last child left home and she could no longer stand up to her controlling husband. My intervention was to get her involved in one of her interests—breeding dogs—which had a salutary effect.

In conclusion, developing a future orientation can enrich the therapist's work, as well as increase effectiveness with patients. Structural interventions are not necessarily tied to the here and now, and change does not often occur overnight. By looking to the future, the therapist can anticipate issues that their patients might face, and design strategies that can be useful at those junctures.

3. Extrapunitive<-->Intropunitive

People might be likened to belly buttons: some are "outies," some are "innies." An intropunitive person is self-critical, directing fault inwardly, while an extrapunitive person often blames the outside world for misfortunes (mildly extrapunitive people seem to report more happiness than intropunitive types).

An intropunitive person who overslept might moan, "Oh no! How could I have done that?" In comparison, the extrapunitive person could exclaim, "What's wrong with this alarm clock?"

An intropunitive person reading this book may think, "I'm not smart enough to absorb all of this information. I should have stayed in school." An extrapunitive thinker may think, "This author doesn't know what he's talking about. He should do more research!"

Since an intropunitive person often wonders, "What am I do-ing wrong?" the therapist could use this common thought in the creation of an induction:

Your conscious mind can notice all the mistakes that you make, but your unconscious mind can make no mistake in enjoying developing comfort.

The therapist could also present an extrapunitive person with something or someone to blame, and still afford this person a con-structive possibility:

Your conscious mind can notice all the mistakes that I make, but your unconscious mind can make no mistake in enjoying developing comfort.

Note that in these two examples the "resistance" is circumscribed to the conscious mind, while cooperation is attributed to the un-conscious.

A therapeutic directive for an extrapunitive client might include elements to reject because extrapunitive people have the need to reject and/or criticize. For example, a therapist working with an ex-trapunitive client who wants to lose weight might say, "As a child you were told, 'Finish everything on your plate and don't play with your food,' which was right for that time of your life, but directives can be challenged. So, this week at every meal, I want you to not finish everything on your plate and assiduously play with your food and be creative, but do it slowly. You say you're interested in archi-tecture, so fashion your food into a model of a building or house. And then get up from the table and rebelliously leave some of the food on the plate." With this directive, the extrapunitive client can have the delight of rejecting one or more of the elements of the cli-nician's complex assignment, while still accomplishing the overall goal of modifying food intake.

Balance is the preferred goal for the dynamic of intropunitive <-->extrapunitive, because having the flexibility to be self-critical can, at times, be helpful. However, overall, criticism and assigning blame are rarely constructive. Like enhancers and reducers, extra-punitive and intropunitive types tend to marry each other. Eventu-ally, marital distress may result from these personality differences.

4. Absorb<-->Emit

We have all seen individuals who, like the sun, emit their powerful "rays" so that it shines on those around them; they fill the room with energy and light. On the other hand, there are those who ab-sorb energy, soaking it up like a sponge. This quality of absorbing or emitting energy is most apparent in social situations.

An induction for an emitter might begin as follows:

Listen, I just read this book by Jeff Zeig, and while I'm not an expert on hypnosis, I think hypnosis could be useful to you, so I'd like to use it. But, I really need your help. Help me help you.

For an absorber:

You're not going to have to do anything. I'm going to do all the work. The experience of hypnosis will be like a psychological massage.

5. Direct<-->Indirect Responsiveness

Some people respond best to overt directives. Those in the military, for instance, are often responsive to direct commands. The same is true for police officers and firefighters, where there is also a chain of command. Others are extraordinarily responsive to minimal cues, so much so that they might unconsciously mimic the behavior of someone in their presence. If a therapist takes a deep breath and sighs, without even realizing it, those most responsive to minimal cues will do the same, perhaps because they have developed mirror neurons.

With the direct responsive individual, the therapist can use a more authoritarian approach. With those responsive to minimal cues, the therapist can use a more permissive, indirect method.

6. Pursuer<-->Distancer

In his systems theory, Thomas Fogarty (1978) discussed closeness in relationships, and focused on the difficulties inherent in developing emotional proximity in relationships. Fogarty points out two movement dimensions in relationships: 1) movement toward objects, and 2) movement toward people. The distancer tends to move away from people and toward objects. The pursuer moves toward people and places little value on objects.

Rather than labeling someone as a "distancer" or "pursuer," clinicians can use these dynamics as motivators to create inductions. For example, for a distancer: "Hypnosis may be of great value to you in accomplishing your goals, but let's take some time and consider things carefully before taking any action." For a pursuer: "Let's get down to work as quickly as possible."

Some people are like monkeys; others, like turtles. If there is a challenge, certain people move toward whereas others shy away. With patients who move toward, the therapist might say: "Let's come up with a plan now." For those who shy away, the therapist could say: "Let's take our time and proceed methodically."

7. One-up<-->One-down

Most dyadic relationships have two roles: one-up and one-down. (But, there are relationships based on maintaining equality.) The individual who is one-up takes charge, and makes decisions based on personal preferences. On the other hand, individuals who are one-down, monitor their environment for cues before acting. They base their decisions on external information, and often respond to the directions (open or implied) from the one-up individual. The therapist can observe both traits by their behavioral manifestations: one-up individuals tend to make steadier eye contact and have a bolder stance; one-down individuals are more tentative.

The Power Dynamic in Relationships:
Complementary and Symmetric Dynamics

In his book *Communication: The Social Matrix of Psychiatry* (1954), Gregory Bateson, observed that all communication contains an implicit message about relationships, and that all relationships could be categorized as either complementary or symmetric. Communication analysts Watzlawick, Beavin, and Jackson (1967), and Haley (1963), further developed Bateson's theories.

In a complementary relationship, the one-up person controls and defines the relationship, and the one-down person is responsive to the other's initiatives. Complementary relationships tend to be stable. In contradistinction, a symmetric relationship is one in which the participants insist on equality, and this type of relationship tends to be unstable.

Depending on the circumstances, a person can ideally fulfill both one-up and one-down roles in a relationship, because having the flexibility to do so is essential to a functional affiliation. For example, when teaching a workshop, I am one-up, controlling and defining the situation. But during a break, I may be one-down, avidly learning from a student. In teaching a workshop, I might assume a symmetric position with a challenging student, giving us both an opportunity to learn from each other.

Individuals rarely discuss or openly negotiate which position in the relationship they will assume. Rather, we automatically adopt one position or the other within seconds of encountering another individual. Hierarchies are ubiquitous in animal behavior, and are part of our evolutionary socio-biology.

Hierarchical positioning is not confined to the animal kingdom. When I was in my clinical psychology master's program at San Francisco State University the students were invited to spend the day at the Esalen Institute. The instructor, Will Shutz, told students to line up from the front of the room to the back. I was not surprised that some students struggled to be at the front of the line. However, I was surprised that the struggle to be at the back of the line was just as contentious. Most astonishing was the equally combative skirmish to be in the middle.

Sometimes roles in a relationship are set contextually: one partner might assume a one-up position in social situations, while the other takes command when it comes to handling financial matters.

Symmetric relationships, one ostensibly of equals, can be tenuous and unsteady as the two parties attempt to resolve the issue of who will dominate or attain one-up status. Consider this example dialogue in a systemic relationship:

Person A: I've been studying Erickson's work.

Person B: Well, I've been studying Erickson, too.

Person A: I understand that Erickson's most important contribution to hypnosis is the development of the confusion technique.

Person B: But my understanding of Erickson suggests his most important contribution is the interspersal technique.

Person A: Well, Jay Haley said that confusion is a part of every hypnosis induction.

Person B: That may be, but Erickson's paper on the interspersal technique was more important.

This escalation in the conversation can end in one of three ways:

It resolves into a complementary relationship where one person becomes one-up; the other, one-down. Person A might stop the escalation by saying: "What did Erickson say about the interspersal technique?"

There is an explosion and the relationship ends. Person A may eventually lose his temper and yell: "You know *nothing* about Erickson's work! I'm leaving." (In relationships that are physically or emotionally abusive, explosions and concomitant violence can be precipitated by simple things.)

The third possibility involves a governor that is employed in the system and allows the tension to escalate only to a certain degree.

The governor may be as simple as a nonverbal gesture, such as one partner crossing his or her arms. Once the governor is exhibited, the couple may either revert to more complementary roles, or they may change the topic, and thus, tension decreases.

In a functional relationship between two strong peers, a governor is often used, although it may not be consciously recognized. The partners support and admire each other's strength and have implicitly developed systems whereby stress is modulated. Paul Carter (1982) observed this phenomenon in a couple that began having marital problems after the husband quit smoking. It turned out that in this couple's relational system, reaching for a cigarette was a covert signal that there was uncomfortable tension. After the husband quit smoking, there was little to break the tension when it did arise. Without a governor, stress between two people in a symmetric relationship can painfully escalate.

Symmetric relationships that are ungoverned can quickly break down. Some people consistently struggle to dominate in relationships where equality is unattainable. An example of this is the couple who keeps a list of how much money each has spent during a week. At the end of the week, they tally it up to make sure that the exchange is fair. A conversation between individuals in such a relationship could be as follows:

He: All right, last time we went out, you paid for the movie and I paid for dinner. This time, you can pay for dinner, and I'll pay for the movie.

She: Are you sure about that? I think I paid for both the movie and dinner. Now it's your turn.

Symmetric relationships can be fraught with frequent clashes and conflicts. Because many aspects of this type of relationship are open to negotiation, struggles can become pervasive, even in the minutiae of day-to-day life. Many therapists have difficulty working with symmetric couples. Any feedback from the therapist that the couple is involved in a power struggle usually does not resonate. One member of the couple might respond, "Power struggle? I'm not involved in a power struggle. My partner may be in a power struggle, but not me!" Suddenly, the therapist finds him- or herself in an escalating symmetric relationship with that patient.

As mentioned earlier, difficulties can arise when there is an inability to flexibly assume (depending on the circumstances) a one-up, one-down, or symmetric role. People fall into the habit of rigidly assuming a stereotypic role in all circumstances. I once visited a European professor who was so insistent on maintaining a one-up position that he spent much of our time together correcting my English (incorrectly, I might add).

Erickson was consistently one-up in his relationships. I first met him when he was 72 years old, so in my observation, Erickson's one-up position was not just a personality trait, but also due to his professional status, age, and self-confidence. Erickson's wealth of experience and keen perceptiveness led him to control and define relationships. I observed Erickson in the one-down position on only one occasion. I had inadvertently made a pun that threw him off balance, but he quickly regained his composure, and topped me with another pun. His recovery to reinstate his one-up position was so swift that I became confused and startled…so much so, that to this day I cannot remember the pun that I made.

In his work, Erickson was most often one-up, which is a common position for conducting hypnosis and psychotherapy, because in this model the therapist works to elicit adaptive states. However, sometimes it could be beneficial to be one-down as a therapeutic strategy.

The great family therapist, Carl Whitaker, MD was expert at using the one-down position. I visited him in 1980 when he was in residence at the Philadelphia Child Guidance Clinic. The setting was a master class in family therapy in which the students were in the outer circle and the family and Whitaker sat in the inner circle. The identified patient was a psychotic young adult. Shortly after beginning the interview, Whitaker briefly fell asleep. When he awoke he recounted a dream that was somehow relevant to the family dynamic. A few minutes later, he fell asleep again, and when he awoke he reported another dream that resonated with the family. The third time Whitaker fell asleep and awoke, the patient's father asked Whitaker to explain. Whitaker admitted, "I often fall asleep when I get anxious."

Whitaker's admission allowed family members who were initially anxious, to feel more at ease. The psychotic young man started speaking comprehensibly. By the end of the interview, the family was cohesive. They hugged Whitaker and departed.

As students, we were nonplussed. Whitaker, the consummate systems thinker, explained: "Craziness only occupies one space and social system." Whitaker's unusual behavior had a systemic effect: The family members' behavior changed and they pulled together. In this case, change was facilitated by the therapist assuming a one-down position.

Years later, Whitaker told me about his only meeting with Erickson. Erickson was lecturing in Atlanta and Whitaker went to the airport to meet him. Upon getting into the car, Erickson asked Whitaker, "How many children do you have?" Whitaker replied that he had six. Erickson told Whitaker that he had eight children. Whitaker said that from that moment on the roles were set: Erickson was one-up and Whitaker was one-down.

Erickson was consistently in the one-up position, working to create evocative experiences. His position was like that of many religious leaders. As a hypnotist, his role was to elicit changes in state in patients and students, which required a one-up role.

I once asked Erickson if he ever got tired of teaching similar themes. Taken aback, he answered, "No, I'm purely interested in what I can learn." Being in the one-up position does not exclude learning. When a client is inflexible and insists on maintaining a specific position, change can be impeded, or even impossible to achieve.

Telling an inflexible one-up person that he or she strives to be one-up is ineffective in bringing about change. It might not be central to the complaint that the client brings. Moreover, the response from the patient could be a meta-communication with the person saying, "That's an interesting comment," because this type of individual has developed skillful maneuvers for parrying overt challenges to the steadfast position of being one-up.

Some people insist on being one-down, often presenting as a long-suffering victim of exaggerated shortcomings and others' insensitivities. For example, the grandmother in this hypothetical dialogue:

Grandson: Grandma, how are you doing?

Grandma: Oh, I'm lonely.

Grandson: Why don't you go out and meet some people?

Grandma: Oh, my bones ache and it's too far to walk out into the neighborhood.

Grandson: Why don't you call a few people and have them come over?

Grandma: I would, but you don't understand, this place is such a mess and I don't have the energy to clean it up.

Grandson: Why don't you call people and just talk on the phone?

Grandma: I would, but I can't hear too well. And it takes so much energy.

Upon closer examination, there are interesting underlying dynamics of Grandma's seemingly one-down position. While Grandma is clearly presenting herself in a victim role, she's controlling and defining the relationship as much as a one-up person would. Bateson described this position as "meta-complementary." (Haley, 1963) A meta-complementary bind occurs when a person assumes a one-down position to actually become one-up. It is called a bind because the person does not define or experience themselves as one-up. In traditional psychiatric nomenclature, this process is known as "secondary gain."

But discussing secondary gain with someone rarely produces

therapeutic change. If you were to suggest to a rigidly one-down person, such as Grandma, that she was controlling the relationship by using her symptoms, she might reply, "What do you mean I'm in control? *I'm* the one who's suffering!"

During my graduate school internship, I treated a woman who was afraid of venturing into stores. Curiously, her surname was a synonym of "store." Her husband had a one-up personality. The woman's fear placed her more deeply in her in the one-down position. But, because her condition prevented her from doing the family shopping, a task her husband had to take on, she gained a measure of control in her marital relationship, which put her in the one-up meta-complementary position. At the time, I did not recognize the imbalances in the marriage and the wife's struggle to achieve parity and competence. Today, if I were I to treat a similar case, I would suggest couples therapy.

The one-up person not only controls and defines the relationship, he or she also induces roles in the one-down person, which can be functional or maladaptive. The roles implicitly assigned to the one-down person could include being stupid, unlovable, or incompetent. But the one-up person could also "induce" in the other person constructive roles, such as being intelligent or creative.

Because the one-up person can induce roles and adaptive states, there is therapeutic significance to being in this position. Consider a family with a disturbed hierarchy where an acting-out child dominates his parents. By taking control of the relationship, the child has the power to induce roles in the parents of being impotent and incompetent. In her classic book, *Strategic Family Therapy* (1981), Cloé Madanes demonstrated that using strategic therapy to alter family hierarchies is therapeutic and can alleviate symptoms. Rearranging the hierarchy can often be achieved through a "right hemisphere" approach, such as assigning tasks or using metaphoric communication. Straightforward discussions are usually of little value in changing the hierarchical power/status dynamics, since jockeying for position does not wholly occur on the conscious, verbal level, but is navigated implicitly. Upon encountering someone, we don't say to ourselves, "Well, in this situation, I'm going to be one-up or one-down." Nevertheless, as stated earlier, these roles are determined in the first few seconds of an encounter through non-verbal behavior, such as demeanor, tone, posture, etc.

Interventions Using Hierarchies

A heuristic principle (No. 18) is : Psychotherapy can be effected on the same level in which the problem is generated. If a problem is generated at verbal levels, it can be solved through open discussion. If the problem is generated at implicit ("unconscious" or limbic) levels, therapy could be directed there. Communication can be used that is based on our sociobiological evolution. Experiential methods address and activate lower brain centers. Most problems are generated at the level of preconscious associations that are not intentional. Therefore, tasks, metaphors, and other "right hemisphere" methods that use "limbic communication" and elicit new associations and disconnect maladaptive rigid sets can be effective therapeutic techniques. Making the unconscious conscious is not the only road to change. Just as a child who is learning a language does primarily through unconscious processes, other changes in human behavior can be made without conscious mediation.

Paul Watzlawick (1982, p. 150) provides an excellent example of Erickson using a right hemisphere method (also reported in Haley, 1973):

A couple ran their small restaurant together and constantly quarreled about the best way of running it. The wife insisted that the husband should be in charge, because she would rather stay home. The husband pointed out that she would never let him do that because she thought that without her supervision he would ruin the business. After a detailed exploration of this interaction in which cause typically produced effect which bent back on cause, Erickson gave them a behavioral prescription. Each morning the husband was to go to the restaurant half an hour before his wife. This simple change, apparently so "remote" from the "real"

problem, totally threw the ingrained mechanism of their ingrained vi-
cious cycle interaction out of kilter. When the wife arrived at the restau-
rant, she was now hopelessly behind in her routine and the husband had
already completed part of her seemingly irreplaceable functions. She
soon realized that she could arrive an hour late, or even later, and she
also found that she did not have to stay with him until closing time. She
thus found more and more time to devote to their home and he became
increasingly capable of running the restaurant alone.

Erickson was acutely tuned into habitual styles of being one-up and
one-down, and he often used strategic tasks, jokes, and even confusion techniques to disrupt inflexible patterns of behavior. Since
one of the main goals of therapy is to elicit more effective roles and
states, it is important that therapists learn to assess hierarchical
styles.

Moreover, therapists should keep in mind the power dynamics
of the therapist-patient relationship. To induce change, the therapist must be in the one-up position. Besides, the patient is paying
the therapist to guide the experience in an adaptive direction. And,
the conversation in therapy is predominately one-sided, whereby
the clinician focuses on the patient's situation. If the patient is consistently one-up, the therapy will not be successful.

The job of the therapist is to work on the patient's behalf to
elicit change. This can only be accomplished when the therapist is
in the one-up position—controlling and defining the relationship
in a manner derived from professional training and experience.
Moreover, it is the job of the therapist to induce or elicit adaptive
states and social roles, which requires controlling and defining the
relationship. Methods offering experiential realizations are central
to effective therapy, and require the clinician to be in the one-up
position.

Using the Power Dynamic in Tailoring Hypnosis

Using an eye-fixation induction with a one-up person, the therapist might begin by saying: See that figurine on my desk? Just look in that general direction. This strategy gives the patient choices. The one-up person values taking charge and this directive provides the opportunity to do so. Still, the choice offered is confined within the frame of hypnosis and within the parameters loosely defined by the therapist.

An eye-fixation induction with a one-down person can be more direct: See that figurine on my desk? Look at the reflection of the light on the top of it and use that to focus your visual attention.

The therapist can also move away from the preferred polarity. Hypnosis with a one-up person can progress so that the individual feels increasingly comfortable in the one-down position. With a one-down person, the therapist might assume a meta-complementary stance of also being one-down, to implicitly encourage the patient to be more assertive.

In 1964, Erickson conducted an induction with a woman who tended to be one-down. In the middle of the induction, he suddenly said to her in a lilting, childlike voice, "You know my name is Milton. My mother gave me that name a long time ago." By mimicking the voice of a little boy, Erickson was, in part, evoking the woman's understanding of a mother-son relationship, which in effect prompted the patient into a one-up position, and subsequently, she commented that Milton was "a nice name."

Summary

The assessment categories outlined in this chapter are the ones that I most often use in my work, however, many others exist, including: Affiliative/Independent; Spectator/Participant; Defend/ Attack; Abstract/Concrete; Warm/Cool; Open/Closed; Compliance-based/Defiance-based; Consistent/Inconsistent; Introvert/ Extrovert; Global/Specific; Flexible/Rigid, etc. Other practitioners will have different perspectives and create their own list of assessment categories.

Now, these categories are not meant to be definitive, but they can be used in multiple ways:

- As sign posts for guiding the therapist in creating effective hypnotic inductions. To create a subjective difference, working with and against the preferred polarity.
- To more effectively individualize therapy by focusing treatment through the client's lens.
- To speak the experiential language of the patient, thereby more fully empathizing with the patient's situation.
- To tailor motivation. For example, a linear person can be given sequential reasons to do a therapeutic task. An internal person can do the task to feel better.
- To determine how the client does the problem. This entails mapmaking (the topic of Chapter Six). To do depression, a client could be internal, tactile, enhance the negative, move away socially, assume a one-down position, etc.
- To model effectiveness. Modeling is one the most important contributions of NLP. To model Milton Erickson, one might be external, visual, enhance the positive, strive to be in the one-up position, etc.

Once again, there is no absolute measure of where a client may fall along the spectrum of polarities. Interpretations are strictly contingent upon the reference point of the individual therapist. For example, one therapist might assess a patient as being external, whereas another sees the patient as internal. The patient may, in fact, simply be more external than the first clinician—and more internal than the second. In the same vein, a clinician who is highly intropunitive might assess a client as being extrapunative. In both these examples, the distinction made is relative to the therapist's own characteristics. Assessment using these categories is a matter of perception, not science.

Another assessment method involves the use of distinctions that identify characteristic patterns. Some patterns are set biologically.

Fixed Action Patterns

A fixed action pattern is an instinctive response in animal behavior triggered by a specific stimulus. This pattern has been extensively studied by ethologists. Once triggered, the pattern can't be stopped and must play out to completion. An example is the mating dance of some species of birds. Although some experts may not consider fixed action patterns to be a part of human behavior, there are redundant processes in humans that seem strikingly similar.

Imagine for a moment that we are unobtrusively observing a group of people who have just been presented with a serious crisis. Before long, we would notice a response in markedly different ways—responsiveness splintering into characteristic forms.

For example, there could be a physiological response: some might demonstrate a diuretic reaction; some, a peristaltic one. (Yup, in the vernacular, some people might have the "piss scared out of them," and others be "scared shitless.")

There are also characteristic differences in personality style when confronted with limbic arousal. One person could act as a bold lion; another as a skittish gazelle; another as a possum, who "plays possum"; another as a motionless fawn; another as a withdrawing turtle; or another as a young animal who wants to run to mother. When faced with serious difficulty, characteristically some people fight, others flee, some fold, some freeze, some hide, some cling, and some submit and let others take charge. Among animals, the most common response to danger is to flee.

There would also be a characteristic emotional response. Depending on emotional makeup and habit, some people would display fear, whereas others would exhibit anger, excitement, frustration, or even guilt.

If the parents of these individuals were on the scene, it is likely that we could quickly match them to their children, based on both the parents' and an individual's problem-solving strategies. Strategies are often passed down through generations. Problem-solving strategies are probably not a genetic predisposition, but rather the transference of a set of learned behaviors fixed action patterns) that people exhibit when observing and reacting to their worlds. Perhaps some are epigenetic. These physiological, social and/or emotional patterns of behavior or "heirlooms" can also be thought of as "hooks."

Hooks

Patients cannot only be evaluated according to assessment categories, but a therapist can also consider the patient's characteristic position or hooks, which determine how a patient acts and reacts. Specific hooks lead to repetitive and redundant patterns of behavior to which the patient commonly adheres. They have relational value, and are often mechanisms that people use to maintain homeostasis in a relationship.

Fisch, Weakland, and Segal (1983) were the first to write about the concept of "hooks." (In subsequent publications of their work, the authors replaced the term with "positions.") I learned about hooks more than 10 years prior to reading the authors' book in a training seminar I attended at the Mental Research Institute in the early 1970s.

The assessment categories I presented earlier have heuristic value, but there is an inherent risk of a therapist rigidly adhering to the categories. For example, it might be easy to openly categorize someone as an enhancer, but I doubt it would have therapeutic value. Thinking in terms of the patient's hooks is a more fluid and flexible approach. It's a matter of assessing the position that a patient takes. As I indicated earlier, Erickson was not interested in labeling or categorizing patients, but he implicitly used hooks to advance the therapy.

A hook does not have to be judged as being either positive or negative; a hook simply represents a person's position. Here are a few examples:

- Being tentative
- Providing only partial information, unless prodded
- Being overly analytical and slow to respond
- Always taking charge of a situation; being a leader
- Being selfless and giving
- Telling people what one thinks the other wants to hear
- Constantly needing assurance
- Being careful and fastidious
- Being oblivious to the effect one's behavior has on others
- Always telling the truth
- Lying
- Moving slowly
- Wearing stylish clothing

Positive or negative, hooks are what people value. For example, some people may be hooked to lying, valuing it for what it can bring them, perhaps even feeling entitled to engage in deception, whereas others may value honesty and take pride in always telling the truth.

Hooks encompass more than just personality traits. Erickson once autographed a book for me with the statement, "Just another book to curl your hair," because he knew I was proud of and valued my curly hair.

Hooks may have had value for a client in the past, but they may not be adaptive in the present. Still, once a pattern of behavior is initiated, it tends to continue until the pattern is played out.

The concept of determining a patient's hooks works on two levels: 1) It offers the therapist an assessment about the patient, and 2) it can be used to tailor directives, with the therapist using hooks as a tool for individualizing treatment.

There is a tendency for people to behave in the way they value and value the way they behave. Once the client's value system is determined, therapy can then be tailored to fit that system, in other words, focused through the patient's lens. For example, if the patient values selflessness, therapy can be hooked to that value by encouraging the patient to change for the benefit of others. For a selfish individual, therapy can be framed solely for the patient's personal gain.

Hooks are generally preconscious patterns. Most people give them little thought, or are completely unaware of them. Patients may ignore their hooks in the same way we ignore steady state information such as music being played in a grocery store, restaurant, or elevator, or the drone of an air-conditioner or car engine. Therapists, however, should be aware of hooks because utilizing them can advance the therapy.

There are an infinite number of hooks to which patients may be attached. I will provide eight categories that I have identified and frequently use to guide my assessments. These distinctions may help clinicians answer the meta-question: "What position does the client take?" The best possible orientation is to minimize the rigid use of distinctions and focus on the meta-question, but the following distinctions may be useful to therapists to determine the best treatment.

1. Personality Patterns/Social Roles

Personality patterns are often easy for clinicians to assess. I once had a patient who was an only child. One parent had a severe physical handicap; the other had serious emotional problems. From an early age, the patient had been taught to be "quiet," "careful," and "responsible." He learned his lessons well and became hooked to these behaviors, and was thus highly competent in situations where the behaviors were valued and necessary. Unfortunately, his personality pattern hampered his ability to loosen up in situations that required a different repertoire, such as being playful with his family. To help him, I also valued his hooks, and emphasized through therapeutic directives (including hypnosis) the usefulness of processes that were quiet, careful, and responsible, but led to adaptive results.

Other personality patterns that patients display could include feeling inadequate, being judgmental, loyal, confident, and so forth. These personality patterns are social roles to which one becomes habituated.

2. Language Patterns

To establish rapport and to offer directives, it is valuable for clinicians to understand linguistic hooks. Certain language patterns often accompany personality patterns. For instance, a highly organized person may be exceedingly precise in her speech, choosing her words and phrases very carefully.

Linguistic patterns can be therapeutically useful, but they are sometimes difficult to discern because they seamlessly blend into the client's communication, and, as mentioned earlier, we tend to ignore steady state information and redundancies. Some clients may repeatedly use minimizing qualifiers such as: "a little," "somewhat," "just a bit," or "it seems." Also, language patterns can indicate the nature of the patient's problem. For example, anxious patients may go to default phrases such as, "What if…?" Depressed clients may use phrases such as, "If only…" A patient's communication may be peppered with filler words and phrases such as, "Okay, so…," "I mean…," "…like…," "So anyway…," and "…you know?" These may seem like useless utterances, but to develop rapport, a clinician can subtly mirror and effectively use the patient's familiar and comfortable redundant words or phrases. Using the patient's language patterns can also make ensuing suggestions more memorable and effective.

Other linguistic patterns clients use, include figures of speech and metaphors. Clients may be formal in their language, or use slang or colloquialisms. And again, the therapist can pick up whatever expressions the client uses to advance the treatment.

Language patterns can facilitate hypnosis. When an individual habitually answers "no" when presented with a "yes" or "no" question, the therapist can utilize this pattern by using a double or even triple negation for a therapeutic directive:

It's not that you don't want to exercise this week, is it not?

Symptom descriptors can be hypnotically reframed. For example, if a patient describes his physical pain as "burning, pressure, and tenderness," in a hypnotic induction, the clinician can reframe symptom words as hypnotic words:

There is no need to experience the pressure...of sitting comfortably in the chair. Your inner mind can monitor the pressure...of your hands resting on your legs, and make any adjustment that can increase your sense of evolving comfort. And you can suddenly realize comforting moments as a child, remembering how you had a burning desire to play with friends, and how the tenderness of your friends made you feel so comfortable.

Micro methods, such as reframing symptom words as hypnotic words, are not beneficial alone, but they can work synergistically in combination with other methods.

When I began my career as a therapist, I would write down what the patient said in the first session so I could later analyze language redundancies. Eventually, I became attuned to redundancies and no longer needed to record the first sessions, but it was helpful at the beginning.

3. Conspicuous Absences

With training, therapists can attune themselves to notice behaviors that are conspicuously absent in the patient. Of course, "conspicuous absence" is an oxymoron. But, be aware: What is absent is often more difficult to perceive than an actual aberration.

Conspicuous absences can be psychological or physical. Psychologically, someone might have a conspicuous absence of assertiveness or another emotion. Some people have a physical absence. I had a friend whose fingers were amputated, but it was weeks before I noticed.

Erickson told numerous stories about students who did not recognize things that should have been obvious. For example, one of his students brought his wife with him to see Erickson and Erickson pointed out that the student's wife had webbed toes. The student had not previously noticed that his wife had webbed toes, but even more curious, the wife didn't recognize it until Erickson pointed it out.

To compensate for inattentional blindness, Erickson instructed his students to notice conspicuous absences in patients upon meeting them, so that the patient's behavior and problems might be better understood. Erickson said students should be aware if a patient had good eyesight in both eyes; could hear clearly out of both ears; had 10 functioning fingers, etc.

There can also be conspicuous absences in verbal language and body language. Someone may not use adjectives or adverbs, or body movements might be constrained. Perhaps a prosocial behavior is missing, such as smiling or laughing. Some people may value not having a certain quality or behavior in their psychological (emotional/behavioral/social) makeup. For example, they may feel proud that they rarely get angry or cry.

4. Nonverbal Patterns

Nonverbal patterns can include intense eye contact or the avoidance of eye contact. Some individuals enjoy being touched while others shy away from it. Clients may use characteristic gestures when speaking; the gestures may be large or small, expressive or cryptic. Proximity maneuvers, such as moving closer or moving away from people and requiring more personal space, are nonverbal patterns. The therapist can become adept at noticing characteristics, and more.

5. Security Operations

I use the term "security operation" to describe a specific subclass of verbal or nonverbal behaviors that people use to promote psychosocial comfort. Such behaviors might be as simple as someone scratching her head, playing with his hair, stretching her legs, crossing his arms, or mumbling "uh-huh." However, security operations are not necessarily effective in achieving psychological comfort. Perhaps a security operation was effective in the past, but in the long run, security operations rarely have an adaptive function. For example, a compulsion such as hand washing (considered a neutralizing activity) may initially alleviate a person's fear of contamination, but when continuously done, it no longer circumvents fear, but instead promotes anxiety.

Therapists should pay close attention to a patient's mannerisms, especially in stressful situations, i. e., early in the first session. This is a time when patients feel most uncertain, and will therefore actively display security operations. Therapists can constructively utilize a patient's security operations when conducting a hypnotic induction or guided fantasy. For example, if a client always crosses his arms on his chest, the therapist can offer a story in which the protagonist surmounts a problem and then triumphantly crosses his arms on his chest.

6. Time

People tend to be past, future, or present oriented, and the way in which someone orients to time could contribute to the presented problem. If it does, the therapist can create a treatment plan using the patient's orientation. Consider the patient whose conversation is filled with references to the past. Being overly involved with an unchangeable past can contribute to depression. Likewise, someone who intensely anticipates the future, often experiences anxiety. When creating an induction for a patient who is obsessed with either the past or future, the therapist can attempt to reorient her to be more present-focused. By its very nature, a hypnotic induction tends to absorb a patient in the immediate experience (see Zeig, 2014), and is therefore present-oriented.

But someone can also be too present-oriented. For example, if an adolescent is only interested in "what's happening now," he might fail to consider the lessons of the past or be aware of possible future consequences. This adolescent would be living "in time." But, the ideal position is living "through time," where one lives in the present, directed toward the future, but still considers past lessons and future consequences.

Assessing how someone relates to time can also include noticing whether a person prefers to do things slowly or quickly. Some problems are exacerbated by the way in which individuals use time. Both overeating and anxiety are often based in doing things rapidly. For more information, see *The Time Paradox; The New Psychology of Time That Will Change Your Life* by Philip Zimbardo (2009).

7. Relational Requirements

Relational requirements are processes by which individuals overtly or covertly require something of another person. It's easier to notice a relational requirement when working with couples or families than it is when working exclusively with an individual client. Examples of relational requirements would be one person unreasonably requiring another to speak in a certain way (slowly or distinctly); needing the other party to express vulnerability; consistently interrupting in couples therapy to comment on and explain a partner's behavior; demanding explicit advice; and obsessively needing to know why something is the way it is.

It is often the case that relational requirements are an indicator of psychological distress; the more intense and demanding the client is with relational requirements, the more severe the personality problem. Hence, it is important for therapists to identify relational patterns.

Many clinicians find it difficult to describe interaction patterns and discern the implicit rules that govern relationships, especially those that are intimate. Our vocabulary is designed around person-centered descriptions, not interaction patterns. Love and anger are primarily described as internal states, but those emotions could also be patterns of interaction between people. For example, an interactional definition of love could be described by using the acronym, TOPIAH, meaning: Take Obvious Pleasure In Another's Happiness. Love is an interaction pattern in which the partners openly take pleasure when the significant other is engaged in something he or she enjoys. Once a therapist is experienced in family and/or couples therapy, systemic understanding of patterns often emerges.

8. Sequences

When deconstructed, hooks consist of both components and sequences; they are not static entities. Hooks are repetitive and redundant patterns of behavior that happen over time. In *Games People Play* (1964), Eric Berne gives a brilliant description of sequential patterns he called "games."

Here is Berne's sequential formula for games: Con+Gimmick-->Response-->Switch-->Confusion-->Bad Feeling Payoff.

An analogy to explain: A fish swimming in a lake sees a worm dangling on a hook. The con is the dangling worm designed to capture attention and the "gimmick" in Berne's vernacular is the weakness (perhaps inattention or hunger) that allows the fish to overlook the hook. The fish wants the worm, so the response is to bite it. The switch occurs when the line is pulled up. There is a moment of confusion because the fish did not expect the switch. In this analogy, the bad feeling payoff is the demise of the fish.

Here's a business analogy: Person A tells Person B that she would love to open a business but does not have the money. Person B offers to provide financing. Person A accepts the offer, but when she moves forward with her business plan, Person B suddenly withdraws the financial support, to the dismay and confusion of Person A, who was so caught up in her enthusiasm that she did not consider Person B's history of offering help in new business ventures, but then abruptly pulling out of the deal. Person A's business plan falls through and she suffers financial difficulties.

Games people play are composed of sequential steps. Now, one sequence is not enough to assess a pattern, but an experienced therapist will eventually recognize a pattern and be able to use it therapeutically.

Here's an example of a sequence:

Patient: I'm feeling stressed out, teetering on the edge of exhaustion.

Therapist: I would say it's about time for a vacation.

Patient: What an excellent idea. But, I can't take a vacation. I think I'll take a weekend off.

Therapist: Sounds good.

Patient: Wait a second...we can't take a weekend trip because my wife is working on an important project. It will be quite some time before we can get away for even a day. I'm never going to get any rest. Things don't seem to work out for me. Everyone else takes vacations but I guess I don't deserve a real vacation.

This patient's sequence can be broken down into six steps:

    i. Asks for advice by implication.
    ii. Compliments the therapist for providing excellent advice.
    iii. Modifies the advice given.
    iv. Finds a flaw in the advice.
    v. Feels frustrated.
    vi. Assumes an intropunitive, self-berating "victim" stance.

In transactional analysis, this pattern might be labeled a "Yes-But" game.

This sequence can be used constructively, for example, in formulating a hypnotic induction. The utilization principle (No. 19) dictates that whatever the client does to create a problem could also be refashioned to create a solution. The sequence of a problem can be incorporated into a hypnotic procedure, whereby elements are constructively reframed and the outcome is constructive.

The following is a hypothetical sequence induction for this patient:

    i. You might find yourself becoming comfortable as effortlessly guided by your inner mind...

ii. *...and you can take time to really appreciate the advice, the supervision of your inner mind as it finds a focus for comfort...*

iii. *...although there might be another experience like a memory or an image that you think will help you to better realize comfort.*

iv. *But, you can find that it is impossible to generate comfort in all parts of your body...*

v. *...and your conscious mind may be frustrated with your efforts.*

vi. *And, your conscious mind can be the victim of its struggle to realize comfort...but your inner mind can realize comfort within...in your way, the way that is right for you.*

In addition to creating hypnotic inductions, there are other ways of utilizing sequences. And, the effect of combined utilization strategies can be synergistic. It's the therapist's job to gift-wrap concepts in such a way that the client realizes them and then assumes adaptive states.

Laying out the steps of a sequence offers insight for clinicians as to how the sequence can be disrupted. A common objective is to interrupt the sequence at a weak point. This can be done by adding a step. For instance, in the earlier example, at the point where the patient becomes enthused about the therapist's advice, the therapist might interject the suggestion that the patient pause, take a deep breath, stroke his face, or engage in some other seemingly innocuous action. Any directive could be valuable at that juncture, because a small modification in the sequence can have a snowball effect in eliciting change.

The therapist might also bring the sequence to the patient's attention, and then both patient and therapist can devise ways to disrupt the overall pattern. In psychotherapy, there is certainly a place for insight, and some patients may benefit from the awareness of an unconscious pattern.

The eight distinctions can be useful in making an assessment and understanding the position that the client takes. The "hooks" can also be considered constituent elements of the assessment categories. For example, a person who is one-up in a relationship has specific ways of relating to time, and uses specific language forms, nonverbal patterns, sequences, conspicuous absences, relational requirements, and security operations. There are also elements of any personality pattern—adaptive or maladaptive.

In summary, creating an assessment is basically structural, that is, addressing patterns that exist in the present that can be instrumental in deciding treatment goals, gift-wrapping methods, and even therapeutic processes. A structural assessment is a comprehensive way of determining how the client does the problem. To accomplish assessment, the therapist can create a map in which elements can be targeted to more effectively promote change.

While assessment categories and hooks are a foundation, more complex maps can be created to further improve treatment outcomes. In the next chapter, we return to depression as an example used for complex mapping.

The principles in this chapter:

17. Suggest-->Motivate
18. Psychotherapy can be affected on the same level in which the problem is generated.
19. Whatever the client does to create a problem could also be refashioned to create a solution.

CHAPTER SIX

Advanced Mapmaking

Introduction

A phenomenological orientation to "depression" leads to the view that depression can be considered a social construction, rather than a disease of insufficient neural transmitters. Tabbing depression as a social construct is valuable because it allows the therapist to create social, rather than medical, interventions.

A radical conclusion to viewing depression as a social construction is that depression does not exist—at least not as the disease commonly understood by professionals in the mental health field—and neither does anxiety or any other psychosocial problem.

My purpose in making such a heretical assertion, which is clearly at odds with prevailing tradition, is to be practical, not provocative. Do I believe that depression does not exist? Well, yes and no. My answer depends on what is clinically expedient. Something that is true in one context may not be true in another context.

There are big truths and little truths. Little truths are absolutes; big truths arise when both the assertion and its negation can be equally true. For example, in physics, light is not a singularity; it can behave as both a particle and a wave. Similarly, psychological problems, such as anxiety and depression, are not singularities and can assume various forms.

For example, a psychological problem can be considered a state, an interaction pattern, a redundant temporal sequence, a skill set deficit, a physiological process, a psychological style, or as a system that includes several of these factors. How a clinician "maps" the problem defines the treatment approach to be used. To effectively navigate the complex terrain of depression, a map is necessary, as it will provide relevant choices. In this chapter, I encourage clinicians to create complex maps of a client's presenting problem as doing so can lead to quicker, more effective treatment.

In this chapter, I focus on depression, but all psychological problems can be mapped. A therapist can map anxiety, a bad habit, an unfulfilling relationship, and so on. A client's strengths can also be mapped, something that could be useful in establishing solution-focused goals.

In this chapter, I outline models of phenomenological assessment and include concomitant indications for treatment. I also expand on the idea of phenomenological maps to better understand a client's subjective reality. Both therapists and clients already have maps before treatment begins. These maps are the therapist's and client's subjective reality of the problem, which can be limiting. However, if a therapist creates a more complex map of a problem, it provides more options for social intervention.

Patient Maps

Patients have simple titles for the complex, implicit maps they use for negotiating life and creating order in a chaotic world. However, titles are often static nominalizations that can lead to rigid rules of social conduct. "Nominalization" is turning a word that is not a noun, into a noun. The use of nominalizations allows one to speak concisely. But, nominalizing something complex can turn it into a label, which can obscure underlying, dynamic processes. Nominalizing places limitations on both the patient and therapist. Metaphorically speaking, it is imprisonment for both parties. But, defining a problem as both a complex of elements and processes, and treating it as such, can be a get-out-of-jail card. If the problem is physical, for example, treating a condition with medication is fine. But, when using a social intervention, addressing underlying components and processes is a better approach.

Depression is a nominalization of the verb "to depress," or its gerund, "depressing." Depression is not a single entity, and labeling it as such can subsequently evolve into the static belief that it is "a thing." Believing explicitly or implicitly that depression is tangible is not helpful in composing psychotherapy.

People often refer to themselves as "depressed," without realizing that their depression is a complex, dynamic process. Moreover, being depressed can become a codified lifestyle; it can become one's identity. Now, as a clinician, I empathize with a client's description of an emotional state, and I don't discount a limiting self-definition. However, I strive to create a different label—one that has utility in promoting desired change. To do so, I think in terms of how a patient "does" a problem. For example, how is the client "depressing" himself or herself? By thinking this way, I change the nominalization of depression into both components and processes.

Viewing a problem, such as depression, as consisting of components and processes is helpful because a component or a process is easier to change than an entity. Patients often present problems to therapists as if they were things to be modified. Clients also overtly or covertly request that the therapist cure the presenting problem, as if the therapist has special powers and the client has little or no control over the situation. Therapy is more effective when the therapist helps a patient to experientially realize that he or she is the author of his or her own life script, not merely a passive victim of an unchangeable disease.

The Disease Model

Categorizing depression as a disease may have utility to nosologists, demographers, statisticians, insurance companies, clinical researchers, physicians, psychiatrists, and, of course, the pharmaceutical industry, but to frontline psychotherapists making social interventions, such categorization has limited heuristic value. A diagnosis is a treatment plan. Diagnosing a patient with the disease of depression implicitly limits the treatment to medical intervention. Therapists, however, can treat people by helping them alter their experience. And they can do this by first creating a more constructive, malleable label for a patient's problem. At the very least, the therapist could posit that the patient is to some extent "depressing" himself or herself through action or inaction, because this implies possibilities for personal agency.

A common contemporary perspective is that depression is solely due to a brain dysfunction or chemical imbalance. In psychotherapy, it is not practical to have such a restricted view because it limits choices for social intervention. I prefer a teleological perspective, orienting first to therapeutic flexibility and effectiveness. From this vantage point, I can deconstruct a problem into components, each of which can be changed by social intervention. Deconstruction creates distinctions that have therapeutic and heuristic value; however, it necessitates understanding the patient's phenomenology: the implicit meaning of his or her lived experience.

Before I explain phenomenological maps, I want to offer some reflections about the contemporary practice of cognitive behavioral therapy (CBT) because it will provide an orientation to heuristics and algorithms.

Cognitive Behavioral Therapy

CBT, the application of behavior therapy techniques to cognitions, is a popular psychotherapeutic model for the treatment of depression. Research studies on CBT abound that show that CBT can physically change the brain. This is not surprising, considering that the mind can change the brain. For example, when we fall in love our brain changes: the limbic system goes into overdrive; lots of dopamine is released; the hypothalamus lights up; and there is reduced activity in the amygdala, which is linked to fear and learning from mistakes.

In the case of depression, CBT can be more effective than medication because the learned skills do not require reliance on the method of treatment, which is often the case when antidepressants are used. From a phenomenological viewpoint, the primary effect of CBT is changing subjective experience. Once subjective experience changes, the client can have a new map, a more positive label, and a better way of organizing the complexities of social/psychological life.

However, CBT is still focused on a medical model whereby interventions are algorithms and a decision tree leads to an outcome. Now, there is nothing intrinsically wrong with medicalizing psychotherapy into manualized approaches; in fact, many clinicians favor an algorithm approach over phenomenologically-based heuristics. But, CBT focuses on modifying automatic thoughts, and since automatic thoughts are not always central to a patient's experience of depression, they may therefore not be central to treatment.

Phenomenology

Heisenberg's uncertainty principle posits that knowing the location of an atomic particle sacrifices information about momentum. When asked what was complementary to "clarity," the great physicist, Niels Bohr, replied, "precision." Phenomenology is complementary to science. Scientists use algorithms, whereas phenomenology is based on heuristics. Science is about precision; it investigates facts about the physical world. Phenomenology is about experiential realization; it is the study of lived experience. Science works with algorithms that have finite conclusions. Phenomenology applies heuristics: simplifying assumptions that are known from experience to advance goals.

People use both algorithms and heuristics to negotiate their worlds. However, using science to explore a state such as happiness has limited utility because happiness is not a finite endpoint; it is an evolving process. Reading poetry, however, could elicit happiness because poets address phenomenology to promote experiential realizations.

My emphasis on phenomenology is due in great part to practicing hypnosis for decades, building on the innovations of my mentor, Milton H. Erickson, MD. Studying hypnosis has been my lodestar to understanding states and the implicit meaning of lived experience. Treatment can be more easily affected when a therapist understands the implicit structure and composition of the patient's depressive state.

Therapists committed to social interventions can create phenomenological maps that illuminate goals that can be addressed socially. The current discussion is focused on assessment rather than treatment strategies, because appropriate assessment leads to effective treatment. When a therapist creates useful distinctions in the assessment phase, common sense can guide the intervention.

To be clear, an assessment is not a diagnosis. Diagnosis concerns pathology. Remember that assessment considers both assets and liabilities. Psychotherapy works best when the therapist assesses the position the client takes, because psychological assessment can lead to psychosocial interventions. Assessment can focus on creating useful maps of the problem and the solution. One of my first phenomenological maps was called, "Elements of Communication." (Zeig 1980 b) The Elements of Communication model is primarily focused on how a person maintains an adaptive or a maladaptive state.

Elements of Communication

All communication consists of a constellation of elements. Thomas Szasz (1954) pointed out that every symptom is a communication. The following table lists primary and secondary elements of communication. The secondary elements are composed of—and modify—the primary elements. The number of secondary elements is endless because they are distinctions made from a therapist's unique vantage point. This table can be used to understand the phenomenology of a problem. A therapist can assess how a patient does the problem, and then create a map for intervention.

The elements of communication encompass 14 components. There are six primary elements: cognitive, affective, behavioral, perceptual, relational, and physiological, and eight secondary elements: attitudinal, contextual, qualitative, symbolic, ambiguous, historical, cultural, and spiritual.

Communication consists of a cognitive element (thought content), an affective element (the way a person feels, which could be covert or expressed), and concomitant behaviors. For example, if a person exclaims, "It's really a beautiful day!" the cognitive element concerns the weather, the affective element is the individual's apparent good feelings, and the behavioral component includes gestures and other para-verbal behavior that the person exhibits when making the statement.

The perceptual element concerns the sensory channels used that inform the communication and the way in which they are internally represented. A beautiful day can be recognized visually and/or felt physically. And, internally it can be represented visually or felt emotionally.

Communication happens in a relational context, and indicates the nature of the relationship, e.g., that it's positive, negative, or benign. All interactions contain an implicit statement about the meaning of the participant's relationship to another person or persons. "It's really a beautiful day!" may communicate, "I can be excited in this relationship," or "I need to be superficial in this relationship and only talk about things like the weather." And, all communication is a physiological event based on biochemical processes.

If the six primary elements were as complex as communication gets, life as a psychotherapist would be a breeze. However, even a simple statement like, "It's really a beautiful day!" could be simultaneously overlaid with secondary elements, such as attitudes that can modify the communication. Attitudes consist of concomitant behaviors, feelings, and thoughts. The person's attitude could be positive, negative, or neutral. If a client says, "It's really a beautiful day," he or she could be thinking, "I love being positive and happy," or "That was a stupid and boring thing to say," or "I'm just letting everyone know about the weather."

Moreover, communication happens in a specific and unique context: occurring only at a precise moment and in a specific place. Qualitative aspects, such as verbal intensity, tone, and tempo, further modify the primary elements. "It's really a beautiful day" is different from "*IT'S REALLY A BEAUTIFUL DAY!*" or "It's *really* a beautiful day."

Communication is symbolic. The word "day" is a symbolic verbal representation of a concept. Communication can also be ambiguous by not being fully specified. Saying, "It's really a beautiful day" in Phoenix, Arizona might mean that it's cloudy and rainy, because in Phoenix there are approximately 300 days of sunshine a year.

Ambiguity can take many forms. What is said on one level might mean something else on another level. Most communication (words and gestures) have multiple meanings. As a result, communication can occur at levels that both sender and receiver are unaware of, but to which they may unconsciously respond.

All communication has historical elements because it is an idiosyncratic representation of the history of the person. And, communication is also a representation of the culture in which the person lives. Some would maintain that there is a spiritual element to communication, perhaps representing the person's place in the "bigger picture" of life.

While any communication, symptom, or therapeutic response contains the elements mentioned earlier (behavioral, cognitive, affective, perceptual, relational, and physiological—and attitudinal, contextual, qualitative, symbolic, ambiguous, historical, cultural, and spiritual), different schools of therapy stress or value specific elements over others. In Rogerian therapy, the feeling aspect of communication is emphasized; in cognitive behavioral therapy, mental elements are most important; followers of B.F. Skinner focus on behavior; family therapists concern themselves primarily with relational elements; Jungians are concerned with symbolic elements; rational behavior emotive therapists primarily address attitudes; Ericksonian therapists value ambiguity; and psychoanalysts focus on historical antecedents that cloud the present. There are contextual schools of psychotherapy. So, it seems that if you want to invent a new stream of psychotherapy, the only thing left is to set up a qualitative school!

Patients often emphasize one aspect of their communication to the exclusion of others and are habituated to their central understanding of the problem. Any problem, in its totality, is a communication containing an evolving constellation of elements. However, patients who define themselves as being "depressed," for example, often emphasize only certain elements. In answer to the question, "How do you know you are depressed?" some may describe feeling sad; others say they lack motivation; and still others know by their "bad" thoughts. Some clients report seeing "dark images." Some patients say they know they are depressed because they are inactive. Some say their depression is physiological (which is true in some cases). Some believe they are depressed because they have bad relationships, and some explain that they are depressed because they judge themselves harshly, and thus, have low self-esteem. For some, the depression is circumscribed to a specific time and place. Depression can be attributed to past trauma and negative memories. A client can have ennui or feel she is in existential or spiritual crisis. Depression can be described in symbolic or metaphoric terms, such as, "falling endlessly into a black hole." By its very nature, the word "depression" is symbolic because words are symbolic representations of objects, facts, experiences, etc. The word "depression" is derived from the Latin word *depressionem* or *deprimere*, meaning "to press down," which is fitting, because some patients report feeling a heaviness, or say they feel weighed down.

Heuristics for Depression

A simple therapeutic principle (No. 20) is to work from the periphery in by assessing the elements of communication that the client uses to describe the nature of the problem. The therapist can choose a peripheral element, and then elicit a modification. The idea is to make a change in an element that is less central to the person's experience. This is a systemic approach in which peripheral changes can quickly snowball and have a generalized effect.

Where should a therapist begin treatment? Not with the aspect of the communication the patient emphasizes because that aspect is more resistant to change; it is more habituated, more concretized. If the patient describes his depression as thinking bad thoughts, I might intervene by suggesting an alteration in perception: The client can frequently notice intricate patterns of light and shadow in the environment. Or, I might suggest that he develop the affectation of cleaning his glasses every hour. I might also suggest that he regularly offer someone a compliment. A seemingly small change in perception, symbolization ("clearing one's vision"), and/or relationship can create positive momentum.

Another heuristic principle (No. 21) is to offer directives that are geared to making minimal changes in the patient's pattern, which can have a cumulative effect. Depression is a complex system of elements, some of which are not recognized by the person who presents with it. If the clinician helps change a significant number of elements in a patient's pattern, it can have a systemic effect and the state of depression could change.

Another heuristic principle (No. 22) is to use parallels. Patients have unrecognized resources for change that can be elicited. When depression is deconstructed into elements, it may become apparent to the therapist that the patient has history of changing thoughts, feelings, behavior, and so forth. The therapist can then set up a series of constructive parallel experiences that help the patient experientially realize a personal history of modifying thoughts, feelings, and behaviors. Working parallel to the problem allows patients to extract meaning from the parallel, and subsequently come to a seemingly autonomous realization.

Dividing any problem into components can change the clinician's understanding of its essential nature. To create interventions, it is best to understand the complex of phenomenology that leads a person to label his or her state as "depression," "anxiety," or even "bad relationship."

Depression as a Social Construct

Depression is a construct of convenience that describes a certain phenomenology—a series of implicit events and relationships that leads to the label of "depression."

As mentioned earlier, patients often emphasize certain aspects of the human experience, which can lead them to label their state as "depression." It's apparent that there is not just one "depression." Problems change over time. The elements that are phenomenologically described by a patient evolve temporally. At one juncture, a client might describe depression in terms of thoughts, and then at another point, in terms of feelings.

I never know what a patient will need to experience to declare, "I'm depressed." Any one of the elements that normally constitute depression, or a combination of elements, could lead a person to label him- or herself as "depressed." However, depression as defined by the patient may not match the therapist's definition of the state. Therefore, a therapist must understand what the patient means when he or she claims to be "depressed."

To understand a patient's experience, psychotherapists can think of themselves as cartographers, creating phenomenological maps. A proper assessment can answer the questions: "What is a phenomenological map of this person's depression?" and "How does this person do depression?" Of course, the same questions could be asked when dealing with any other psychosocial problem. Creating maps helps users get to where they want to go. The goal of the mapmaking process is to improve therapy by specifying more easily obtainable goals.

Examining depression as a social construction and creating distinctions by using elements of communication is only one way to divide the territory. Other useful distinctions can be made that help to facilitate treatment, including mapping solutions phenomenologically.

Mapping Solutions

Phenomenological maps can help therapists devise strategies for eliciting solutions. If the therapist can determine the map of the problem, one heuristic is to create a solution map by inverting the elements. For example, in contradistinction to a depressed person, a happy person would be external, present, active, positive, hopeful, socially engaged, open to new experiences, goal-oriented, visually oriented, positive in interaction with others, and in a state of positive arousal. The happy person would also acknowledge accomplishments, emit social energy, use positive self-talk, neither engage in self-blame nor blame the world for problems, live meaningfully, and socially assume the role of a victor. And, of course, the chances are good that connecting with any number of these elements will lead a person to exclaim, "I am happy!"

In Chapter Four, we discussed a generic map of depression and happiness and how therapy choices could be accomplished in the following four ways: 1) destabilizing components of the problem, 2) eliciting components of the solution state, 3) using hypnosis as a bridge between the land of the problem and the land of the solution, and 4) using the therapist's state as a bridge between the problem and the solution. Destabilizing a problem can elicit change, because most people naturally desire a sense of well-being and will move in that direction without much prompting.

Complex Maps

Over the years, my assessment procedure has become more refined. I now create five maps: 1) a map of the phenomenological states of the problem; 2) a map of the phenomenological states of the solution; 3) a map of the somatic sensations of the problem; 4) a map of the process of the problem; and 5) a map of the interaction pattern. These maps provide more options in determining my therapeutic strategy.

Thus far, I have focused on phenomenology, mapping the components of problem states, and eliciting solution states. But somatic sensations, sequences, and social patterns can also be mapped. If a therapist ascertains from the patient's description that a significant portion of the problem involves the patient's physicality, then the therapist can work somatically, perhaps by prescribing walking or yoga. A patient with depression may display vegetative symptoms, including weight loss (or even anorexia), insomnia, fatigue or low energy, or inattention. If this is the case, the therapist can focus on promoting feelings of physical well-being.

Problems can be conceived of as linear sequences: a repetitive series of events over time. When the process of the problem is discerned, pattern disruption can be applied, which can entail adding or changing steps. Any of the steps can be modified, or a new step can be added to see if the addition changes the sequence. A complaint, such as "depression," is not the endpoint of the sequence, because changing what happens before and after can modify the central element.

Interaction patterns can also be mapped. If the patient's social pattern is significant in the maintenance of the problem, the therapist can promote interactional solutions by involving others. We live in a social world and our behavior is a product of our interaction patterns.

Maps and Strategies

A clinician's map determines the strategy for therapy. Therapists who focus on problems due to lapses in psychological development will use psychoanalytic techniques, including interpretations. If one maps deficits, psychoeducation might be a method of choice. Mapping biology leads to the use of medication. Experts often tout their maps as absolute truths. But, maps are lenses that both focus and distort. Although any map can be valuable, the more maps that therapists have at their disposal, the greater the likelihood for constructive change. This could be considered principle No. 23.

Following is a table that illustrates how a map often leads to proscribed interventions.

Table 6-1: Using Maps to Establish Treatment Strategies

MAP	STRATEGY
State (Phenomenology)	"Flip It" (elicit opposite components)
Somatic Signs	Somatic Work
Sequence (Process)	Pattern Disruption
Social Pattern	Interactional Solution

Traditional Maps

History	Meta-Comment; Interpretation
Physiology	Medication
Deficits	Psychoeducation
Behavior Analysis	Desensitization; Conditioning

An exercise to improve therapist effectiveness: Take the problem of "depression," and using each map, work out hypothetical assessment schemes and concomitant interventions.

Advancing the Use of Maps in Clinical Practice

Having a wide array of distinctions can lead to more effective assessment and treatment.

The following table includes four general components: 1) state, 2) somatic signs, 3) sequences, and 4) social patterns. It adds numerous distinctions, all of which are facets of human experience.

Table 6-2: The Phenomenology of _____
(How to "do" the problem and/or solution)

I. INTRAPSYCHIC
INTERNALIZED
Attention:
Sensory System:

Internal Imagery:

Perception:

Perceptual Process:

COGNITIVE

Internal Vocabulary/Incantation:

Grammar:

Primary Question:

Cognitive Distortions:

Metaphor/Analogy:

BEHAVIORAL No. 1/No. 2/No. 3/etc.

Posture/Gesture:

AFFECTIVE

Affective Process:

ATTITUDINAL

Belief System:

Self-Esteem:

Existential:

Spiritual:

PHYSIOLOGICAL (SOMATIC SIGNS)

Biological/Health:

Energy/Activation Level:

Sensations:

TEMPORAL

Tempo:

Expectation:

Memory:

Memory Process:

PROCESS No. 1/No. 2/No. 3/etc.

ABSENCE No. 1/No. 2/No. 3/etc.

II. SOCIAL / INTERPERSONAL

Social Expression:

Social Distance:

Blame: Intropunitive / Extrapunitive

Role:

Control: One-Down / One-Up

Social Energy: Emit / Absorb

Triangulation:

Direction: Pursue / Distance

Relational Requirements:

Responsiveness:

Interpersonal Sensitivity:

Contextual Sensitivity and Awareness:

Systemic Functions:

Functional Age Level:

Birth Order and Upbringing:

Resistance:

When creating maps, the primary questions a therapist should ask are: "How does this person do depression?"; "How does this person (or any person) do a converse state, such as happiness?"

Using the template, a therapist can create two maps to guide the therapy: one for the problem and another for the solution. Creating maps for individual patients is an "action assessment"; directions for treatment become obvious.

The following is a map I created for a patient's depression. It helped me to organize my thinking, and subsequently discover avenues for experientially eliciting change.

Table 6-3: The Phenomenology of Patient X's Depression
(How Patient X "does" depression.)

I. INTRAPSYCHIC

INTERNALIZED

Attention: Internal

Sensory System: Tactile, hyper-aware of body sensations

Internal Imagery: Dark

Perception: Suppresses positive input

Perceptual Process: Enhances the negative and reduces the positive

COGNITIVE

Self-destructive, defeated, indecisive

Internal Vocabulary/Incantation:
  "What is wrong with me?"
  "I can't do anything!"
  "What if things don't change?"
  "I can't cope!"
  "Why is it taking so long!?"
  "Everything is such a big effort!"
  "Why am I not having a good time?"
  "Why can't I _____?"

Grammar (Punctuation): Most of the complaints were punctuated by exclamation points. Her verbal emphasis was such that it seemed as if she were using exclamation points.

Primary Question: "Where is my energy?"

Cognitive Distortions: "I need something magical to make me better...and I need it now!"

Metaphor/Analogy: "I am pushing against the tide."

BEHAVIOR NO. 1
Lazy

BEHAVIOR NO. 2
Often forces herself to do things

BEHAVIOR NO. 3
Weepy in the morning

Posture/Gesture: Inward, constricted

AFFECTIVE
Feels empty, sad, listless

Affective Process: Inflexible mood

ATTITUDINAL
Feels shame, insecurity, hopelessness

Belief System: "I can't cope," "I can't do things"

Self-Esteem: Low, feels inadequate, indecisive

Existential: Nothing is meaningful

Spiritual: Questionable faith, spiritual doubts

PHYSIOLOGICAL (SOMATIC SIGNS)
No energy

Biological/Health: Doesn't enjoy food, weight loss

Energy/Activation Level: Decreased activity

Sensations: Arms feel heavy

TEMPORAL
Worried about the future

Tempo: A little slower than usual

Expectation: "What if I cannot _____?"

PROCESS NO. 1
Underactive, compared to normal

PROCESS NO. 2
Overwhelmed and shut down

PROCESS NO. 3
"Fogged over"

```
┌─────────────────────────────────────────────────────┐
│              ABSENCE NO. 1                          │
│  Assertive behavior                                 │
│                    ABSENCE NO. 2                    │
│  Goals                                              │
└─────────────────────────────────────────────────────┘
```

```
┌─────────────────────────────────────────────────────┐
│            II. SOCIAL / INTERPERSONAL               │
│  Social Expression: "Forced" with people            │
│  Social Distance: Withdrawn, lack of social involvement │
│  Blame: Intropunitive / Extrapunitive (Hard on self)│
│  Role: Helpless, more childlike                     │
│  Control: One-Down / One-Up                         │
│  Social Energy: Emit / Absorb (Primarily absorbs energy) │
│  Direction: Pursue / Distance                       │
│  Relational Requirements: Covertly requests help, then rejects it │
└─────────────────────────────────────────────────────┘
```

Once I mapped this patient's problem, I could see that her lived experience of the problem was contained in her (mostly) internal vocabulary. Hence, my initial interventions were directed to components that were not so charged with personal meaning.

If map as complex as the one that I am proposing is not enough, other templates can be used.

Levels of Depression

The following is a list of eight levels (separate distinctions) of "depression," roughly presented in order of increasing severity.

1. Situational Determinants
2. Existential Perspectives
3. Denial of Depression
4. Belief Systems
5. Identity Disturbances
6. Disorder of Desire

7. Suicidal Concerns and Self-harm

8. Physiological Disorders

I can present this list to clients to determine the level at which they perceive themselves, or I use it to help conceptualize the case. The first level identified is situational determinants. Grief could be considered a situational determinant, although it is not considered depression per se. However, patients may talk about depression when they are experiencing situational grief. And in life, there are frustrating events that could be depressing, like losing an opportunity. Patients may generalize and report "depression," but they can be reminded of the situational cause.

A client's existential perspective affects mood. Depression can be reported by patients who feel they are not living a meaningful/purposeful life. In such cases, logotherapy could be a good choice.

Depression can be unrecognized by a patient, or denied altogether. These patients may exhibit their underlying angst by acting out, abusing alcohol, and/or using drugs. Some assiduously avoid depression by hypomanic activity.

Some "depressed" patients have problematic belief systems that may consist of pessimistic projections. For some, depression is an identity, and therapy can address that level of human experience. Then there are the "wanna, wanna" patients with disorders of desire. These patients may plaintively offer, "I want to want to be happy." "I want to want to be freed from depression." "I want to want to feel like I'm living again." In such cases, the emphasis can be on eliciting motivation and desire for change.

Even patients with moderate depression may be at risk of suicide. Therefore, therapists need methods of assessing the severity of the risk and providing treatment. Mapping a patient's suicidal tendencies can provide useful inroads. Finally, some depression is due to a brain dysfunction or chemical imbalance, and if this is the case, it needs to be treated as such.

Summary

This chapter focuses on systemizing assessment models that shed light on the nature of a problem. Therapists can create maps that empower psychosocial interventions. The best maps are road signs that indicate pathways for effective, commonsense solutions. To create psychosocial interventions, it is best to consider depression a social construction, not a disease.

Once a clinician creates a map to compose a goal (what to communicate), the clinician needs a way to present a goal (gift-wrapping), which is the subject of the next chapter.

The principles in this chapter:

20. Work from the periphery inward.
21. Offer directives that are geared to making minimal changes in the patient's pattern.
22. Use parallels
23. The more maps that therapists have at their disposal, the greater the likelihood for constructive change.

CHAPTER SEVEN

Gift-Wrapping

Preview

It is patently impossible to produce a comprehensive list of gift-wrapping techniques. However, in this chapter, I outline 19 methods that can be used to gift-wrap therapeutic goals. I also suggest how each procedure might be used in the case of depression.

Introduction

Once a therapist has a goal in mind, the next question is: "How can I effectively present this goal to the client?" If the therapist gift-wraps the directive appropriately, it will maximize patient-based change. Proper gift-wrapping enhances the presentation and elicits activation as conceptual realizations are "stimulated into play." Again, therapeutic techniques are simply vehicles to kindle realizations; in and of themselves, they do not cure.

The 19 interventions presented in this chapter are designed to activate dormant capabilities in the client—resources that the client has successfully used in the past. The state that the therapist accesses when offering interventions is instrumental in promoting client adaptation. The client presents a problem that may be "gift-wrapped" in a symptom. Thus, the therapist gift-wraps constructive possibilities within a technique. The client activates by "unwrapping" the proposed solution contained within the intervention. Because goal-setting is so important, I offer a brief review.

Goal-Setting: A Review

To review: To gift-wrap possibilities, the therapist must first have a specific goal in mind. Therapeutic goals can be established in several ways: the goal can come from the client and/or the clinician. Goal-setting is highly dependent upon the therapist's preferred theoretical orientation, and it is often idiosyncratic. Remember, a behavioral therapist may attempt to decondition the client of anxiety, even though the client complains of depression. A transactional analyst might want to discuss a life script with the same patient. A family therapist might target interactional patterns. Even therapists who subscribe to the same theoretical orientation can have different methods for goal conceptualization. Thus, the components of change are not written in stone.

In science, experts define fundamental elements, but in psychotherapy there are no fundamental units. Physicists agree on the existence of fundamental particles, such as protons, neutrons, and electrons. Psychotherapists do not agree on the fundamental units of change, which could include behaviors, perceptions, memories, relationships, cognitions, attitudes, emotions, and so on. (For further information on different schools of psychotherapy and fundamental differences among them, see Zeig & Munion, (Eds.), 1990.)

Psychotherapy would be a more rational and scientific process if goals could be formulated by using clear uniform standards. However, given each patient's unique perspectives and life experiences, a universal standard is impossible to establish. Add to the mix the therapist's professional perspectives and life experiences, and a highly individualized interaction occurs. Through this interaction, the therapist and patient essentially co-create therapeutic goals.

Oftentimes, goals are initiated by clients because many problems are within the realm of the client's awareness and understanding. A client may want to overcome depression or a bad habit, or have more enjoyable relationships. In many cases, the therapist accepts the patient's goal. However, problems and goals presented by the patient tend to be generalizations, whereas the therapist's goal could involve addressing the components of a patient's problem. In addition, a patient may not be fully aware of the nature of the problem. In such cases, since therapists perceive a patient's situation from an observer's standpoint, the therapist can take an active role in establishing goals.

Therapists can also reshape goals because in psychotherapy goals are malleable: If the problem is depression and the client wants to be happy, the therapist can reshape the goal by suggesting changes in perception, relationship, understanding history, and by searching for exceptions.

In psychotherapy, there are no set rules about whether to make goals explicit to the patient, but I advise clinicians to check the ethical requirements of their discipline. In Chapter Nine, I will discuss a case in which Erickson recognized that the patient did not fully understand her problem. In that instance, he continued therapy without making his goals explicit to the patient.

Some therapies eschew establishing specific goals, maintaining that the patient/therapist contract should be open-ended and serve as a growth experience for the patient. Gestalt therapy and some humanistic/existential approaches support this idea.

In this book, three orientations of goal-setting have been presented: 1) Dividing the problem into components; 2) creating a map of how the client does the problem, and 3) assessing the position that the client takes.

In brief therapy, the therapist should strive to create clear, concrete, positive goals, orienting the client to experientially access adaptive states. Many people seek therapy because of their inability to be flexible in accessing positive states—states such as sociability, which could promote a more enjoyable life. Accessing the state of sociability could involve eliciting components until such time that change "just happens." Components of sociability could include remembering previous examples of being social, engaging others in conversation, accessing sufficient energy to be social, placing oneself in a social environment, extracting meaning from a social situation,and being positive. Each one of these components could be gift-wrapped within a chosen method and presented to the patient as a mini-goal, which can lead to a synergistic effect. In this way, states are "redintegrated" through the assemblage of partial cues.

When enough elements are stimulated into play, a different state can suddenly emerge.

However, there are potential limitations in promoting goals. The therapist can only establish a climate that enhances the patient's ability to attain a phenomenological goal or sub-goal. By gift-wrapping a goal within a specific technique, the therapist creates a "social magnetism" that draws the patient into a more desirable state. Therapeutic methods are meant to awaken potential and possibilities; they are not designed to trick or manipulate the patient into relinquishing symptoms. Gift-wrapped goals are presents from the therapist to the patient, and the patient can delight in unwrapping the gifts, and then choose how to use them.

Locating Goals

Let's continue the review. A utilitarian phenomenological perspective would be that therapeutic goals can be established by a process of deconstruction: dividing the patient's presenting problem into components, and then devising solution components that the patient can engage to counteract the problem components and ultimately access a different state. (Remember the heuristic: Treat components, not categories.) Identifying the components of a problem is not an exact science; it's more a matter of consequence. The components of the problem (and/or solution) are co-created through the interaction between client and clinician. This process is utilitarian; it serves an important purpose. The components, however, are not empirical—they are not truths. Therefore, therapists should strive to ascertain components that have heuristic value in effecting individualized treatment. Subjectivity can trump objectivity as practical perspectives may be more important than objective truths.

The therapist can also check the validity and pragmatism of the deconstruction. In the case of depression, the therapist could deliberate: "Would I classify myself as depressed if I were inactive, internally preoccupied, ruminating about the past, overly critical of self and others, and enhancing negative experiences while reducing positive ones?" If the answer is yes, the therapist could establish solution components that are directly opposite to problem components. But first, the therapist could consider this question: "Would I classify myself as happy if I were active, externally oriented, present, accepting of self and others, and enhancing positive experiences while reducing negative ones?" If the answer is yes, then the therapist can compose gift-wrapping methods that could stimulate into play solution components. Since the synergy of combined elements creates the solution state, a goal could be to elicit the minimal number of solution components that would allow the client to reclassify his state as "happiness."

The following table reviews how the problem of depression could be broken down into components. On the left, are the components of the problem, which can create the negative state of depression; on the right, are the reciprocals, or the opposite components. (In mathematics, a number, X, can have a reciprocal, which is $1/X$.)

TABLE 7-1. Components of the Problem and Their Opposites.

Components of "Depression"	Reciprocal Components of "Happiness"
Being inactive	Being active
Being internally oriented	Being externally perceptive
Ruminating about the past	Being present, directed to the future
Being overly critical of self and others	Having a constructive view of self and others
Enhancing negative or reducing positive experiences	Enhancing positive and reducing negative experiences
Reducing positives, generally	Enhancing positives, generally
Inflexibility in mood	Flexibility in emotional adaptation
Global thinking	Specific thinking

If the patient can achieve a significant number of the reciprocal components, then he or she could report being happy. Once therapists formulate a list of reciprocals, he or she may realize that a depressed patient has a history of doing things that are on the reciprocal list. For example, a depressed patient who is inactive currently may have been active at times in the past. The job of the therapist is to gift-wrap constructive realizations so that the patient can reconnect with potentials. Patients do not need to be taught skills; they need to be awakened to dormant resources.

After the therapist creates a table of the components of a problem and the reciprocal components, then he or she can gift-wrap the reciprocal components. For example, the therapist might decide her initial goal is to gift-wrap the idea of being active. She could begin by offering a direct suggestion (the first on the list of interventions). If that works, there's no need to continue with another technique. Therefore, it can be efficient to attempt direct suggestion first.

The following interventions are primarily experiential methods for awakening clients to dormant resources. Hypnosis is just one of many experiential gift-wrapping techniques, and again, the purpose of hypnosis is to awaken the client to adaptive states, not to put the person to sleep.

Remember—in the field of medicine, an intervention or technique can cure. For example, a specific surgery technique can correct a physical problem. Social interventions are ways of eliciting empowerment. For example, hypnosis is a way of gift-wrapping that at its core, promotes a conceptual realization that a person can change a state, which can be a step to other adaptive changes in state.

Gift-wrapping Interventions

In Chapter Two on the meta-model, I listed 19 different interventions a therapist could use to elicit resources. The interventions are common to an Ericksonian approach, but they can be used to promote empowerment in any school of therapy. Again, here is the list of interventions, presented roughly from most direct (No. 1) to most indirect (No. 19).

Table 7-2. Main Interventions

1. Direct Suggestion
2. Hypnosis
3. Indirect Suggestion
4. Directives/Tasks
5. Ambiguous Function Assignments
6. Symptom Prescription
7. Reframing/Positive Connotation
8. Ordeals
9. Displacement
10. Fantasy Rehearsal
11. Future Orientation
12. Change History
13. Confusion
14. Metaphors
15. Symbols
16. Anecdotes
17. Sculpting
18. Parallel Communication
19. Interspersal Technique

These interventions are either microdynamic or macrodynamic ways of gift-wrapping possibilities. Direct and indirect suggestion (No. 1 and No. 3) are microdynamic because they are the building blocks of the more complex gift-wrapping methods, which can be categorized as macrodynamic and consist of an assembly of microdynamic forms.

To appreciate the differences between the various forms of intervention, I will discuss each one, again using depression as the example.

A caveat about clinical applications and employing any of the interventions discussed: Therapists can ask themselves, "If I were a patient, would I be comfortable if my therapist used this particular intervention?" If you would not feel comfortable, then don't use it with your patient.

1. Direct Suggestion

The most direct suggestion that could be made in the case of depression is, of course, "Be happy." Since this directive is unlikely to be effective, it might be better to suggest changing a component. For example, since physical activity has been shown to be an important factor in surmounting depression, perhaps the clinician can suggest: "Be active this week." Or, more specifically: "Take a 20-minute walk every day."

If the patient responds to the direct suggestion, there may be no need to continue therapy. If the patient does not respond, the therapist could offer a more elaborate direct suggestion: "Well, I know that you were active when you were a child, so this week I want you to remember how much fun you had back then, and recreate those experiences." If the patient still does not comply, the therapist could try a direct suggestion with a rationale: "You can be active because we're having beautiful weather and there's a lot going on in the city and I think you'd enjoy getting outside more, perhaps walking or riding a bike." Or, the therapist could provide a different rationale, perhaps suggesting the patient read an article about exercise and how it relates to depression.

Continuing to offer direct suggestions with more rationale is somewhat like titrating the dose of some medicine in which "more" increases the effect. For example, more sedative results in more sedation. The principle in physics is that more force creates more reaction. But in a social relationship, "more" may not have the same effect. Gregory Bateson quipped that if you kick a rock you can compute the acceleration, velocity and trajectory, but if you kick a dog, it is a different story. Social and physical systems work differently.

If altering the "dosage" of a direct suggestion does not have an effect, the therapist has reached a Choice Point: Continue with more direct suggestions, or try another gift-wrapping method, such as hypnosis. A direct suggestion gift-wrapped within a hypnotic experience may be more effective than direct suggestion alone.

2. Hypnosis

In using direct suggestion with hypnosis, the therapist might first try traditional methods. (See Zeig, 2015 for information about the traditional model.) After creating an induction and eliciting hypnotic phenomena, such as arm levitation meant to convince the client that he or she is in trance, the therapist can then suggest, "Now, this week you will become more active and exercise." The implication is that the power of the patient's unconscious has been influenced by hypnosis so that the subsequent therapeutic suggestion is enhanced.

Using hypnosis as a frame can be powerful. Consider the effect a direct suggestion could have on a client who wants to stop smoking. When the patient is in trance, the therapist can offer a direct suggestion and the client might be exhorted to realize: "Cigarettes will taste bad. Cigarettes will smell bad." Without the frame of hypnosis such suggestions would be ineffective and ridiculous. (Further information about direct suggestion in traditional hypnosis can be found in Kroger (1977).

By increasing the level of direct suggestion, with or without hypnosis, a therapist understandably is thinking linearly—where more leads to an enhanced effect. But, social/emotional systems adhere to logic that is specific to changing states, which is counterintuitive to linear systems. In social/emotional systems, experiences lead to changes in state. And when a change in state is the goal, an algorithmic approach or linear instruction is not effective. Linear thinking will not help someone have faith, find motivation, or experience humor.

If neither direct suggestion with hypnosis nor direct suggestion alone is effective, the therapist can then apply indirect or incongruent methods, either by using indirect suggestion (microdynamic gift-wrapping), or some of the more complex forms of evocative communication (4-17 on the interventions list). More simply stated (principle No. 24): When congruent methods, such as direct suggestion, do not work, incongruent methods can be used. When the goal is to elicit a change in state, incongruent methods are more effective.

States are altered and elicited by orienting toward, not by informing. For example, poets and composers do not explain the themes they are exploring. They want their audience to discover the implied messages. Artists orient toward; their imperative is: "Show, don't tell." As a result, states are elicited.

When compliance or adaptive changes in state are not forthcoming, the therapist can use an indirect method. A relatively benign indirect or incongruent method of intervention is indirect suggestion.

3. Indirect Suggestion

The concept of exercise, any type of exercise, may be daunting to some clients. Therefore, a directive could be offered in which the activity of "walking" is "couched" in a directive. For example, the therapist could say, "I happen to know there's a park in your neighborhood. Walk over there and watch some children play, and then tell me what you encounter." Hence, the directive is indirect.

Simple, formal, indirect suggestions consist of embedding a suggestion so that compliance is implied. If the goal is to become more active, a presupposition could be: "I don't know when you will exercise this week." In this case, exercise is presupposed—it is just a matter of when. A more complex presupposition would be: "You really don't consciously know how much you will enjoy taking a walk next week. You may be surprised and delighted."

It is unlikely that one simple indirect suggestion can prompt a patient to achieve a therapeutic goal or mini-goal, but it does happen occasionally. Franz Baumann, MD (personal communication), a renowned pediatric practitioner of hypnosis, described an incident in which Erickson effected change with one simple, indirect suggestion. This occurred in the 1960s in San Francisco where Erickson had been invited to lecture. As part of his presentation, Erickson was to conduct a hypnotherapy demonstration with an adolescent (perhaps a patient of one of the attending doctors) who had been acting out.

Erickson seated the boy on the stage beside him, facing the audience. Erickson then directed his lecture to the medical audience and ignored the boy. He offered no direct hypnosis or therapy. At the end of the lecture, Erickson finally turned to the boy and dramatically intoned, "I really don't know how you will change your behavior. I really don't know how."

Baumann reported that this one simple indirect suggestion prompted change in the adolescent's behavior such that he went on to make a satisfactory adjustment.

Indirect suggestion has the greatest potential when the suggestions are recursively stacked together in support of a specific goal. This builds the patient's range of associations until the mass of representations elicits adaptive change. (Forms of indirect suggestion are covered in *The Induction of Hypnosis*, Chapter 11, Zeig, 2015.)

Macrodynamic Methods

As mentioned earlier, the interventions are listed roughly from most direct, to most indirect and complex. There is no empirical measure of intangibles, such as indirection, but I attempt to identify in broad terms, techniques that I believe are more indirect, to the extent in which they orient toward rather than inform. These techniques, moreover, do not need to stand as single entities, but can be merged or nested within each other. For example, a symptom prescription could be embedded within reframing.

4. Directives/Tasks

Directives and strategic tasks have been extensively developed by Jay Haley (1963, 1973) and Cloé Madanes (1984). (Any serious student of psychotherapy should become familiar with their work.)

Human behavior is context dependent. In offering tasks to patients, therapists take advantage of the subtle ways in which alterations in context and relationship modify behavior, as task-directed therapy can be used to stimulate realizations.

As an example, Erickson used this type of therapy with a wealthy woman who was suffering from severe depression. Her son had told Erickson that his mother belonged to a church, but that she had no friends in the church even though she attended services regularly. The woman had a housekeeper and a gardener, but she rarely spoke to them. The son asked Erickson to visit his mother and see what he could do for her.

When Erickson went to the woman's house, he noted that she had African violets in her sun room. He knew that African violets take a great amount of care, so he gave the woman what he described as "medical orders." He instructed her to send her housekeeper to the florist the next day to purchase as many African violets in as many colors as she could find. Erickson told the woman that those would be her violets and that she should take good care of them. He also said the housekeeper should buy 200 flower pots and 50 potting pots and potting soil. The woman was to take cuttings from her violets and propagate them until she had enough violets to send to every family with a newborn in her church. Erickson also instructed her to send an African violet for a christening, in the event of illness, then there was an engagement announcement, wedding, funeral, and so on. Erickson told her to send them on every possible occasion and that she should contribute a dozen or more violets to any church bazaar. The woman followed Erickson's therapeutic task and her depression lifted. When she died nearly 20 years later, she was known as the "African Violet Queen of Milwaukee." Erickson commented, "Anybody that takes care of 200 African violets is too busy to be depressed." (Zeig, 1980, p.286)

A similar case was reported to me by one of Erickson's students. The client was depressed due to the routine nature of his life. He read books all day, taking breaks only for meals. Erickson was concerned about the man's physical health as well as his mental well-being, and therefore prescribed exercise. The man was to walk to the library in the morning and bring his lunch. There was no need to bring books because there was plenty to read at the library. The section on ornithology fascinated the client, and gradually he interacted with others who frequented that section of the library. Eventually, they all formed an ornithological club and the client's ennui evaporated.

Sometimes Erickson's tasks had intrinsic meaning. For example, he frequently encouraged patients to hike "Squaw Peak" (renamed Piestewa Peak), a landmark in Phoenix, or to visit the Desert Botanical Garden. When climbing Piestewa Peak, a hiker would follow a rocky path to reach an elevated view, and thus, a different perspective. At the botanical gardens, a visitor would encounter evidence of adaptation and the ability to survive and thrive in a harsh environment.

5. Ambiguous Function Assignments

Patients often seek growth and adaptation and have the capacity to find constructive meaning in benign tasks; they learn by doing things.

Erickson's proclivity to give ambiguous function assignments was identified and written about in *The Answer Within* (1983), by Stephen Lankton and Ann Lankton. This method consists of giving the client a benign task that has the potential to elicit adaptive realizations. For example, a depressed client could be instructed to light a candle every evening when the family gathers for dinner, and at the next session provide the therapist with an explanation of why the assignment was given. Now the therapist might not have an explicit rationale for the assignment, but he or she understands that the task could stimulate something constructive in the patient.

Perhaps the patient would report, "That was a great assignment. Thank you. Our family realized that we were no longer doing rituals like lighting a candle or telling jokes at dinner, and we missed that. Those things had so much meaning. We decided to start doing them again. And now that I think of it, lighting a candle is symbolic of bringing light back into our family. How did you know to tell me to do this task?" "It was obvious," the therapist might reply, "but you did not extract all of the meaning in my assignment. So, continue doing this, and the next time you're here you can tell me what you further realize."

6. Symptom Prescription

In its simplest form, a symptom prescription is a directive to continue some aspect of the symptom complex. A depressed patient might be told to act depressed, feel depressed, and/or think depressing thoughts. A compliant patient who follows these suggestions might gain a measure of control over the symptom. A defiant patient might rebel against the prescription and, consequently, engage in more effective behavior. (Rohrbaugh, Tennnin, Press &White, 1981)

With the oppositional patient, the investment in self-direction may be greater than the investment in the symptom. In either case, a change in the symptomatic pattern may be achieved. Symptom prescription can be more complex by adding a reason for complying. For example, a depressed patient could be told, "You can continue to be depressed because it's not the right time to change. Think of what a sprinter often does in a track meet: before he begins running, he first pulls back to push off. In a similar way, you need to spend more time this week pulling back and being inactive before moving ahead into new territory. You don't know what you will discover because pearls are found in the mud."

Remember, therapeutic methods such as a symptom prescription, are designed to stimulate unrecognized capabilities, not to manipulate the patient so that he or she does not experience symptoms. Moreover, there are contraindications with symptom prescription. For example, I would never prescribe suicidal thoughts to a suicidal person. (Before using any technique, clinicians must be adequately educated in their use.)

Although other names have been used for similar approaches, I prefer the generic term "symptom prescription." The method has been described as "massed practice" in behavior literature, and as "paradox" in other schools. In logotherapy, Viktor Frankl (1963) called the approach "paradoxical intention." He used it to stimulate humor, which would block anticipatory anxiety.

Symptom prescription has been extensively examined in psychotherapeutic literature. A classic work on this subject is *Paradoxical Psychotherapy* by Weeks and L'Abate (1982). An Ericksonian conception of symptom prescription appears in Zeig (1980 a & b).

7. Reframing/Positive Connotation

Reframing is a term used by Watzlawick, Weakland, and Fisch (1974). Selvini Palazzoli, Boscolo, Cecchin and Pratta (1978) used the descriptor "positive connotation."

Reframing involves changing the meaning of the problem, which offers clients an opportunity to alter their attitude about symptomatic elements. For example: "Depression can be quite important. It can be a time for reflection. So, when you are feeling 'depressed,' you might consider it a time of 'deep rest,' in which you can recharge your batteries."

Reframing can be combined with symptom prescription. For example, if the depressed person has a partner and it was appropriate, the therapist could offer: "It would be helpful if you could stay inactive this week and continue to dwell on your painful past. If you stop, your partner would have to think about his own past and it would bring up painful memories. Right now, your partner is not strong enough to deal with his past, and he is using your depression as smoke screen to avoid it. Therefore, this week, try to remain depressed and inactive until we can help your partner become stronger." In this directive, depression is reframed as a caring act: protecting a partner from confronting his own vulnerability. The combination of symptom prescription and reframing can change the interactional function of the symptom. (For additional information on reframing, see Bandler and Grinder, 1982.)

8. Ordeals

Jay Haley developed some of the most important concepts on the use of ordeals in psychotherapy (1984). Erickson conducted a prototypical case of ordeal therapy, which was reported by Haley in his seminal book, *Uncommon Therapy* (1973). The case concerned a client suffering from insomnia. After assessing aspects of the man's life, including his hobbies, likes, and dislikes (one of which was polishing floors), Erickson asked him to sacrifice eight hours of sleep to overcome his insomnia. The man was appalled at this incredulous request, telling Erickson that he had only been getting two hours of sleep a night as it was. Erickson said he could relinquish the eight hours of sleep over four nights, which seemed more reasonable to the man. The client was told to put on his bed clothes at bedtime, but instead of going to sleep, he was instructed to spend the night polishing the hardwood floors in his home. The man followed Erickson's directive for three nights. On the fourth night, after he got ready for bed, the man decided to rest his eyes for a few minutes before polishing the floors. That night he slept for eight hours. Erickson reported that the man kept the floor polish on his mantel, knowing that if he ever had insomnia again, the solution would be to polish floors. "That man would do anything other than polish his floors all night..." Erickson said, "...even sleep."

In a case of depression, an ordeal might entail asking the client to write an extensive list of reasons for being depressed. For example, the therapist could say, "After each meal, I'd like you to sit for 20 minutes in the smallest room of your house and write a list of reasons for being depressed...and it would be helpful if you wrote complete sentences with good penmanship. Make a new list each day. When you bring this list to me, we can analyze it and create an appropriate treatment."

There is automaticity to symptoms; they must "just happen." Scheduling a symptom or symptoms alters that function, which may have constructive results. Moreover, sitting in the smallest room of a house (most often the bathroom) can add a bit of irony, because depression is sometimes due to the patient believing that his or her life is "in the toilet." When well executed and shared with the patient, it can be helpful to be ironic about the problem, but I would not advise being ironic about the patient.

A case example of the use of my use of ordeals is presented in Chapter Twelve.

9. Displacement

Displacement is often accomplished under formal hypnosis and involves changing the location of the symptom. Erickson (1958) used displacement to move a patient's extreme dental sensitivity from his mouth to his hand. In one of my early professional papers (Zeig, 1974), I described displacing the auditory hallucinations of acute schizophrenic patients by first using them as focus for hypnotic induction, and then displacing them into physical discomfort. Eventually, I returned the hallucinations to the client, moving them from their original location to a different place in the patient's body, during which time I redefined the hallucinations as voices that could have benefit.

On the surface, displacement techniques may seem to border on the bizarre, but closer examination reveals that displacement is merely a utilization method. Patients displace their problems. For instance, when faced with an emotional difficulty, one person could develop a headache; another could develop a backache; another, an upset stomach. If displacement is an aspect of a problem, it can also be harnessed as a solution. In Chapter Ten, I discuss in-depth Erickson's treatment of a phobic patient, part of which involved the use of displacement (moving a woman's phobia to a chair).

Similar techniques can be used to displace aspects of depression. Perhaps overall physical inactivity could be hypnotically moved to a specific part of the body that is seemingly inactive, such as a toe.

10. & 11. Fantasy Rehearsal and Future Orientation

The imaginal techniques of fantasy rehearsal and future orientation are closely related. Using vivid mental imagery, with or without hypnosis, a patient can use fantasy rehearsal to practice a solution or a component of a solution. The patient can also project himself or herself into the future to a time when some aspect of the symptom has changed. Erickson (1954) called this technique, "pseudo-orientation in time." Employing a future orientation, the depressed patient could imagine becoming more active, for example, visualizing playing tennis with friends.

12. Change History

The technique of changing history, developed by Erickson in the case of the February Man, was described by Haley (1973) in *Uncommon Therapy* and extensively developed by Rossi (Erickson & Rossi, 1989). In the February Man case, Erickson established age-regression under hypnosis, and then made regular visits to the patient at pivotal points in her life, serving as a surrogate parent (called the February Man) who provided the "child" with parental advice that would help her adapt more successfully when she became an adult. This technique is a way of changing the narrative, not changing the past. What is changeable is the patient's perspective on that history.

The technique can also be modified for depression. For example, let's say the depressed patient was socially isolated in childhood. A nurturing, positive introject (such as Erickson's "February Man") could go back in time hypnotically and leave messages for the child that promote sociability during different developmental stages.

13. Confusion Technique

Erickson considered both the confusion and interspersal technique his most important contributions to hypnosis. These techniques are extensively discussed in Erickson (1964) and Gilligan (1987). In the most basic conception, the confusion technique is used to disrupt rigid thinking patterns. A period of psychological confusion (undifferentiated arousal) is first created. Next, a concrete suggestion is offered. The response to the suggestion may be enhanced because most people dislike the feeling of uncertainty generated by the confusion technique, and therefore carry out the first concrete suggestion they hear to resolve their discomfort.

A simple illustration of this technique is juxtaposing opposite concepts, such as understanding a misunderstanding in what could become a mind-boggling affiliation: "Your unconscious mind has ways of understanding things, and your conscious mind has ways of understanding things. And the kind of conscious understandings that can be unconsciously understood are different from the kind of unconscious understandings that can be unconsciously understood. And there are basic misunderstandings. And the kind of conscious understandings that you can unconsciously misunderstand are different from the kind of conscious misunderstandings that can be consciously understood. But you really can't understand until you...set aside time this week to be more active."

As he invented it, Erickson's confusion technique was an aggressive attack on a patient's entrenched resistances. In his later work, he modified aggressive confusion into mild destabilization. He would create slight disruptions during an induction or when doing therapy that would raise tension, and then follow with a concrete suggestion. In comparison, with traditional practitioners of hypnosis who create inductions that are soporific lullabies, Erickson's inductions were like symphonies with consonant and dissonant passages that modulated levels of arousal. And, as in symphonies, Erickson's unstable harmonies eventually led to a stable harmony.

14. Metaphors

Metaphor is a figure of speech that makes an implicit, implied, or hidden comparison between two seemingly unrelated things. The use of metaphor can be a valuable therapeutic tool. For instance, if a patient says, "My depression is a heavy stone," the therapist might offer a metaphoric story in which the stone comes alive and loses much of its weight. Alternatively, the therapist might offer: "Your depression may be one of many stones that build walls, but it can also be used to build bridges." Or, "Your depression is a whetstone against which you can sharpen yourself."

But metaphors need not be limited to verbal techniques—actions can also serve as metaphors. A visual metaphor can be powerful because it creates an image in the person's mind. For example, when working with a depressed client, I might sit up in my chair as straight and tall as possible, and say, "One of your goals is to feel like this." A theme that underlies many of my seminars for therapists is the use of metaphor. Aristotle once said, "The greatest thing by far is to have a command of metaphor." And indeed, metaphor is a fertile field for therapists to explore.

Erickson preferred to use real-life anecdotes rather than fabricated metaphoric stories. Some therapists, including Gordon (1978, Gordon & Meyers-Anderson, 1981) do not distinguish between metaphor and anecdote, and use the terms interchangeably. Another valuable reference is Gene Combs and Jill Friedman: *Symbol, Story, & Ceremony* (1990).

15. Symbols

Symbols and rituals are extremely valuable agents of change. Erickson used symbols in a case of a woman who had lost a child to crib death (Zeig, 1980, pp. 287-288). To overcome her grief, Erickson urged the woman to plant a fast-growing eucalyptus tree in her backyard and name it "Cynthia," the name of her deceased child. Erickson said to her, "I want you to watch Cynthia grow. I want you to look forward to the day when you can sit in the shade of Cynthia." A year later, the tree had grown tall and the woman, who had been so despondent she was suicidal, was able to sit in the sanctuary of the shade and comfort of "her daughter." The woman also transformed her once plain backyard into a resplendent display of blooming flowers and budding trees.

I had a patient who suffered from what I thought was depression (Zeig, 1992). However, she explained to me that she had psychosomatic problems. I did not interpret that her psychosomatic problems were masking depression. So I asked her to carry around a black rock for 10 days, and we set a return appointment for two weeks later.

At the second session, she told me that she had completed the assignment. I asked what she had done with the rock after 10 days and she replied, "I didn't know what the rock was for, so I put it in my husband's library." I said, "I think would be a good idea if we did some couples therapy and get your husband involved in the next session."

I traded symbols with this client. She gave me a symbol (her psychosomatic problem) and as a matter of kindness, even as a matter of politeness, I returned a symbol: the black rock, which I thought would symbolize her depression. As it turned out, the problem was not so much depression as it was a couples' issue. She symbolically corrected my misinterpretation when she chose a place to put the rock.

My intervention utilized a symbolic process. I could monitor the response to my symbolic tasks and appropriately adjust my method. (Zeig, 1992) A videotape featuring Erickson conducting symbolic hypnotherapy is available at www.Erickson-foundation. org. Rituals are complex symbolic tasks. More information can be found in Van der Hart (1983) and Madanes (1981, 1984).

16. Anecdotes

Therapeutic stories were a mainstay of Erickson's therapy and teaching. Most of his stories were about cases in which he felt successful, but he also drew from interesting events in the lives of family members, friends, and patients to create hypnotic inductions and teaching tools, and to embed therapeutic advice.

Stories are a foundation of human communication. By design, we are natural storytellers; we also remember and respond to stories. Erickson used storytelling throughout his career as a therapist and instructor. Yet, storytelling is not commonly taught in graduate school training programs. When I first began doing psychotherapy in the 1970s, I was shy about telling stories, but gradually storytelling became central to my practice. Patients share stories with therapists, so it's only natural for therapists to also use stories to offer treatment.

Storytelling is an experiential method of gift-wrapping that can prompt conceptual realizations. The client "unwraps" the message in the story, and can effectively change. The story is a context for how to think/feel/act/relate differently.

Anecdotes can be used to guide associations. The intent is to elicit constructive associations that will drive more effective behavior. For example, if a patient is having difficulty experiencing a range of feelings, perhaps he or she would benefit from stories about emotional flexibility. The technique could be reversed for an oppositional patient. The therapist could tell stories about people who are extremely rigid, with the intent to awaken the patient to his or her own rigidity, and subsequently promote change. Such methods prompt autonomy: change is stimulated from within and initiated by the client. (Erickson's use of anecdotes is extensively described in Zeig (1980), Rosen (1982), Zeig (1985), Lankton and Lankton (1983), and Gordon and Meyers-Anderson (1981).

Anecdotes are one form of parallel communication. They might have themes that correspond to the patient's themes, but since they are one step removed, the patient may find them more engaging and helpful.

17. Parallel Communication

Parallel communication occurs when the clinician communicates one thing to create an association to another. A metaphor is parallel communication. When Romeo says, "Juliet is the sun," he creates a metaphoric parallel.

Other forms of parallel communication include simple and complex analogies. For example, parallel communication with a depressed patient could involve talking about trimming dead branches from a tree, and how removing them is necessary for new growth. Games and riddles are also forms of parallel communication. Erickson often used mental games in therapy and teaching. For example, to introduce the idea of a flexible perspective, Erickson once asked me to describe all the possible ways of getting from his office to the next room. After I felt that I had exhausted the possibilities, Erickson said I had missed one way: I could go out the back door of his office into the main house, take a taxi to the airport, board a plane to New York, then one to Rome, Hong Kong, Honolulu, and Los Angeles, then back to Phoenix, where I would taxi to his home and enter the room next to his office from a side door. This was a playful, analogical way of encouraging flexible thinking to surmount learned limitations.

Some years ago, I was working in a hospital with a schizophrenic patient. The patient believed that because he was in the hospital, it meant he was "crazy." He reasoned that if he were released from the hospital, it would mean that he was sane. Unfortunately, his behavior was such that he could not be discharged. He had full-blown psychosis and was a danger to himself. I showed him a graphic image and asked him to read the words printed inside the triangle.

"Paris in the spring," he read.

"No."

"Paris in the spring," he said again.

"No."

"Paris in the spring!" he said angrily.

"No." I said again. "Read it word for word."

"Paris in the... the spring," he finally read correctly.

"Yes, you've been overlooking the obvious," I replied.

From then on, when I felt he was overlooking the obvious, I'd remind him to look at other possibilities by saying, "Back to the triangle."

18. Sculpting

Sculpting is a technique that I often use in both assessment and treatment; it was not something that Erickson practiced. Family sculpting was commonly used by experiential family therapists, including Virginia Satir and Peggy Papp. Family sculpting is a method whereby the therapist asks a family member or members to make a representation or sculpture of another family member, or of the whole family and how they see themselves in relation to their family. Externalizing a problem or solution can have decided effect. Much of our brain processing is dedicated to vision. Therefore, creating a three-dimensional image can be a constructive therapeutic step.

I sometimes use what I call "therapist sculpting." For example, I ask the patient to figuratively "sculpt" me into a symbolic representation of his or her depression. I stand straight with my arms at my side and then ask the patient to give me instructions so that I can rearrange my body in such a way that it creates a representation of the problem; a sculpture that can be static or kinetic. I explain that I want to more accurately understand the client's situation. The patient may instruct me, for example, to fold my arms tightly across my chest and sway from side to side, or to crouch down and curl up tightly, not moving. Then, I might ask the patient to sculpt me into a symbolic representation of a solution or solution component. The patient may see the solution as me raising my arms up and out, or even twirling around in a joyful manner. My goal is for the patient to create an externalized, memorable visual representation that can prompt change.

19. Interspersal Technique

The interspersal technique was one of Erickson's most important contributions to the practice of hypnosis. In a case involving pain control, Erickson used this technique when he metaphorically spoke about tomato plants, while he continually interspersed suggestions of comfort: "One puts a tomato plant into the ground," Erickson began, "and he will hope that it will grow into a tomato plant and it will bring satisfaction by the fruit it has. The seed soaks up water with not too much difficulty in doing that because of the rains that bring peace and comfort." (Erickson, 1966, p. 203) Erickson marked his suggestions of comfort with shifts in his tone of voice, converting them to implicit directives that could stimulate into play a train of associations that would alleviate pain as the client became absorbed in Erickson's patter.

One way of using the interspersal technique is to create an anecdote or description of something that parallels the patient's problem, with the therapist providing covert suggestions about how the patient might see/think about/do things differently. The interspersal technique can be extraordinarily complex, in that it can encompass anecdotes, metaphors, and forms of indirect suggestion, such as embedded commands and presuppositions.

Here is an illustration of the interspersal technique in the case of depression. The therapist might offer:

You're familiar with the experience of walking down a path. You have a goal...a place you want to get to...a destination that seems attainable, but unexpectedly, a storm appears with its dark, ominous clouds. Then, there's a sudden downpour that makes it difficult to continue... but...you want to get to your destination...and you reason... "Just wait

it out; the storm will pass." So you...find a safe place...find a comfort-
able place...and brace yourself while you...wait out the storm. And as
you...are cocooned in your darkened shelter...you can look outside...
and see that the clouds are lifting and you remember that storms do pass.
And you can enjoy the realization...that the storm will clear the air...
there will be a freshness and beauty in the world.

Here again, the therapist's goal is to build constructive associations
to stimulate effective adaptation.

Other Techniques

Erickson used other techniques, including harnessing hypnotic
phenomena, such as amnesia, age-regression, and post-hypnotic
suggestion. He also used shock, drama, boredom, and oxymoron.

An example of Erickson's use of an oxymoron is in the case of
a woman who had been sexually molested by her father. She told
Erickson that she felt "soiled" and could not enjoy sex, participating
only passively. She was also terrified of an erect penis. Erickson told
her, "Your vagina can take a *vicious pleasure* in reducing a *penis to a*
helpless dangling object," (Rosen, 1982, p. 37) which empowered the
woman to both enjoy sex and satisfy her vengeful feelings toward
men.

Conclusion

Erickson invented the confusion and interspersal techniques; he
did not invent all the methods described, although he did contribute a great deal to their development. And, at the time Erickson was exploring their usefulness, most of these techniques were
avoided by traditional therapists. Today, these techniques are cor-
nerstones of many clinical practices. Erickson rarely taught specific
techniques, but he did write about them, including in his work with
Rossi (Erickson, Rossi, & Rossi, 1976; Erickson & Rossi, 1979;
Erickson & Rossi, 1981 and Erickson & Rossi, 1989). Erickson

primarily explored the parameters of responsiveness, working to maximize constructive and cooperative responsiveness through his utilization methods. Erickson formulated a three-step process for therapy by answering these questions: 1) What is the patient's current position? 2) What resources does the patient have in his or her situation? 3) What can be utilized to help the patient discover inner resources?

The 19 techniques discussed in this chapter are among the primary interventions used by Erickson. It is not necessary for therapists to use all the techniques with one patient; in fact, doing so could result in a mechanical, contrived relationship with the patient. The novice psychotherapist, however, may find the list of techniques helpful when deciding how to gift-wrap a goal. If a patient doesn't respond to one form of gift-wrapping, the therapist can refer to the list and choose another method.

The key component is not the structure of the technique itself, but its contribution to eliciting a desirable response. No matter how elegant the technique, it must be received by the client so that it can be put into action.

At their best, techniques are utilization strategies. The utilization dictum is: Whatever the patient uses to maintain a position can be used by the therapist to promote effective living. For example, if a schizophrenic patient speaks in an erratic way to distance himself, the therapist can speak in the same manner to promote closeness (See Zeig, 1987).

Bear in mind, these main intervention techniques can be used to elicit therapy goals or hypnotic goals. A metaphor, for example, could be used to address the therapy goal or a hypnotic goal, such as focused attention.

As suggested earlier, it can be a useful exercise for therapists to choose a therapy goal or hypnosis goal for a hypothetical case, and then devise gift-wrapping methods utilizing each of the 19 techniques.

To emphasize once again, these interventions are not intended to trick patients out of their symptoms. The purpose is to help patients recognize dormant capabilities and inner resources. The techniques convey the therapist's implicit message: "Through this therapeutic experience, we can experientially elicit adaptive conceptual realizations."

The process of presenting an intervention influences its effectiveness. This process is further developed in Chapter Nine.

In the next chapter, gift-wrapping and tailoring will be combined. Using the exercises suggested in Chapter Eight can help clinicians improve therapeutic results.

A principle from this chapter:

24. When congruent methods do not work, incongruent methods can be used.

The Tailoring Grid

Introduction

The tailoring grid is a tool designed to assist the clinician in combining gift-wrapping techniques and assessment to enhance effectiveness. With this tool, the clinician can learn to tailor an intervention to the unique aspects of the client.

The Tailoring Grid

An intervention can be enhanced by framing it within a patient's
worldview. This grid is not the therapy intervention itself, but rather a mechanism for evaluating what intervention strategies are most
appropriate, given the individual characteristics of the client.

As discussed in Chapter Five, assessment categories and hooks
can be used: (1) as road signs for both hypnosis and therapy; (2)
as resources; (3) to speak the patient's experiential language; (4)
to ascertain how the person "does" the problem; (5) to present
the therapy through the patient's lens; (6) as motivators; and (7)
as ways to describe the microdynamics of excellence. In Chapter
Seven, 19 types of interventions were listed according to their level
of indirection.

Combining tailoring and gift-wrapping facilitates focusing the
therapy through the patient's lens. Let's see how merging the two
might be accomplished with the tailoring grid in our hypothetical
case of depression.

A sub-goal for treating depression might be to increase activity.
The therapist's task would be to elicit in the client recognition of
untapped potential, which subsequently would prompt the client
to utilize that potential. To the client's own credit, potential ener-

gy would become kinetic energy. In the last chapter, we saw how a therapist could begin such an intervention with a direct suggestion. From there, the therapist could modify the gift-wrapping by offering the direct suggestion under hypnosis. There is another choice: If the intervention was not successful, the therapist would not need to switch gift-wrapping techniques, but could instead refine the tailoring. This step could involve using the patient's experiential position.

It then becomes a matter of triangulating three parameters: the goal, the technique, and the position. The following diagram provides a simple example.

Table 8-1: Tailoring Grid. Example One.

GOAL	CLIENT'S POSTURE	GIFT-WRAPPING
Activation	Internal Attention	Direct Suggestion

In this example, the goal is to elicit increased activity. The selected technique is direct suggestion. The patient's posture is internal attention, so the gift-wrapped technique can be presented through the patient's position of being internally oriented. If this were the case, the clinician might offer to the patient: "Take a moment to go inside. If it helps, you can even close your eyes. In this quiet time when you are alone with your thoughts, you can get in touch with some things that you can do that would be of personal value. I think you will find that one of the things that can be a decided benefit is to realize ways in which you can become more active this week."

Another possibility would be to use the client's position as a motivator. For example, "I would like you to realize that you can take a one-hour walk alone this week because it's a good way to privately reflect upon and resolve things." (Discussion of supplying motivators for suggestions is found in Zeig, 2015. There is also a discussion of language forms that can be used without the application of formal trance.)

Now, let's change one of the parameters: the client has an external orientation.

Table 8-2: Tailoring Grid. Example Two.

Goal	Client's Posture	Gift-Wrapping
Activation	External Attention	Direct Suggestion

In this case, the therapist could suggest that by looking around, the client can realize the benefit in recognizing how others engage in activity before she carries out the assignment to become active herself.

An external orientation can also be used as a motivator with the patient enjoined to take a one-hour walk because he can notice "tremendous variations in sights and sounds." In carrying out the assignment, the client may even notice enhanced visual acuity.

When working with a client with a "linear orientation," the therapist might ask her to take a walk on a straight path—and to notice just how straight she can walk along that path.

For a mosaic thinker, the task could be to take a walk on a path with many twists and turns, or to just meander along. Perhaps this client would spend time window shopping, daydreaming, or listening to music. An enhancer could be prescribed a walk in which she could take note of all the fantastic, incredible, and amazing things. A reducer could be asked to take a walk and look for one small thing, such as a special rock, leaf, or seashell that might have a little meaning or value. An intropunitive person could be assigned a difficult walk, because the challenge could mollify this person's need for critical self-judgment. The extrapunitive person could be asked to find three significant flaws in her environment, for example, a littered area, clogged street drains, and inadequate signage—things that this person could change to make a difference. A one-up person could be asked to personally decide where he wants to walk, perhaps to a convenient location, a busy grocery store or bustling coffee house. A one-down individual could be instructed to walk to a specific place at a specific time.

As for hooks, if a person values caution, she could be asked to notice potential hazards on her walk, as well as any preventative measures she takes to avoid them. An adventuresome person could be encouraged to take a walk to discover new things.

Of course, the range of assessment categories and hooks is as extensive as are variations of human thought, feeling, behavior, perception, and relationship. Moreover, they depend on the therapist's position or orientation (discussed earlier). The process of assessment involves the idiosyncrasies of the therapist and how the therapist interacts with the patient's position or orientation. It's the therapist's job to decide what is most relevant to the immediate situation and to use the assessment categories and hooks as lenses and motivators in tailoring gift-wrapped goals.

Having technique, gift-wrapping, and position as aspects of the palette means that the therapist has a wealth of treatment options from which to choose. If a gift-wrapping or tailoring technique doesn't work, the therapist need not become frustrated or feel at a loss. He or she can simply select from the grid another method or combination of methods. It is important that the clinician utilize whatever response results from the directive (good, bad, or indifferent) to strategically advance constructive clinical outcomes.

Altering the Gift-Wrapping

To tailor the approach to fit the patient, the therapist will be flexible when it comes to making alterations. The therapist could maintain the goal of eliciting activity, for instance, and then modify the gift-wrapping method by using a presupposition rather than direct suggestion. If the client is internal, the therapist could say, "You really don't know how much you can enjoy one hour of solitude when you take a walk this week...do you? For the external person: "You really don't realize how beneficial it can be to get outside yourself when you take a walk this week...do you? And you can enjoy seeing things quite differently on morning walks than you would on afternoon walks." (See Zeig, 2015, for information on creating presuppositions.)

If the patient is extrapunitive, the therapy can be focused

through that lens. Since an extrapunitive person needs to reject something in the therapy, the therapist could present a method that allows the client the satisfaction of using a well-developed judgmental lens and yet still therapeutically activate. For example, the therapist could say, "This is what I want you to do this week to become active, and I want you to do it exactly as I prescribe. My experience has been that this is, without a doubt, the best way to do it. Perhaps it is the only way to do it. At 8 a.m. on Saturday, I want you to hike [name a place]. Be sure to take a carton of yogurt with you. Also, take an orange. It's best to get one that is medium-sized. When you have completed the hike, spend half an hour writing a list of 10 benefits that you derived from the experience. And if you decide on a different activity, please list the 10 benefits you gleaned from that experience."

This type of directive contains numerous smaller directives for the client to reject, while at the same time implicitly motivating him or her to perform an activity—one that the client personally chooses. Now, the client might tell the therapist in a later session, "I didn't climb that mountain, and I don't like yogurt. But I did spend a few hours doing my hobbies on Saturday morning."

Similarly, I advise students submitting their dissertation to insert grammatical mistakes so that the dissertation committee has something to criticize. After all, the committee needs something to correct, and if the grammar is perfect, the committee might take aim at the content.

Aspects of a client's position or orientation can be ascertained and utilized by the therapist. For example, an instruction to an inactive, tactile client might be, "This week, sometime midweek, either take a one-hour walk, or say three nice things to your spouse (or to a friend, family member, stranger). Do whatever you think might feel best."

Note that the directives presented in this chapter are minimal goals. To elicit change, it's a matter of the therapist determining the minimal strategic step that the client is willing to take. Remember the concept: Address components not categories. The idea is to divide the goal into components and small steps, and then strategically build upon those steps, which can alter the larger system. If progress does not ensue, perhaps the goal can be further divided. A principle (No. 25) to abide by: If the problem is difficult to surmount, and/or the resistances are hard to overcome, divide the goal into components and encourage the client to take small steps. Resistance can be countered by modifying the goal, selecting a different method of gift-wrapping, and/or by tailoring.

The following exercise can help therapists become more effective communicators:

Select a goal and state it in concrete and positive terms: For example: "Meditate five minutes each day" or "Smile more around your spouse" or "Exercise."

If need be, a negatively stated goal, such as "eat less," can be used. Create a tailoring grid and list several client assessment categories and hooks across the top. Down the side, fill in several possible gift-wrapping methods. Now, design a tailored directive that merges the patient's position with the gift-wrapping method. Once you've completed the grid and established strategies for all the combinations you have identified, you can quickly and easily modify your treatment by either altering the assessment category or the gift-wrapping method. Any combination may be pertinent to an individual client. You can further experiment with fine-tuning your goal-setting abilities by changing the goal, perhaps by breaking it down into smaller components.

The limitless number of corrections, modifications, and alterations that can be made to a simple suggestion such as "be active" might seem overwhelming to a novice, throwing the person into a kind of mental paralysis. However, keep in mind that a new way of thinking that at first seems impossible, often becomes fundamental later.

Let me illustrate with a personal experience. Years ago, I took up piloting gliders. My flight instructor's first task was to teach me to level flight. Like most beginning pilots, I overcompensated at first. It took some time to learn how to avoid overcompensating and maintain a level flight pattern at a constant altitude.

The next step was to learn how to turn or bank the plane. A pilot must learn how to control a plane's flight in three dimensions, whereas driving a car is done in two dimensions. My instructor taught me how to bank by breaking the task down into smaller parts. He also listed the numerous undesirable side effects of incorrect actions. To bank a plane, it's necessary to properly adjust the aileron, rudder, and flaps. Of course, I discovered firsthand what happened when I did not do this correctly. I was overly conscious of every step, and again, I overcompensated.

The same thing can happen in golf or tennis when someone starting out is overwhelmed by the nuances of learning the basics, even though most instructors teach by breaking the process down into manageable segments. But it is only when the movements or patterns move from working memory to procedural memory that we really begin to attain true proficiency—what professional athletes call being "in the zone" or "in the flow." Today when I fly sailplanes, I don't consciously think about the changes that must be made. Rather, I effortlessly respond to the changing conditions.

A therapist trying to work the dimensions of the tailoring grid may initially feel like a juggler with too many balls in the air. But, over time, with experience in modifying the various aspects of the grid, conscious decisions will begin to flow to procedural memory and the therapist will soar to new heights, just as I do now almost automatically and effortlessly in a sail plane.

Summary

In a brief therapy approach, it is essential that clinicians have a clearly defined goal in mind. The strategic approach focuses on individualizing treatment toward a specific goal (Haley, 1973), and this is best accomplished when the therapist accesses the client's world view, applying techniques that utilize the patient's position, such as the client's assessment categories and hooks.

However, this method of combining goals, gift-wrapping methods, and tailoring requires some homework on the part of the clinician.

The principle in this chapter:

25. If the problem is difficult, divide the goal into components and take small steps.

CHAPTER NINE

The Process of Ericksonian Therapy

Overview

Psychotherapists should attend not only to assessing a patient's problem and applying techniques, but to the process of treatment itself. This chapter examines the strategic aspects of Ericksonian therapy in the three-stage model of the Set-up, Intervention, and Follow-Through (SIFT), which is illustrated with a hypothetical timeline of psychotherapy.

Introduction

Since the latter part of the 20th century, Erickson and his therapeutic techniques have gained significant cachet. Erickson's interventions were meticulously and logically planned, and he is perceived by many to have been an extremely intuitive practitioner. Erickson was facile at improvisation, but his spontaneity was a byproduct of years of deliberate practice. He was one of history's most strategic clinicians, thoughtfully attuned to creating steps that advanced a process. His interventions were teleological, oriented to a constructive future.

When I first visited Erickson in 1973, I was wedded to a Rogerian model of psychotherapy. My response to clients was brief, usually consisting of a simple phrase that mirrored what the client had told me. For example, if the client said, "I am sad," I would respond, "You do seem down." I gradually began to realize that Erickson spoke in a more complex way, and he often spoke in triplicates. He would do this by entering, offering, and then exiting. I often use this process in therapy by pacing, suggesting, and then motivating. Once I realized how effective Erickson's method was, it changed my way of communicating, both personally and professionally.

The SIFT Model: An Outline

The Three-Stage SIFT Model

The Set-Up, Intervention, and Follow-Through (SIFT) model of processing is illustrated in Table 9-1, repeated for convenience from Chapter Two. Solutions to the patient's problem can be recursively suggested in each of these three stages; they need not be limited to the main intervention. The SIFT model is a simplification, and once mastered can be incorporated into a robust strategic process to promote change. This process can be used to elicit in the client small steps toward change, and it can serve as a structure for an entire therapy session.

The therapist can first decide what to communicate, whether it's a comprehensive goal or a sub-goal that will lead to a comprehensive goal. The question then becomes how to communicate the goal or sub-goal, which can, for example, be gift-wrapped within a main intervention. Goals are, moreover, tailored to the uniqueness of the individual. With a gift-wrapped and tailored goal in mind, the therapist can begin the SIFT process.

Stage I: Set-Up

To establish rapport, the therapist first paces the client. Perhaps the therapist does this by speaking the client's experiential language and meeting the client at his or her frame of reference. Rapport is especially important in hypnotherapy because clients often feel vulnerable to the perceived intimacy of hypnosis.

For example, the therapist might validate/reframe a client's depression by saying, "I understand why you're feeling down. You've been through a lot and suffered loss. It's now time for self-reflection and mourning the past. But you came to this appointment, and that is a first step toward change." By identifying something positive in the client's symptomatic experience, the therapist can elicit motivation and positive expectations.

Table 9-1. SIFT

STAGE I SET-UP	STAGE II INTERVENTION (*Main Intervention to Elicit Resources*)	STAGE III FOLLOW-THROUGH
Therapeutic assessment	Direct suggestion	Ratify changes
Pace	Hypnosis	Promote amnesia
Establish rapport	Indirect suggestion	Process instructions
Establish empathy, which can be accomplished experientially	Directives/tasks	How to use the elicited resources
Establish a positive frame	Ambiguous functions assignments	Test the therapy in session, symbolically or with fantasy rehearsal
• Appreciate the patient's position	Symptom prescription	Tasks to consolidate and practice learning
• Elicit motivation	Reframing/positive connotation	Hypnosis
Destabilize habitual sets	Ordeals	Letters and other post-session contact
Seed intended targets	Displacement	
Frame interventions	Fantasy rehearsal	
Move in minimal strategic steps	Future orientation	
Initiate drama	Change history	
Access cooperative responsiveness to minimal cues	Confusion	
Use hypnosis	Metaphors	
Deal with resistance	Symbols	
Utilize	Anecdotes	
	Sculpting	
	Parallel communication	
	Interspersal technique	

Rapport can harness nonverbal methods. For example, the therapist could covertly mimic the client's posture with a slight delay, a process called social mimicry.

Next, the therapist can work to establish a positive frame, possibly by reframing or redefining the client's problem, which could change the meaning of it. For example, "Perhaps you are not depressed. It seems that you are disappointed with yourself."

Several strategies, including storytelling, can be used to establish a positive frame and to prompt motivation. The therapist might recount the experience of learning to swim, emphasizing "getting a sense of buoyancy" and "knowing it can be done."

The confusion technique can be used to destabilize habitual sets (for more information, see Erickson, 1964). As developed by Erickson, the confusion technique appeared to be quite aggressive because it was initially designed to "attack" resistances, but it was gradually replaced by a "softer" method of destabilization. The technique involves utilizing mild arousal states followed by concrete suggestions. Destabilzation is a "spice" that can improve a recipe, if properly used. As an advanced method, it requires training prior to using it in practice.

The therapist can also seed the intended target, foreshadowing it before the main intervention. Foreshadowing is a powerful and extremely valuable tool that often proves successful in increasing the response to the future target. Erickson often seeded, or "primed," future directives. For example, if he intended for a patient to experience arm levitation, he would lightly touch the patient's arm at some point before suggesting the levitation. He was, in effect, orienting the patient to attend to the arm and develop feelings of lightness in it. (For information see Zeig, 1990)

The therapist need not move directly toward the intended goal or main intervention, but can instead take minimal strategic steps, while creating a background drama of change that inexorably increases in intensity. Eventually, the main intervention would take shape.

In hypnosis, arm levitation, a dissociative phenomenon, can be used as an induction technique, or as a convincer that a client is experiencing trance. A therapist conducting an arm levitation induction can move in small steps and use destabilization throughout the induction:

Your eyes are closed and you are sitting comfortably, and you can wander...wonder about what would be enjoyable to experience next. You might notice the position of your arms...so that you can... attend to the sensations in your arms. And that can glide (sic) you...guide you to your hands so that you can notice...notice in your hands a sensation, perhaps a sense of lightness, and that can be so interesting.

And then you can be curious about the way in which things can move from one place to the next. And you can be interested in the development of the present...pleasant sensations of movement, and you can have those sensations at the tip of your fingers, so that you can notice, to your own delight, how your hand can begin to...lift...up...in small stepwise movements, so that it can surely touch your face, which is a moment when you can take a deep breath and feel yourself even more comfortably absorbed.

Erickson often took minimal steps with his patients. Moreover, he relied on multilevel communication. He created a smooth, even flow to his work. By moving in incremental steps, Erickson increased the chance of a positive response to his targeted intervention. He would weave suggestions together, lining them up so that one suggestion became the set-up for another. By the time Erickson presented the main intervention, the patient would only have to take one other small step in a series of constructive movements.

Another set-up intervention is to access responsiveness to minimal cues. Building responsiveness to innuendo is central to hypnosis. This can be accomplished through offering an induction, one component of which involves responding to implication. In the process, the therapist can identify emerging resistances—and utilize those resistances.

Building responsiveness can also be understood within the

context of farming, the occupation of Erickson's father. Before planting a seed, the resistant ground needs to be worked to improve its receptiveness. Fertilizer may be added. Subsequently, the seed needs to be watered.

Throughout this book, I have emphasized the use of evocative communication, which is based on the use of minimal cues. The response to innuendo is central to hypnotic psychotherapy. Eliciting responsiveness can be achieved in two ways: through formal hypnosis or naturalistic techniques. The primary objective is to establish (to the maximum degree possible) cooperative responsiveness. (For discussion on hypnotic induction in eliciting responsiveness, see Zeig, 2014.)

Stage II: Main Intervention

Main interventions are extensively discussed in Chapter Seven. Readers can refer to the list of interventions when deciding on which might be the most effective gift-wrapping method.

Remember, interventions are not intended to trick patients into relinquishing symptoms, rather they are designed to help patients to elicit resources for change. In the case study presented in the next chapter, Erickson uses symptom prescription, displacement, and anecdotes to elicit resources.

Stage III: Follow-Through

It is obvious from a cursory review of the SIFT framework that most of the steps in the process are in the set-up and follow-through stages. The intervention stage may merely contain one gift-wrapped main intervention. However, the follow-through stage contains numerous possible components, which reflects how important this stage is in psychotherapy.

The SIFT process is akin to hitting a tennis ball. The ball comes into the court with a certain characteristic spin. The player first diagnoses the spin (tailoring: the position of the ball), deciding whether it's a topspin, backspin or sidespin. Then the player decides where to return the ball (goal-setting), and what kind of spin to use (gift-wrapping) in the return. The dynamic power of placing a winning shot, however, comes from the follow through.

The same process can be harnessed in therapy. Improper follow-through can lead to therapeutic failure. Commonly, the follow-through involves several components, including ratifying changes. (The Erickson case discussed in the next chapter offers a good illustration of using ratification procedures in the follow-through.)

Promoting amnesia can be another valuable follow-through technique. Amnesia can be used to seal away information from the potentially disrupting scrutiny of the conscious mind. (For more information on amnesia, see Zeig, 1985.)

The therapist can test to see if a certain technique has worked. Some interventions can be tested in the office. For example, with a patient who fears eye contact, the therapist could determine whether there is increased eye contact after an intervention. If a technique for a patient's problem cannot be easily tested—for example, the fear of flying—the therapist might test the intervention strategy by using the patient's imagination; the therapist could have the patient take an imaginary plane ride.

Another Stage III intervention is to offer tasks to consolidate and practice learning. The therapist can give a homework assignment. For example, if a patient has trouble making friends, he or she could be given the assignment to watch children play—to see how they interact with one another and effortlessly make new friends. Suggested tasks can have symbolic meaning. Erickson often asked patients to visit the Desert Botanical Gardens in Phoenix, which contains a vast variety of desert plants. This task afforded numerous symbolic interpretations: thriving in a difficult arid environment, finding beauty in unexpected places, and being vigilant about hidden threats, surviving on sparse resources, etc.

The Timeline of Psychotherapy

Therapists should be aware that providing an assessment in therapy and employing an appropriate technique is no guarantee of a successful outcome. A therapist may use one of Erickson's brilliant techniques in a similar case for his or her own patient, only to discover a less than satisfying outcome. The reason could well be the lack of strategic set up of the intervention; timing is a crucial variable.

Diagram 9-2: Timeline of Psychotherapy

This timeline graphically shows how a therapist can move from one stage of the SIFT process to the next. Common steps are listed. "Build responsiveness" is a euphemism for offering a formal or naturalistic induction. Keep in mind that even though the interventions on this timeline are presented in a linear fashion, the inherent vagaries of therapy will, by necessity, alter a straightforward approach

The timeline, gleaned from an actual session, presents descriptions of Erickson's movement through the three stages of the SIFT process (see: *Marital Therapy*, which can be purchased with commentary at: www. ericksonfoundationstore.com.)

The actual session, a peerless example of strategic development in therapy, is approximately one hour. But Erickson, a consummate dramatist, used the first 25 minutes as the set-up to build toward the main intervention (a story told to the husband and wife) so that it would have maximum impact. The story he told is approximately five minutes long. Erickson devotes the last half hour of the session to following through.

The case presented in Chapter Ten exemplifies the strategic process of change. The interventions may strike the reader as intuitive and irrational on the surface, but are, in fact, quite logical and intentional when understood as the evocative approach they represent.

Therapy for a Flying Phobia

Originally reported in *A Teaching Seminar with Milton H. Erickson* (Zeig, 1980, pp 64-70), this case depicts a patient with an "airplane phobia." Erickson's main intervention was hypnotic displacement, in which he suggested to the patient that her phobia slide out of her body onto a chair. Erickson's main intervention may seem eccentric, but his keen understanding of the patient allowed him to succeed. Although displacement seems dysfunctional, the mechanism can be used adaptively. Moreover, the client's problem is illogical; therefore, an illogical solution based on emotional logic could be effective.

The Dramatic Process to Elicit Change

Within every session, therapists can formulate a series of steps to elicit change, and the SIFT process can be a dramatic, strategic method to energize therapy. Again, there are three sequential stages: 1) Set-up; 2) Intervention; and 3) Follow-through. The process is akin to what artists use to create film, theater, poetry, and literature. These arts involve a sequence that unfolds from beginning to end. For example, a filmmaker understands that every element of the film advances the story; a playwright uses the idea of "set-up" and then "pay off," by interspersing clues that merge in the denouement; a poet creates a strategic development of a theme; and a novelist foreshadows elements in the storyline to increase dramatic intensity.

Establishing drama is an evocative tool in therapy, when the goal is to elicit changes in state: a process that awakens the recipient to dormant capabilities is imperative.

Analyzing a case report is not the same as dissecting a video or a transcript, but there are similarities. Even when reporting a case, Erickson chose his words and his nonverbal communication with the precision of a surgeon; every word and physical nuance contained meaning.

This detailed analysis of Erickson's case is a template designed for those who want to understand the microdynamics of his strategic method. Moreover, it provides a roadmap for reading Erickson's works.

Erickson was a psychotherapeutic artist who poetically improvised and staged a drama of change. His strategic communication was often nuanced with innuendo and signification; he did not use an empirically validated protocol. The evocative apparatus that any artist uses to create drama is often invisible to the viewer of the art. The art therefore remains experiential rather than informative.

The case that follows is but one example of how Erickson conducted his therapeutic art.

The "Airplane Phobia"

In 1979, Erickson held a week-long teaching seminar with a diverse group of therapists. I attended part of this seminar. The case was presented at the end of the first day.

Erickson: And now, in 1972, a 35-year-old woman, married, very pretty rang the doorbell. Her statement to me when she came in was: "Dr. Erickson, I have an airplane phobia. And this morning my boss told me, 'On Thursday you fly to Dallas, Texas, and you fly back on Saturday.'" And he said, 'Either you fly both ways or you lose your job.' Dr. Erickson, I am a computer programmer, and I have programmed computers all over the United States.

In 1962, ten years ago, a plane I was on crashed. There was no real damage done to the plane and nobody on board the plane was hurt. And for the next five years I rode planes, Phoenix to Boston, New York, New Orleans, Dallas, everywhere. Each time I was on a plane and riding through the air, I got more and more fearful. And finally, my fears were so great that I would shake visibly all over my body. (*Erickson demonstrates.*) And I'd have my eyes shut. I couldn't hear my husband speaking to me and my phobia is so strong that by the time I got to the place where I would do my work, even my dress was wet with perspiration. It got so bad that I had to go to bed for eight hours and sleep before I could do my work. So I began going to my different jobs by train, by bus, and by automobile. My airplane phobia is so peculiar. I walk on the plane all right. I can taxi to the end of the runway. But the moment the plane lifts off the ground, I start my shuddering, and I am so full of fear. But when the plane lands at an intermediate stop, as soon as the plane is on the ground, I am very comfortable. I taxi to the airport, and back to the runway.

So I began using cars, buses, and trains. Finally, my boss got tired of me using my vacation time, my sick time, and my allowable absentee time in order to travel by bus, or car, or train. This morning he said, 'You fly to Dallas or you lose your job.' I don't want to lose my job. I like it."

This was the information that Erickson provided his students. He thought it was all therapists needed to know to help this woman solve her "airplane phobia."

From this passage, let's consider aspects of assessment using tailoring distinctions that were discussed earlier, starting with intrapsychic processes. The problem is presented in tactile terms and the patient enhances her negative physical sensations. She reports neither internal dialogue nor visual components; both these elements are conspicuously absent. There is also a dissociative component in that her preoccupation with her phobia is so great that she cannot hear her husband speaking to her. From the interpersonal perspective, she is more one-down: ready to respond to situational determinants, rather than being one-up: controlling and defining the situation.

He continues:

Erickson: I said, "Well, how do you want your phobia treated?" She said, "By hypnosis." I said, "I don't know if you are a good hypnotic subject." She said, "I was in college." I said, "That was a long time ago. How good are you now?" She said, "An awfully good one." I said, "I'll have to test you."

With his first intervention, Erickson agreed with the patient that she had an "a phobia," although he did not specify what he meant by using her descriptive term. He implied that he would treat her phobia; it was a matter of "how."

Erickson challenged the patient's motivation by using an indirect method of parallel communication: he tested her possible resistance to hypnosis, not to the phobia treatment. If she was motivated and cooperative in achieving hypnosis, then in a parallel fashion, she could be motivated and cooperative in the treatment of her problem.

Whereas most hypnotherapists conduct hypnosis at the end of a session, Erickson began with hypnosis. Erickson used what could be called "The Beethoven Principle." He jumped into action just as Beethoven did in presenting the theme of the Fifth Symphony. Erickson's method prompted the woman to immediately engage in constructive steps and not merely recount details about her complaint.

In a first session, a traditional therapist may encourage the client to talk about the history and details of his or her problem and begin therapy by gathering a history, determining a diagnosis, and collaborating with the client on a treatment plan prior to starting treatment. But this information may not inform future therapy. Erickson "cut to the chase," leaving little time for discussion about the problem. Sometimes treatment can begin without extensive information. Erickson would begin a session with an intervention, and assessment would be a byproduct of that intervention.

In medicine, a diagnosis must precede intervention. A physician performs an exam, obtains a history of the problem, and often orders medical tests to determine a diagnosis before offering a treatment plan. This is not necessarily the case in a social intervention such as psychotherapy, where the response to the intervention shapes the direction of treatment.

In this next segment of Erickson's case description, we learn that the client was more compliant than defiant.

Erickson: She was a good hypnotic subject. I awakened her and said, "You are a good hypnotic subject. I really don't know *how you behave* on a plane so I want to put you in a hypnotic trance and have you hallucinate being on jet plane 35,000 feet up in the air."

As Erickson emphasized the word "behave," he indirectly initiated a distraction. The patient's problem was primarily affective, but Erickson distracted her from focusing on feelings and instead turned her attention toward another element of her experience: behavior.

In the initial stages of therapy, a therapist can engage the patient in simple activities—the intention being that once a patient undertakes one action, it's easier to successively perform another, and then another. Erickson was not asking much of the patient when he first requested that she go into trance. Then, he complimented her ("you're a good hypnotic subject") and asked her to take another small step: to go into a second trance and hallucinate being on a plane. His stated motive was to ascertain how she might behave on an airplane.

But the second intervention is a hypnotic symptom prescription. Erickson was directing the patient to experience symptoms of the problem. The patient, at that moment, did not experience her symptoms while on a plane; she experienced them in a chair in Erickson's office. Thus, Erickson seeded the main intervention of the therapy: namely, changing the location of where the patient experienced symptoms of the problem. This small modification of changing the location altered the context of the "airplane phobia," and paved the way for future spatial modifications. Remember: Make a minimal change that can have a strategic effect.

Note that Erickson did not immediately offer the hypnotic symptom prescription. It was one of a series of small strategic steps. The patient complied. She showed her motivation to go into hypnosis; then she demonstrated her hypnotic ability. These small steps seamlessly linked together eventually formed a chain of cooperative responses. When the patient's symptomatic behavior emerged in trance, she was taking a small, logical step in a sequence of strategic steps that would eventually lead to the main intervention.

Erickson: So she went into the trance and hallucinated being on a jet plane at an elevation of 35,000 feet. The way she bobbed up and down, trembling all over, was a horrible sight to see. And I had her hallucinate landing the plane.

When Erickson had the patient land the plane, her phobic symptoms subsided. This confirmed what she initially described about the actual nature of what she called an "airplane phobia."

Erickson: Before I can help you, I want you to understand something...

This directive, which was a framing intervention, abruptly changed the flow of the communication. By commenting, "Before I can help you..." Erickson implied that his prior interventions were more diagnostic than therapeutic. The purpose of this comment was to prevent the patient from analyzing the previous steps. Such analysis could impede experiential realizations that promote change, just as analyzing a joke prevents the experience of humor. Erickson implied that the patient could disregard (have amnesia for) his actions up to that point, and for the things he was about to say that would precede the "real" therapy. Once she "understood something," Erickson would begin the therapy. Through this subtle method, Erickson constructed a frame for the patient that marked the beginning of the therapy as something that had not yet occurred. The therapy had, in fact, begun the moment Erickson and the patient met. Each step that Erickson took thereafter that was meaningful, and advanced the process of therapy.

Erickson: You are a rather beautiful woman in your mid-30s. Now, I am a man, and while I'm in a wheelchair, you don't know how much I am handicapped. Now, I want a promise from you that you will do anything, good or bad, that I ask of you. And, bear in mind that you are an attractive woman, and I am a man whose handicap you don't know. I want an absolute promise that you will do anything and everything, good or bad, that I suggest.

This unusual intervention was designed to destabilize the patient and increase dramatic tension. Therapists do not commonly use arousal states to advance therapy. Most often they rely on inducing relaxation and affect regulation; arousal is avoided. Erickson frequently created arousal states, both in therapy and hypnosis, which heightened the affective processes. Again, he used The Beethoven Principle. Like composing a symphony, Erickson's inductions and therapy used both dissonance and consonance in concert.

Erickson asked the woman to promise to "do anything," which was an aggressive request that if carried out could have proven stressful or even unpleasant for her, especially since his statements were freighted with sexual innuendo. The woman came to Erickson with a phobia, and he presented her with something else over which she might feel even more anxiety. Erickson was also taking advantage of the inertia he had just established in which she said "yes" to the two hypnotic directives, thereby increasing the likelihood that she would comply with his new request. This intervention—prescribing anxiety—could be considered an affective symptom prescription. Keep in mind that if Erickson could increase affective arousal, he could also decrease it.

Erickson: She thought it over about five minutes and then said, "Nothing you could ask of me or do to me could be worse than my airplane phobia."

Note that the patient took five minutes to agree to this request. She was not as quick to agree as she had been in the previous steps.

Erickson: "Now that you've given me that promise, I'm going to put you in a trance and ask for a similar promise."

In the trance state, she gave me the promise right away. I awakened her and told her, "You promised both in a trance state and in a waking state—your absolute promise."

I said, "Now, I can treat you for your airplane phobia."

This maneuver reaffirmed Erickson's faith in unconscious processing. He wanted the patient's unconscious agreement; a conscious promise wasn't enough. Her conscious mind might have had reservations, but her unconscious promise was immediate; her unconscious was eager to trust the process and to respond positively, without hesitation.

Artists often add subtle elements to their work that are overlooked by the untrained eye. True mastery often involves innovation and levels of subtly that go unrecognized. For example, although Haydn authored 100 symphonies compared to Beethoven's nine, Beethoven's mastery surpasses Haydn's because of the complexities and innovations that Beethoven stimulated into play. Evocative complexities can alter state, but they must remain implicit. Readers do not attend to the linguistic devices used by novelists.

Erickson's request that the patient give a hypnotic promise reflects his mastery. This request alone is a relatively small element. But, in context, as we will see, it's a brilliant step.

After the patient responded favorably, Erickson implicitly reinforced the frame of the therapy, suggesting that she should view the next intervention as the formal beginning of treatment—as if the previous steps were irrelevant.

But the previous steps form a "Yes-Set." (For information on Yes-Sets and other grammatical forms frequently used in hypnosis see Zeig, 2015.) She had said "yes" to Erickson four times: Yes, to the trance. Yes, to demonstrating the phobia. Yes, to the promise. And, yes to the promise in the hypnotic state. Now, having said "yes" four times previously, creates an inertia that most likely lead her to say "yes" to the next directive: the main intervention.

Erickson: "Go into a trance and hallucinate being 35,000 feet up in the air, traveling 650 miles per hour ground speed.' She was shuddering frightfully, bent over, her forehead touching her knees. I said, 'And now, I want you to have the plane descend, and by the time it reaches the ground all your fears and phobias, anxiety, and devils of torture will slide off your body and into the seat beside you."

Since Erickson had established the patient's compliance with his prior directives, he could be more certain that she would accede to the new directive. And because the patient had already agreed to several smaller tasks, it was not such a big step for her to agree to one more: letting the fear slide off her body onto a nearby green chair.

The green chair was the patient's chair in Erickson's office. It was not especially comfortable. If a patient's goal was to be comfortable, the client would create those sensations. It was not going to be a function of the furniture.

Remember that Erickson seeded the idea of having the phobia in the chair. The client had previously demonstrated the ability to change the context of her phobia by hallucinating being in an airplane while in Erickson's office. Her fear thereby emerged in the green chair under hypnosis in Erickson's office, not in an airplane. Moreover, this act of displacing the phobia mirrored the patient's own account of her customary behavior, because when the plane landed, her fear dissipated. Requesting that she allow her fear to slide onto the chair was Erickson's strategic method for the patient to experience displacement.

As illogical as the method seems, it was just one additional step in a chain of strategic steps. The patient had accomplished several other tasks: going into trance; demonstrating the phobia in trance; making the promise; and making the promise in the hypnotic state. Having agreed to all of Erickson's prior requests, yielding to one more—allowing her phobia to slide onto the chair—was not likely going to be a daunting task for the woman.

A pivotal component of the response to this intervention was the reduction in tension created by Erickson's unconventional, sexually nuanced statements to the patient, and then, his emphasis on eliciting a promise from her to "do anything" he asked of her. The effect of this was two-fold. First, it raised tension in the woman due to the unknown action she would have to take to fulfill her promise to Erickson. Second, when the request to let her fear slide onto the chair was presented, it seemed a relatively simple thing, and possibly even a relief, compared to what she might have to do for Erickson. This all transpired so quickly that the patient did not have the chance to consciously examine Erickson's intent, which was designed for her benefit. (If one knows what the magician is doing, the effect is minimized.) Finally, Erickson's use of the word "now" and his vocal emphasis on it made his subsequent suggestion more of a command.

Erickson: And so she hallucinated landing the plane, awakened from the trance and suddenly leapt out of the chair with a scream and came rushing to the other side of the room saying, "They are there. They are there!" (*Erickson points at the green chair.*)

Because the patient accepted Erickson's suggestion to displace her fears, it might appear that the therapy was complete...but it was not. Erickson expertly provided the set-up and the main intervention, but he was also aware of the need for follow-through.

Now this case could have had an additional contextual effect, since Erickson presented it to the student therapists at a week-long seminar. The green chair was situated next to him, and throughout the seminar, whenever he conducted demonstrations, he would have individuals sit in that chair. Perhaps one of the students would think, "This is ridiculous. There's no fear attached to this chair." Or, someone might wonder, "What will I leave in Erickson's chair, in Erickson's office?"

Erickson often guided associative processes that would stimulate implicit responses. Implicit techniques for awakening representations underlie the creation of all art, which is conceptual and not informative.

We can also confirm assessment information. The client's response to the displacement indicated that she enhanced, rather than reduced, experiences.

After the main intervention was set up and carried out, Erickson then began the follow-through.

Erickson: I called Mrs. Erickson into the room and said, "Betty, sit in that chair." (*Erickson points*) And the patient said, "Please Mrs. Erickson, don't sit in that chair." Mrs. Erickson continued walking toward the chair and the patient rushed forward and physically prevented Betty from sitting in the chair.

Why did Erickson involve his wife in this case? Hypnotic induction often uses a procedure called "ratification." (Zeig, 2014) Ratification is a method that presupposes that the client has constructively responded in a desirable direction. In this case, Erickson ratified the patient's alteration in vivo: the patient demonstrated that she had undergone a change through hypnotherapy. By bringing in his wife, Erickson demonstrated ("ratified") to the patient that her phobia had been removed, not just in the presence of Erickson, but also with a stranger.

Yes, it seems uncommon, perhaps unethical by some standards, to involve one's family in treatment, but Erickson's family was often utilized. There was an effect he wanted to achieve, and his wife was available, and she had been called into sessions to help on other occasions.

Erickson: So I dismissed Betty and turned to the patient and said, 'Your therapy is complete.'

Just as Erickson had delineated the starting point for the therapy, so too, he signaled the end of therapy—when the frame was to be closed. This implied that what followed next would be insignificant. The patient needn't pay close attention to it. And the next statement was, according to Erickson, intoned softly. But, it represented an important therapeutic step.

Erickson: "Have a good time flying to Dallas and flying back to Phoenix, and call me from the airport and tell me how much you enjoyed the plane trips."

Erickson gave his patient a directive to enjoy flying to Dallas and back to Phoenix—placing the emphasis on her having a good time. His statement contained a presupposition: "Call me (the directive), and tell me how much you enjoyed the plane trips" (presupposing that she took the trips and enjoyed them). Erickson's method is akin to a "presumptive close," commonly used by salespeople, e.g., "Tell me how many you would like to buy," which presumes a purchase.

There was an additional level to the communication. The woman had promised to do anything Erickson asked, which could include calling him to let him know how much she enjoyed the plane trips.

Erickson's follow-through, however, did not end there.

Erickson: After she left, I had my daughter take an overexposed picture of that chair (*Erickson points*), and an underexposed picture, and a properly exposed picture. I put them into three separate envelopes. I labeled the overexposed picture: "The eternal resting place of your phobias, fears, anxieties and devils of torture slowly descending into the oblivion of eternal gloom." The underexposed picture, I labeled: "The eternal resting place of your fears, wholly dissipating into outer space." And the properly exposed picture, I labeled: "The eternal resting place of your phobias, fears, and anxieties."

Erickson provided not only a symbol for the patient's fears, but also a symbol for change. He gave his patient something tangible: an amulet, a symbol containing her fears that could function as a substitute for the void created by relinquishing her fears. She "lost something," but acquired something else in its place. Erickson may have used words like those the patient had used when first describing her problem to him, e.g., "devils of torture." And, there is something subtly entertaining and humorous about the photos, which could have been a method of changing the emotional background of the problem. Change can occur by altering the emotional background, not just by changing obvious elements. Remember, Erickson used a similar method to help me stop smoking a pipe.

Again, a family member was involved in the case. It seems Erickson's style of family therapy was involving his family to help the client!

Moreover, Erickson's gift of the photos was unexpected by the client. It was an indicator of Erickson's implicit presupposition that her problem was treated. Clients appreciate when a professional takes such thoughtful extra steps.

Erickson: I mailed the envelopes to her. She got them Wednesday morning. Saturday, I got an excited call from the airport: "It was magnificent. It was utterly wonderful, the most beautiful experience of my life." I said, 'Would you be willing to tell your story to four students of mine whom I am tutoring for their Ph.D. examinations?' She said, "Yes." I told her to come at 8:00.

At 8:00 she and her husband walked into the house. She walked around that chair, skirting it as far as she could, and she sat in a seat farthest from that chair. The students came about five minutes later and one of them started to sit in that chair. My patient said, "Please, please, don't sit in that chair!"

The student said, "I've sat there before. It's a comfortable chair and I'll sit there again." The patient said, "Please, please don't!" The student said, "Well, I've sat on the floor before and I'll sit there now if it will satisfy you." The patient said, "Thank you very much."

And she told the students the story, including the story about the pictures I sent to her. She said, "I took those pictures with me in the way you carry a good luck charm and a good luck piece, a rabbit's foot, a Saint Christopher's medal. They were part of my traveling kit. The first leg of the trip was to El Paso. I was comfortable and I kept wondering when the air turbulence would begin. There was a 20-minute layover in El Paso. I disembarked and went to a quiet place in the airport and went into a trance and said, 'Dr. Erickson told you to enjoy it. Now you do what Dr. Erickson *told you* to do.' I went back to the flight and the trip from El Paso to Dallas was wonderful. On the trip back from Dallas, high up, all we could see below was a bank of clouds with holes here and there. We could look through those holes and see the earth far below. It was a fantastically beautiful trip."

In this segment, Erickson carefully recounted the patient's description of looking down through the clouds. This event confirmed that the patient had overcome her fears. She was now secure when looking down from above. Also, it didn't matter whether the patient was aware of Erickson's directions or not; she still carried them out and enjoyed the flight.

Erickson: I said, 'Now, I would like to have you go into a trance, right here and now.' So she did. I said, 'Now, in this trance I want you to go down to the airport in Phoenix, buy a ticket to San Francisco, and enjoy the scenery all the way there, especially the mountain scenery.'

In this part, Erickson applied a fantasy rehearsal technique. Once again, he employed presuppositional terminology that had been successful earlier: to enjoy *the scenery; and to especially* enjoy *the mountain scenery. His emphasis on mountains seeded the idea of heights—alerting and preparing the patient's unconscious mind for the task to follow. Priming a future target increases the accessibility of the target when it is later presented. Erickson's seeding method is akin to the literary device of foreshadowing. The use of such subtlety is cumulative; it is the difference between something that is excellent and something that is masterful.*

Erickson: 'When you get to San Francisco, disembark, rent a car and drive out to the Golden Gate Bridge. Park your car and walk out to the middle of the bridge and look down.'

Erickson suspected that his patient had another phobia: being on a suspension bridge. In this case, he seemed to realize that the presenting problem was part of a larger, more encompassing problem, and he determined it was best to address the whole problem.

When Erickson was working with me on smoking, he divided the problem into several components, which changed the emotional background of the problem. If he had determined that my smoking was part of a larger problem, for example, inadequate self-care, he might have proceeded differently.

Diagram 10-1 shows how a patient's problem could be viewed:

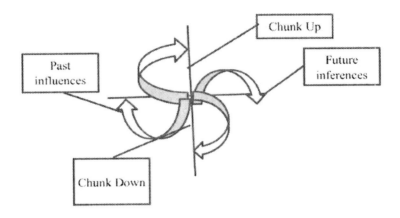

On the Y axis, the therapist could move down, dividing the problem into components (Chunk Down). Or, the therapist could move up on the Y axis to determine if the presented problem is a subset of a larger problem (Chunk Up). On the X axis, a therapist could move to the left—to the past—to find historical antecedents (Past Influences). A move to the right could be the future, and the intervention could be predicated on a prediction of what could result from the problem if it was left untreated (Future Inferences).

As Erickson later reports, the patient feared being in a place without a visible means of support, for example, inside an airplane flying at 35,000 feet, or standing on a suspension bridge. By suggesting that the patient stand on the Golden Gate Bridge (putting her into another situation she feared) Erickson was attempting to confirm whether she had overcome her entire problem. This technique was quickly followed by what Stephen and Ann Lankton (1983) called a "multiple embedded metaphor," or a story within a story.

Erickson: Now I will tell you a bit of history about that bridge. The pylons supporting the bridge were 740 feet high. When the bridge was completed, one of the workmen who painted the bridge had a fish net on the end of a long pole and he caught seagulls and painted their heads red. One day an enterprising reporter published a story in the newspaper about a new breed of redheaded seagulls. His name was Jake. All that is factual.

Erickson's story was designed to create arousal and anger that would block the perceived fear of looking down from the bridge. Clinicians can desensitize a phobia by progressively paring it with relaxation. In contradistinction, Erickson created a reference experience for blocking a heightened phobic response with an angry emotion that was similarly heightened. It is easier to move from one sharp emotion to another than it is to move from a sharp emotion to relaxation.

Erickson: Then, you watch the waves down below, the foam on top of the waves, and you watch the seagulls. Then the fog will roll in. You won't be able to see anything. So you go back to your car and go back to the airport, and use your return ticket to Phoenix, and come from the airport directly here.

Very promptly she awakened from her trance and said to the students, "I must tell you about my trip to San Francisco, and about that nasty Jake." Her husband said, "I knew she wouldn't like that." She was an ecology freak. (*Erickson laughs.*) And when she finished telling the story, she said, "And I came directly here from the airport. Oh my goodness, I was in a trance when I did all that. I didn't really go to San Francisco. I was in a trance and I thought I went there."

Erickson suggested this fantasy rehearsal to offer the patient the opportunity to discover that the therapy had snowballed, and he had dispensed with another problem.

The seagull story was more than just a distraction. It also directed her attention to thinking about "horrible Jake," instead of the empty

space beneath her. Erickson used the patient's value system—her ecolog-
ical concerns—to induce anger that might be more powerful than her
fear. And, perhaps the image of the redheaded seagulls was also meant
to seed anger, since red is often symbolically associated with feelings of
anger.

Structurally, this resembles the previous successful intervention,
which also increased the tension. Then, Erickson offered a concrete idea
that reduced the tension: the fog would obscure her view.

Erickson: And then I asked her an important question. 'What other
problem did you get over on your trip to Dallas?' She said, "I
had no other problem...just my airplane phobia." I said, 'Yes,
you had another problem, a very troublesome problem. I don't
know how long you've had it. Now you are over it. But tell the
students what your other problem was.' She said, "Honestly, I
didn't have any other problem. I don't have any other problem."
I said, 'I know you don't have any other problem now, but what
was the other problem you solved in Dallas?' She said, "You'll
have to tell me." I said, 'No, I will just ask you one question and
then you will know what your problem was.'

At this point, Erickson queried the students in his teaching seminar,
prompting them to guess the patient's "other problem." None could.

Erickson: I told her, 'You had another problem you corrected. Now,
what was that problem? I'll ask you a simple question: 'What
was the first thing you did in Dallas?''

She said, "Oh, that? I went to that 40-story building and I rode
the elevator from the ground floor clear to the top." I said, 'How
did you use to ride an elevator?' She said, "I rode from the first
floor to the second floor, got off, took another elevator and rode
to the third floor, got off, waited for another elevator and went
to the fifth floor. All the way up the elevator, one flight at a time.
I'm so used to doing that that I didn't look upon it as a problem."

Erickson explained to the students that he could deduce the parameters of the woman's problem by her initial description of it.

Erickson: She said, "I can go aboard an airplane. I can ride to the runway comfortably. I can taxi back to the end of the runway. The moment that the plane lifts off, I go into phobic shuttering." She was afraid of enclosed spaces where there were no visible means of support. An airplane is enclosed space with no visible means of support; so is an elevator.

I said, 'Now what was the other problem?' She said, "I don't know of any other problem. If you say so, I must have had another problem." I said, 'You did have another problem. Now it's corrected. Now when you weren't flying, you were in a car, buses, and trains. You had no trouble on the train. And in the car or a bus, what happened when you came to a suspension bridge—a long one?' She said, "Oh, that. I used to get down flat on the floor, keep my eyes shut and shudder. I'd have to ask some stranger, 'Is the bus over the bridge?'"

My students knew that I knew about it because I had her make that hypnotic trip to San Francisco and had her walk out on the bridge.

And now, the patient lives aboard a plane. She and her husband took their vacation flying all over Australia. She goes to Rome regularly, to London, to Paris. And she doesn't like staying in hotels. She prefers sleeping on board a plane, eating on board a plane. And she still has those three pictures. And she is still afraid of that chair. (*Erickson points and laughs.*)

Erickson succeeded not only in resolving the patient's presenting phobia, but in resolving her other fears. He intervened on several levels and continued to work until he was certain that her maladaptive patterns were eradicated. Erickson recognized that the patient did not actually have an airplane phobia, as she was not afraid of getting into an airplane. Her presented phobia was an example of a larger problem.

Once he identified a primary fear—being in a space with no visi-ble means of support—he deduced that she was likely to ascribe phobic reactions to other situations that were structurally similar (being on a suspension bridge or in an elevator).

Erickson respected the patient's unconscious need to dissociate and keep her other fears out of her conscious awareness. He also made sure that her presenting problem was corrected before he brought the other problems to her attention.

Erickson: You see, you didn't listen. She didn't have a phobia for airplanes. She said, "I'm comfortable in a plane, and when it lifts off, I begin shuddering." And I know that when a plane lifts off, it's an enclosed space with no visible means of support. The same with an elevator. The same with a bus on a suspension bridge. You can't see the support at either end; you look to the right and look to the left. (*Erickson gestures to the right and to the left.*) You are up in the air. Onboard a train, she had proof of support—auditory proof—the clicking of the wheels on the rails, so she didn't have any phobia in the compartment of a train. She could hear the outside support.

Two days later in the seminar, Erickson returned to this case:

Erickson: Now the patient with the airplane phobia...I don't have to believe anything that anybody tells me. I don't believe it until I understand her words. When she talked about her airplane phobia and she told me she could walk aboard a plane and ride it comfortably out to the end of the runway, but as soon as the plane left the ground she had a phobia, I could understand that she didn't have an airplane phobia. She had a phobia for closed space where someone else was in charge of her very life, and that someone else was a stranger to her: the pilot.

I had to wait until I understood her words. I made her promise she would do everything good or bad. I got that promise very carefully because it duplicated her life in the hands of a strange pilot. Then I told her, 'Enjoy your trip to Dallas. Enjoy your trip back, and tell me how much you enjoyed it.' She didn't know that she was keeping her promise, but she was. I knew what I intended by that promise. She didn't know. And it was said so gently, 'Enjoy the trip there and back.' And she had promised to do whatever I asked of her. She didn't notice that I asked that of her. (*pg 158*)

It is clear in this case that Erickson did not remove the woman's fear, instead, he displaced it. Yes, the solution was irrational, but so was the problem. And, the fear was still there, as intense as ever, and the patient could return to it whenever she wanted—by going back to the green chair. Erickson changed the character of the fear by changing its location. The patient lost nothing—and she gained the enjoyment of life. A key principal (No. 26) applicable to many therapy problems is to alter choice, not take it away.

After Milton Erickson died, his patient files were destroyed by the Erickson family. But before this was done, I happened to see one of the files from this case. There was identifying information including the woman's complaint of an "airplane phobia." In the file were three copies of the picture of the green chair: one photo properly exposed, one overexposed, and one underexposed. Moreover, I met one of the four graduate students who were mentored by Erickson. (See Zeig, 1985 for information.)

Summary

Therapy is best achieved when the patient discovers previously unrecognized capabilities that can be used to overcome problems. Erickson used indirect and multilevel communication to effectively elicit motivation, cooperation, and therapeutic change. His method was strategic: linking a series of steps together that would seamlessly build a drama of change.

When one studies Erickson, it is important to recognize the process of his orientation to change. First, he seeded ideas; then, he built responsiveness. The foundation of hypnotic induction is building implicit responsiveness (Zeig, 2014). Strategic steps are created that build toward a dénouement. The client accomplishes small tasks that independently seem innocuous and unimportant, but when linked together, they have, in effect, exponential power.

In this case study, Erickson presented his main intervention only when he linked several steps together and built enough responsiveness to pave the way for the main intervention. In choosing a main intervention, he was flexible and creative, not limited by theoretical constructs. Once the intervention was implemented, Erickson followed through and ratified the changes that the patient made. Subsequent follow-through ensured that the patient take the necessary steps to make permanent change in various social situations.

The principle in this chapter:

26. Alter choice, do not take it away.

CHAPTER ELEVEN

Psychoaerobics: Experiential Approaches to Clinician Development

"Tell me and I'll forget. Show me and I may not remember. Involve me and I'll understand."
—Native American proverb

Keep in mind that the book you are reading is one in a series. The first in the series, *The Induction of Hypnosis* (Zeig, 2014), focuses on fundamentals or hypnotic induction. Next is *Psychoaerobics* (Zeig, 2015), which offers practical exercises and insights into therapist development. This book rounds out the series, and although each book stands on its own, I conceived of the volumes as complementing each other to offer a multidimensional education to support the range of therapeutic endeavor.

This chapter provides a summary of *Psychoaerobics* in which I reflect on my evolution as a clinician, with added emphasis on my growth as a teacher. My hope is to stimulate clinicians to use the model for personal growth and development, and apply the experiential method as a tool for clinical practice. Again, Milton Erickson figures prominently. This is not a case of transference (well, maybe a little transference). After closely examining the work of masters from many disciplines, in my final analysis, Erickson is unquestionably the most interesting, complex, and finest clinician I have ever had the privilege of knowing. And, I am not the only one who has come to this conclusion. Many notable practitioners have been profoundly influenced by Erickson. He had an extraordinary ability to therapeutically reach a diverse range of patients because he developed in himself effective therapeutic states.

My interest in hypnosis naturally led me to view things in terms of states. The hypnotic state is a compilation of components. The states that patients adopt—adaptive and maladaptive—are a compilation of components. Therapist states are similar. And states are elicited using experiential methods.

Ericksonian States

To consider components that could become therapist states, I will briefly describe four states that Erickson exemplified: being experiential, utilization, orienting toward, and being strategic. While some would consider these components to be methods, to me they are states that a therapist can intentionally assume to advance treatment goals. The underlying principle (No. 27) is that the state that the therapist assumes is the mother of the technique.

Being experiential:

One state that is a hallmark of Erickson's work is creating experiences. Erickson orchestrated therapeutic encounters whereby a patient would experientially realize adaptive concepts and previously unrecognized abilities to cope and change. He did this by harnessing methods commonly used by artists, including storytelling, metaphor, and symbolic tasks. Erickson understood that insight is not a precursor to change, so in his therapy and teaching, he steered clear of insight in favor of experiential methods to promote realizations.

Utilization:

Another state for which Erickson is known is utilization, which remember, culls qualities from the total weave of the therapy situations to promote therapeutic goals. Utilization is the therapist's state of readiness to strategically respond to aspects of the patient or the patient's environment. However, this cursory explanation of utilization may diminish its place as the foundation of all Ericksoni-

an methods, and as the signature method of an Ericksonian therapist. All of Erickson's cases are based in utilization.

Over the last 40 years, I have sought to master the utilization
state, and most of my writing on Ericksonian methods includes ex-
plications of the process of utilization. Utilization is to Ericksonian
therapy as interpretation is to psychoanalysis, or desensitization is
to behavior therapy. It is true that many great clinicians utilize what
the patient brings to therapy. However, the extent to which Erickson developed his utilization orientation is unparalleled. (For further information on utilization, see Zeig, 1992. See also my lectures
on utilization on YouTube.)

For a moment, let's accept that utilization is a central and defining characteristic of the Ericksonian method, and accede that it has
clinical utility. Still, we may ask, why is it essential for clinicians to
develop a utilization state? One reason is that it speaks to a fundamental aspect of psychological problems. Psychological problems
can be thought of as "believed-in" limitations. Patients often act
as if they cannot change or adequately cope. In contradistinction,
utilization is a philosophy of sufficiency and resourcefulness. Metaphorically speaking, the therapist becomes an alchemist, creating
gold out of lead. Consequently, the patient is encouraged to do the
same in his or her life.

Utilization is a state I assume in every hypnotic induction. I
harness what is in the immediate reality situation to accomplish
four common trance goals: internal absorption, altered intensity,
constructive dissociation, and implicit responsiveness. In offering
hypnosis, it's as if the hypnotist is a feedback mechanism: taking
whatever transpires and utilizing it to elicit goals.

To begin an induction with the reader, I might suggest:

*You are seated here, in the moment, you can realize you are where you
are, and you can realize that there are words you are reading. But, as you
take a deep breath, you don't really need to...focus intently on what is
immediately apparent. Because you don't need to attend to the support
of the chair, or the...back rest...or arm rest..., because you have mem-*

ories of effortless focus. And I don't know if your unconscious mind can suddenly remember a time when you were reading in school, or a pleasant time reading at the beach or being at home…reading. And there you are…. But you can continue to enjoy the developing comfort that can be a part of the evolving experience, and as you do, you can take an easy breath and continue effortlessly.

Note that all four induction goals were contained within the context of talking about reading this book.

Orienting toward:

Erickson is also associated with the state of orienting toward: an indirect method used by the therapist that "nudges" the client toward change, rather than directly stating goals to the client. Therapy is the re-association of internal life (Erickson, 1948), and thus, the therapist can create effective treatment by guiding the client's preconscious associations. A common example of orienting toward would be the parables and stories used in some religions to elicit faith. After all, faith is a state, and to achieve it requires evocative means.

Being strategic:

Many psychotherapists think vertically, ferreting out "deep" dynamics. They are "archaeologists" working to uncover what is beneath the surface. Therapists who do this believe that unearthing a client's pathology, history, or family pattern, and bringing it to the surface, will prompt change and fix the problem. Erickson, however, was more interested in response. He was keenly attuned to the intended outcome of his suggestions. More navigator than archeologist, Erickson was charting a course. An expert in hypnosis, he set his sights on the horizon, and he demonstrated a person's ability to respond to nuance, such as the locus of voice, change in intonation, and alteration in tempo.

Throughout his years of practicing hypnosis, Erickson investigated how people respond to innuendo. He strategically used both verbal and nonverbal implication to indirectly orient patients toward a desired response. Especially important to Erickson was the way in which a person responds without fully realizing the response or the stimulus that elicited it. A similar phenomenon can be seen when a person yawns and another person (or even animal) may be stimulated to yawn in response; mirror neurons simulate the action.

These four states—being experiential, utilization, orienting toward, and being strategic—are core Ericksonian states. Expertise is often a matter of accessing an ideal state. Premier athletes learn how to "get into the zone" to accomplish a given task. Having practiced elements in their working memory, the state becomes a procedural memory. Similarly, I don't think that Shakespeare thought about the technique of creating a metaphor. He had practiced the method until being metaphoric became a state that was fundamental to his writing.

Now, let's further examine the nature of accessing states.

On Experience

The four states that Erickson exemplified could be seen merely as techniques, and they are described as such by many experts. However, I think of them as states that a clinician can access and maintain to promote more effective therapy. And, methods of training differ for techniques and states. Techniques can be taught didactically, but states are accomplished experientially. Therefore, an experiential procedure is needed to train therapists to achieve states that promote positive clinical outcomes.

States are essential for patients because while ideas can be mastered intellectually, concepts such as happiness cannot. Earlier, I spoke of happiness as an experiential reality. It is not something that can be "achieved" via a formula or sequence of preordained steps. Happiness must be realized; accomplished by living experiences.

On Training

My training with Erickson was intermittent and spanned more than six years. He was my therapy teacher; he was also my mentor in facing the challenges of life.

My tutelage under Erickson was as uncommon as his therapy. He never actually saw me do hypnosis or therapy, although he sought out reports on some of the cases he referred to me. He rarely provided didactic input. Not only did he forgo cognitive learning, he seemed to imply that it was often a hindrance more than a benefit. In interpersonal situations, Erickson did not teach content; content could be learned through books. Instead, he oriented to the development of the clinician's experiential state.

There is an implication in Erickson's teaching method that has influenced my training of clinicians: clinicians must develop more than their technical ability. Self-development is not limited to seeking personal therapy. Clinicians should develop states that will improve therapeutic effectiveness. Systematic methods can be used. This is a "bottom-up" approach of living experiences, directed to the right hemisphere, rather than a "top-down" method of training didactically, which is directed to the left hemisphere.

I will outline my training model so that the clinician development section can be understood in perspective. (The complete model appears in *Psychoaeorobics*, Zeig, 2015.)

Distinctions

The meta-model in this book is based on the five Choice Points: 1) goals 2) gift-wrapping 3) tailoring 4) processing, and 5) the position of the clinician. In my workshops, when I teach the first four Choice Points, I use experiential exercises to help students practice and master principles, but when I teach about the position of the clinician, I am almost always experiential.

The position of the therapist can be divided into four categories: lenses, muscles, heart, and hat, each of which has a professional and personal aspect. First, lenses represent our ways of viewing. On a professional level, the lenses learned when studying family therapy differ from those learned in behavior therapy. On a personal level, lenses learned in one's family of origin differ from family to family. Parents teach their children how to perceive the world. Next, muscles influence how we do things. Psychoanalysts, for example, often use their interpretation muscles to the point of hypertrophy, while Ericksonians flex their storytelling muscles. Third, "heart" is a metaphor that represents compassion, the definition of which differs among professions and families. Finally, the "hat" a therapist chooses to "wear" symbolizes the therapist's social role. Some therapies are more formal and bound to rules, and others are more informal and open to improvisation.

On Therapist Evolution

Through training and experience, a therapist can continue to evolve. Many therapists, regardless of their theoretical persuasion, would ascribe their professional evolution to some combination of sources. In querying clinicians about their primary source of growth and development, a common response is: "I've learned the most from my patients." But, if we can think of therapy training like sports training, which requires athletes to develop Ideal Performing States (IPS), then shouldn't there be an experiential, systematic method for training therapists?

Professional athletes possess similar physical skills, including strength, stamina, flexibility, coordination, agility, power, speed, and they can access an IPS that is situation-specific. For example, golfers have an IPS when teeing off, but another IPS is required when putting. Similarly, therapists could regularly train (and cross-train) to grow and develop an IPS that is situation-specific. If this were the case, then the emphasis would be on developing therapist states rather than on techniques. To advance the growth and development of the therapist, I developed Psychoaerobics as a systematic, experiential training system. Perhaps it mirrors the way that

Erickson intuitively trained himself because he had few didactic mentors.

Erickson's Self-Training

Erickson reported many exercises that he used to train himself. For example, to compensate for omissions in his medical school education, internship, and residency, in one of his early jobs, Erickson would get a social history from the social work service and write an intuited mental status examination based on the written history. Then, he would compare his intuited version with the actual mental status examination. Subsequently, he would reverse the process: he would get a mental status examination, intuit a social history, and then compare it with the actual social history from the social work service. Erickson said he did this exercise with numerous patients. He was not trying to learn content, he was trying to master a state: understanding human development.

Erickson also studied nuances in human social behavior. Working like Sherlock Holmes, he would observe a clue and then write a prediction that he would give to his secretary to hold onto until he confirmed it. For example, he once correctly noted that a husband was covertly deceiving his wife. Another time he wrote down that a patient was pregnant before there was any physical evidence. He appeared dedicated to developing the state of extrapolating from minimal cues; he was not merely focused on increasing his base of cognitive knowledge. He was developing a state of inference: "If X, then Y."

Throughout his life, Erickson was devoted to personal growth and development. Just before his death, I asked him a simple question about a therapy case. He answered by using one of his common indirect techniques: he told a story—and I had to "unwrap" the answer. His choice to not directly reply interested me. I had the sense that he was playing—but more so, that he was exercising his orienting toward "muscles," wanting to maintain tonus. His methods solidified his therapeutic state.

On occasion, Erickson would give me personal development assignments, although not systematically. For example, he once asked me to go to a schoolyard and watch children play and then predict which child would go to which toy next and which would leave the group first. The idea of extrapolating from minute details in behavior and then projecting future behavior was important to Erickson, and he promoted this state in his students.

In modeling Erickson, I often adopt a theme of the month—a theme I try to develop on a professional or personal level. For example, I might dedicate time to being more visually perceptive or work on a technical issue, such as using gesture to communicate concepts. Eventually, states transition from working memory and become consolidated states in procedural memory.

In my workshops, I promote the philosophy of self-training and provide pragmatic guidelines for students to also take on a weekly or monthly theme to enhance therapeutic states. An extended application of this training method would be to offer patients specific weekly or monthly challenges to enhance adaptive states.

Historical Reflections on Training

There is an experiential tradition in psychodynamic methods. For example, with Franz Alexander there is the corrective emotional experience. But psychodynamic methods are based in understanding. Metaphorically speaking, experiences should be the main course; understandings, the dessert.

In many contemporary schools of therapy, the primary focus is on understanding the etiology of the patient's problem. In these schools, understanding is the fulcrum, and without it, change cannot happen. Therefore, clinical training focuses on the didactics of learning theory and technique.

The methods of training therapists reflect the history of therapy. Psychotherapy is a relatively new field, beginning at the end of the 19th century. Training methods reflected what was known in the field at the time, which was very little. Therefore, the focus was on theoretical issues, rather than technique. Training empha-sized the development of the therapist by experiencing a personal analysis. To rid themselves of their own distortions (which could have led to countertransference) psychoanalysts-in-training spent years undergoing a training analysis. The thinking was that a thera-pist who was freed of transference was better equipped to promote psychoanalytic treatment.

After World War II, with the burgeoning number of divergent schools of psychotherapy, the focus turned toward alternate theo-ries and specialized techniques, and the development of the thera-pist receded into the background.

I maintain that the development of the therapist should return to its experiential roots, but, this time around, a training analysis is not needed. Instead, the therapist should be experientially trained to develop core therapeutic states. One way of doing this is to use art as a model. If we conceive of therapy as more of an art than a science, then we should train ourselves like artists.

Modeling Art

Modeling art requires an entirely different approach to learning therapy. I explored this theme earlier, but I will expand upon it here because it is central to my practice, teaching, and training. One can learn basic and advanced principles of physics by listening to schol-arly lectures. But learning how to paint or write poetry cannot be accomplished solely by reading or listening to teachers. The same is true when it comes to understanding and working tangibly with concepts like happiness and effectiveness. Some things must be learned from the inside out—by discovering something inside our-selves, rather than learning a specific set of rules.

Many years ago, I became preoccupied with the idea of ther-apy as art and wondered, "Are we centering on the wrong model for training therapists? If so, what would be a better model?" I de-cided to study theater—more specifically, improvisation—with the hope of discovering how artists are trained. Whenever we interact with another human being, we are doing improvisation. And in psychotherapy, communication is more improvisation than static technique.

Now it just so happens that several notable psychotherapists have backgrounds in acting and drama, including Fritz Perls, Peggy Papp, Jacob Moreno, and Virginia Satir. These therapists used what they learned in drama as a tool to help clients. I took a class to learn how theater experts teach improvisation. I joined a small group of students, all in their early 20s, for a six-week adult education class that was led by a woman with a PhD in drama. Later, I took two more six-week courses in acting and improvisation. We began the initial session by introducing ourselves and saying a word about why we had come. The first student gave his name and said, "I'm here because I want to do theater." The next person stated, "I'm here because I want to be in the movies." And the next person shared, "I want to do commercials." When it was my turn, I explained, "I'm a spy. I want to learn how an expert teaches improvisation." After the introductions, we all stood in a circle to do our first acting lesson: la-las. The task was to repeat a vocal pattern (the first time around we used "la la"), while adding a body motion such as hand clapping.

At first, the teacher led the exercise and we were to copy what she did. Soon after, she turned to me, "You be the leader. Pick a different sound. Use the same rhythm. Choose a different motion." So, I chose the vocal pattern, "pa pa" and made a cradling gesture. Everyone copied me. The next student selected "ga ga," and offered a new movement. The teacher stepped outside the circle and gave us feedback. "No, Jeff," she said, "your movements aren't sweeping enough. Watch and listen to the leader closely and copy her. And, it's not ga ga; it's GA GA."

Then, to my astonishment, when the exercise was over, we simply went on to the next exercise. No discussion. No processing of what had just happened. No analysis. When my expectations for follow-up were not fulfilled, I entered a state of confusion. "Wait a second," I silently protested. "Aren't we going to analyze this? Pick apart the meaning of this experience?"

I am a "shredder." Give me something, and I will dissect it; shredding the chaff from the kernel. Patients tell me things and I dissect what they tell me. I reduce what patients tell me to little pieces and feed the components back to patients. I'm very skilled at this regurgitation process: chewing up information, digesting it, and returning it to the patient in a more palatable form.

But in this class, we were not dissecting. I couldn't just automatically chew up, digest, and regurgitate. Suddenly, I had to think, "What is this about? What am I learning? What skills are being taught here? What skills and states are necessary to do drama?" One skill necessary in acting, of course, is articulation. To do any kind of stage work, the actor must be articulate. I recalled the teacher's observation of my inadequate mimicry: "No, Jeff. It's not ga ga, it's GA GA." I was learning articulation.

In addition, a stage actor often needs to make exaggerated gestures, not subtle movements. As a psychotherapist, this element was most foreign to me. I had always sat when I worked as a therapist, restraining my body motions as much as possible. Suddenly, I was being asked to use gestures for effect. Now, this was something I could apply when offering therapy.

The last thing I learned from the acting exercise was the importance of modeling. To act you must model. If you are going to become a character, a taxi driver, let's say, you should observe taxi drivers and model what they do. Perhaps you're required to get into character as a physician. The best way to do this, of course, is to observe a real-life physician and model his or her behavior.

I concluded from the acting exercise that these three skills—articulation, big gestures, and modeling—are important in acting, but the teacher never actually said that. She did not begin the class with a lecture on the three skills. Rather, we did an exercise, and somehow it was understood that once we got on stage we would be articulate, use big gestures, and model. We would seamlessly access desirable states and bypass conscious processing.

After the first acting exercise, we did many more improvisation exercises. Some, including vocal exercises, were presented as warm-up exercises. Other exercises, including scene work, prompted specific acting states. It was not the kind of learning to which I was accustomed. It was more like learning how to ride a bicycle for first time—straddling it, pushing off, and hoping it would somehow make sense. The amazing thing is that it eventually does. You don't learn in your left hemisphere how to ride a bicycle. Studying the physics of riding a bicycle would not help you ride one. Learning to ride a bicycle is a visceral experience. To learn about momentum, you must be on the bike trying to balance, and develop an implicit awareness of all the ways your body movements affect the direction and stability of the bicycle. You try it and you fall. Then, you try again. And after a while, you can do it. Your body learns and you've "got it." Remember the breathless "Aha!" when you suddenly learned how to ride a bicycle—when you were simply riding? I think psychotherapists should foster that breathless "Aha!" in patients. And, psychotherapy training should foster a similar feeling in students. Moving something into procedural memory is an experiential process.

Psychoaerobics

Psychotherapy is more subjective than objective, and it is affected by the state of the clinician. Therefore, psychotherapy tends to be highly idiosyncratic. The therapist's state is projected into the therapy situation and forms part of its core. A therapist whose state is didactic will expound teaching methods, whereas a therapist whose state is experiential will use this orientation as a therapeutic core, and so on.

Therapists should develop their state/style/selfhood/orientation/ways-of-being, and a systematic, experiential program is not only helpful, it is vital. All therapies should expand training to elicit core states. As I evolved as a teacher, I added a core component to my teaching: I teach experiential states. They are primarily Ericksonian states, but the scope and implications are wider.. In doing this, I have developed the Psychoaerobic system, which can be used as a template to develop states in any arena of human expertise. The idea is to examine the components that comprise expertise in an area and then create exercises to elicit those components as states. In the Psychoaerobic system, there are two sets of exercises: warm-up exercises that can be used in many schools of therapy, and Psychoaerobic exercises that develop states specific to Ericksonian practice.

A few of the exercises follow.

Warm-up Example

This Warm-up exercise is conducted in a group. Sitting in a circle, one group member becomes the Pitcher and the other members become Receivers. The Pitcher is required to tell an emotionally revealing personal secret to the Receivers using normal gestures. However, rather than communicating the secret verbally, the Pitcher is instructed to communicate the secret by either mouthing the words, or using only a single sound such as "ba" to represent each syllable. The Pitcher is to use the same nonverbal behavior he or she would normally use when speaking. Exaggerated pantomime is prohibited.

Group members are to realize the states of "experiential assessment" and "experiential empathy." In response to the Pitcher telling the secret, the Receivers are prompted to move continuously, allowing their bodies to resonate with the perceived emotions. The Receivers are to turn off their analytic process and allow their bodies to feel and express the Pitcher's emotions.

Consider two tuning forks placed on a conductive surface. If one of them is struck, the other vibrates or resonates, albeit to a lesser degree. Similarly, each Receiver should allow his or her body to resonate, reflecting the emotion the Pitcher feels when telling the secret. When the Pitcher is finished, the Receivers hold their final postures so that the Pitcher and other Receivers can subtly examine and discern how the message sent approximates the message received, and how different Receivers respond.

Why are we doing this exercise? It is because therapists can experientially assess a patient's emotional state by monitoring their own physical responses. If the clinician notices herself slumping in the chair, perhaps she is responding to the patient's depression. Most therapists learn verbal empathy early on in their career. Experiential assessment can be considered a therapist state.

This warm-up is also designed to stimulate openness, cooperation, and playfulness. Moreover, this exercise prepares the therapist for the Psychoaerobic exercises. Before presenting these exercises, I want to reflect on the way in which this Warm-up Exercise can be generalized into a treatment session to add an experiential component.

Warm-up Exercise Options for Treatment

The Psychoaerobic exercises are not limited to improving therapist states. They can also be used to create clinical options to benefit clients. For example, the preceding warm up could be experientially used in the therapy of a regressed patient who lacks the ability to discern others' feelings. Practice could occur in individual, group, or family therapy. One person could "tell" an emotional story without making a sound. The others could physically identify and perhaps articulate the expressed feeling, thus improving emotional recognition. The exercise could also be given as an assignment. For example, a disengaged family known for emotional rigidity could do the exercise, taking turns as Pitcher and Receiver at dinner and sharing events of the day with each other using the syllable, "ba," thereby stimulating the state of playfulness.

Furthermore, the exercise could be used with children in a group. One child could be secretly given an instruction to enact related emotions such as frustration and anger using sub-vocal speech, or by just using "ba." The group members would be asked to guess the emotion. This process could help them develop verbal empathy skills. The exercise could also be used for training therapists, perhaps in a supervision group with novice therapists.

The underlying motive for this type of exercise is help people realize and access the state of empathy. Empathy is best learned experientially, and it can be accomplished as a state rather than a technique. It cannot be learned didactically any more than one can learn to swim by sitting on a sandy beach, or learn to be a chef by reading recipes. Empathy must be learned by living the experience, and only practice will lead to improvement.

The following is Warm-up Exercise 3 as it is printed in my book *Psychoaerobics*.

EXPERIENTIAL EMPOWERMENT
PSYCHOAEROBIC^{SM} Exercises
www.psychoaerobic.org
Copyright 2015 Jeffrey K. Zeig

WARM-UP EXERCISE 3

Clinician Posture to Develop: Resource states of empathic attunement (resonance) and experiential assessment.

Format: Group of five to eight participants.

Roles: One person is the Pitcher; the others are Receivers.

Method: The Pitcher tells an emotional and personally revealing secret in four or five sentences, but speaks subvocally, using normal gestures, postures, and facial expressions. The person does not pantomime. He mouths the words using complete sentences, but does not speak aloud. The secret can be negative, such as something terribly shameful, or it can be positive, such as a profound intimate experience. The secret needs to evoke strong emotions.

The Receivers attend and allow their bodies to empathically resonate with the Pitcher's emotion. The Receivers should stay kinetic, moving constantly in response to their body's intuitive perception of the Pitcher's emotions. Cognitive processing to determine the emotions should be limited as much as possible. The Receiver's body can seamlessly portray the feeling of the Pitcher. The empathic assessment of emotion is realized by the Receiver's responsive postures.

The Receivers do not look directly at the teller of the secret. They use indirect eye contact or peripheral vision only, perhaps focusing on the Pitcher's knee and watching with a soft focus. When the Pitcher finishes telling the secret, then and only then, will the Receivers freeze and become statues. Maintaining a stylized posture they hold their final pose so that the Pitcher can see each Receiver's physical portrayal of empathy. The group members can also look at each other's statues to see how other group members resonated, but, movements should be minimal and the final pose should remain unchanged as much as possible. The Receivers should not openly guess the emotion behind the secret.

The next Pitcher tells a secret and the Receivers "resonate" with the Pitcher's emotion. It may be beneficial for the Pitchers and Receiver to do something physical between sets to de-role—stretch, walk around the room, etc.

Variations:

1. Tell an emotional story rather than a secret.
2. Conduct the exercise in dyads.
3. Tell the secret in gibberish, rather than subvocally.
4. Tell the secret using only one syllable, such as "Bah," "Ru," or "Lee."
5. The Receiver(s) can guess the emotion, naming it in one word.
6. The Receiver(s) can gently mirror the Pitcher as a technique to discern the underlying emotion. To avoid making the Pitcher self-conscious, three methods can be used:
(a) The Leader secretly provides mirroring instructions to Receivers prior to the exercise.
(b) Use a one-second delay before mirroring.

(c) Obscure the mirroring by using approximations. (If the Pitcher makes an open gesture, the Receivers minimally open their posture.)

7. Each person successively describes his or her state of empathic attunement after completing the entire exercise. "I know I was empathically attuned because I..." I know I was empathically attuned when I...

Purpose: To develop a state of implicit emotional resonance/empathetic attunement. To develop experiential empathy.

Attitude: The ideal attitude for participating in PSYCHOAEROBIC^{SM} Exercises is playful, cooperative, and nonjudgmental.

Another Warm-up Exercise is conducted in dyads with a Pitcher and Receiver. The Pitcher is required to offer several compliments to the Receiver, who is asked to discount them and increasingly display defensiveness, perhaps crossing his or her arms tightly across the chest or looking away, or even silently discounting the compliment. When the Receiver adequately accesses a defensive state, the Pitcher asks the Receiver, "Specifically, how do you know that you are defensive?" The partners are prompted to focus on small changes. For example, if the Receiver says, "I know that I am defensive because my arms are folded across my chest," the Pitcher says, "Unfold your arms a little." If the Receiver says, "I know I am defensive because I am thinking negative thoughts," the Pitcher could say, "Think less negatively." The Pitcher should continue to refute the responses until the Receiver reports he or she is no longer able to maintain a defensive state.

Then, the Pitcher and Receiver reverse roles. The new Receiver discounts the new Pitcher's compliments and becomes increasingly defensive. Then Receiver's responses are refuted until he or she can no longer maintain defensiveness.

The ability to easily access states is valuable for therapists to learn. This exercise can also work in the therapy context with the therapist acting as the Pitcher and the patient being the Receiver. A client who is mildly depressed can be asked, "Specifically, how do you know that you are depressed?" After the patient responds, the therapist can suggest a counteraction. For example, if the patient says, "I know I'm depressed because I don't see friends anymore," the therapist can counter this by saying, "Make it your goal to get together with at least one friend this week." If this is deemed too big a step, the client can be instructed to watch happy people, and then report on the experience. In the case the depression, if the patient were to follow the therapist's suggestions to counteract depression, there may be a point at which the patient is unable to maintain a depressive state. Therefore, dividing the problem (depression in this case) into components is vital.

The Warm-up Exercises are also primers for the Psychoaerobics exercises, which were designed for therapists to develop Ericksonian states.

Psychoaerobic Exercise 1

Exercise 1 is designed to help clinicians develop the Ericksonian style of orienting toward rather than informing. The subsequent technique of indirection was an emergent quality of being in the orienting toward state.

This exercise is conducted in a dyad with a Pitcher and Receiver. It begins with the Receiver studying the Pitcher for a minute or two. The Receiver is then asked to write five questions that could be answered yes, no, or sometimes. The Receiver should ask questions that do not have an obvious answer. For example, if the Pitcher is a meticulously dressed and groomed, the Receiver wouldn't ask, "Do you like when you get a food stain on your jacket?" or "Do you like to take your time getting dressed?" However, the Receiver could ask, "Do you like classic movies?" The answer to this question would not be obvious to the Receiver.

The Pitcher is to reply to the questions not by answering yes or no, but rather by telling a story that orients toward the answer. The

Pitcher should speak in a slow, measured monotone, making no obvious gestures. The story should be short and simple. For example, the Pitcher could talk for a couple of minutes about walking to the movies with a friend. The story must infer that the Pitcher has a feeling about classic movies: liking them, not liking them, or sometimes liking them. Nonverbal cues cannot be used.

The Receiver is to attend to the Pitcher via experiential assessment (a state primed in a Warm-up Exercise), rather than through conscious deliberation. The Pitcher will carefully attend to the Receiver's physical responses. If the Receiver nods or shakes his or her head, indicating either yes or no, that answer can be accepted by the Pitcher. If the Receiver shrugs or tilts his or her head, this could indicate that the Receiver believes that the Pitcher sometimes enjoys classic movies. Responses can be as subtle as a change in proximity: either moving closer or farther away. Once the Pitcher is satisfied that the Receiver demonstrates a noticeable response that indicates either yes, no, or sometimes, the participants proceed to the next question.

The Pitcher and Receiver should not discuss the correct answer to the question or why the Receiver interpreted the answer one way or another. The correct answer is not important. Instead, the participants should strive to discuss their respective states during the exercise. The Receiver could talk about what it was like to extract meaning from the story and access the state of "gift-unwrapping," and the Pitcher could discuss the state of orienting toward by gift-wrapping the answer using a story. This is where the second Warm-up Exercise comes into play, as the skill of fluidly entering and exiting states is accessed and harnessed. Both the Receiver and Pitcher can provide feedback. For the example, the Receiver could offer, "When you were gift-wrapping by telling the story, you had a relaxed demeanor." The Pitcher could say, "When you were listening to my story trying to unwrap the gift, you leaned toward me, as if to listen more intently."

Like many of the Psychoaerobic exercises, Exercise 1 is meant to develop core states. For the Pitcher, Exercise 1 primes the state

of orienting toward, and for the Receiver it primes the state of resonance or "unwrapping a gift." These states can only be learned experientially and viscerally, in the same way that swimming or riding
a bike is learned.

Indirection may be the technique, but orienting toward is a
state that the therapist can access, like compassion and empathy.
Through practice, these states can be more easily accessed and fully
developed. Once the therapist understands specific markers for entering a state, those markers can be used to access the state during
clinical practice.

The Psychoaerobic exercise process is akin to physical exercise in
that muscle groups can be isolated and developed. In Exercise 1,
directly communicating an answer with words and gestures is restricted so that latent skills can emerge. It is similar to the treatment
of amblyopia (lazy eye) in which the ophthalmologist patches the
good eye to foster development of the eye that is not functioning
well. Also, in Exercise 1, the Pitcher's actual answer to the question
is not important. The reason for this is so that participants can more
fully focus on accessing states. In Exercise 1, those states are orienting toward and gift-unwrapping.

Psychoaerobic Exercise 2

In Exercise 2, the roles are reversed, and the exercise is a bit different. In the first condition, the Pitcher begins by describing an imaginary object, such as a tennis racket. The description should reflect
a negative emotion, for example, guilt, anger, or fear. The Pitcher
should identify the emotion prior to imparting the description and
not state it out loud. Also, it cannot be changed while the person is
describing the object. It is best if the Pitcher gradually eases into the
emotion and progressively orients toward it. Again, gestures and
changes in tone and tempo are restricted. The description should
orient toward the emotion.

The Receiver accesses a state of experiential assessment and discerns the projected emotion and mirrors it back to the Pitcher with minimal cues. For example, the Receiver might grimace slightly, indicating fear, or furrow his or her brow, indicating anger. The Pitcher continues the description until an emotional response can be discerned in the Receiver; the"correct" response is unimportant.

In the second condition, another object is described, for example, a glass half filled with water. A positive emotion, such as happiness or excitement, is pitched. In the third condition, a tennis racket could be used to describe a positive emotion, and in the fourth condition, a half-filled glass of water could be used to describe a negative emotion.

At the end of the exercise, participants are asked to describe their respective states. They are not to compare answers as to what emotion was embedded in the description. Again, the goal is to elicit states: orienting toward and resonance (gift-unwrapping). It is not important that the Receiver guess the correct emotion embedded within the description.

Describing a state is difficult, but it is valuable. It is also highly individual. For example, how would you describe the state of curiosity? Possibly, "I know that I am curious because I'm leaning forward, my hand is touching my face, my eyebrows are slightly lifted, and I have a feeling of excitement and anticipation. I'm waiting to know what comes next and I'm thinking, 'This is fascinating!'"

To further understand the purpose of these two Psychoaerobic exercises, consider a technical method that we discussed earlier that Erickson called the "interspersal technique." (Erickson, 1966) The case involves Erickson working with a pain patient who was a florist, and he talked about the growth of tomato plants, interspersing suggestions of comfort into the description. In another case, he told stories to an anorexic and interspersed suggestions of hunger while also eliciting a range of emotions.

Let's assume the interspersal technique is valuable. In training therapists to use the interspersal technique, it could be broken down into technical components. For example, indirect forms of communication that are components, such as truisms and presuppositions, could be taught. I also teach how a therapist can alter the tone and direction of his or her voice to mark out suggestions. Alternatively, I teach that the interspersal technique is a part of a larger experiential method—the experiential state of orienting toward. Exercises 1 and 2 could be used to access that state, in which case the technique would be a byproduct of the state that the therapist assumes.

The object of Exercise 1 is for the Pitcher is to orient toward a thought (yes, no, or sometimes). In Exercise 2, the Pitcher orients toward an emotion. The interspersal technique is based on orienting toward a thought, emotion, and/or behavior. Eventually, preconscious associations elicit constructive action by what is called the ideodynamic effect, which has to do with the ways in which associations stimulate actions. In the interspersal technique, the patient is induced into a state of resonance, of gift-unwrapping.

Experiential assessment is integral to hypnosis. In fact, hypnosis does not have to be considered trance; it could be defined as a state of experiential resonance. Hypnotic suggestions might be conceived as ways of guiding associations. In Ericksonian therapy, associations are not analyzed; they are elicited and utilized.

Like physical exercise, the Psychoaerobic exercises should be practiced regularly.

Over the years, I have taught both technical methods and experiential states, but recently I have been more inclined to teach the latter. I even use group hypnosis before and after the exercises to further experientially solidify learning states.

Orienting toward is an essential therapeutic state. Other states used in Ericksonian practice include developing acuity, communicating for effect, and utilization. Keep in mind that I am describing these concepts as states, not as techniques. My goal is to help therapists better access states when they are on the therapeutic stage.

Acuity Exercises

Acuity exercises outnumber other exercises in the Psychoaerobic system, as it is imperative that therapists develop their lenses, or ways of viewing. There are several sub-states of acuity, including visual or auditory attention and concentration, detection of patterns, extrapolating from minimal cues, and noticing conspicuous absences. Specific exercises are provided for each of these sub-states. One of the acuity exercises to access visual perception is as follows:

Two participants, one Pitcher and one Receiver, face each other. The Receiver "memorizes" the Pitcher and then closes his or her eyes. The Pitcher then makes three physical changes. For example, removes a watch, changes the location of jewelry, or unfastens a button. The Receiver then opens his or her eyes and identifies the changes. The ensuing discussion focuses on identifying the state of visual attention.

Another exercise is designed to enhance perception of pattern. In this exercise, one member of the group, preferably one who is a native speaker of a foreign language, tells two brief stories using that language, one that is true, and the other, containing an emotionally significant lie. (Using an unfamiliar language focuses students on behavior rather than content.) The group works at discerning cues that represent the speaker's pattern of lying. Group members identify the state of pattern recognition. Again, achieving the intended state is most important; being correct is not the goal.

In an exercise based on the state of extrapolation, two participants make inferences about each other, based on minimal information. For example, one participant might say, "You don't like crowds," or "You spend a lot of time outdoors."

After each of the exercises, participants should discuss accessing and developing a robust acuity state. Similar exercises could be offered to patients. For example, for a depressed patient it could stimulate an external awareness that is antithetical to the inward pressures of depression, thereby disrupting the depressed state and eliciting a more external positive state. A depressed patient could be given the task of perceiving images of animals, faces, or objects in cloud formations (called "pareidolia"), just as he or she might have done as a child. Likewise, exercises could also be practiced in families.

When my daughter, Nicole, was an adolescent, she and I played a game at restaurants. After being seated at a table I would close my eyes and she would make three changes on the tabletop, for example, rearranging the salt and pepper shakers. I'd open my eyes and try to discern the changes she made. Then, we would switch roles.

I once asked a researcher in neuroanatomy if there were changes in the brain when practicing such exercises for an extended period. He replied with something I often recall: "Most definitely. After all, the mind creates the brain."

Communicating for Effect

There are many exercises to develop the state of communicating for effect. In one Psychoaerobic exercise, I have participants conduct hypnosis using gibberish. The purpose is to understand that states can be elicited through nonverbal and para-verbal behaviors, not just through words.

In another exercise, I have a participant induce hypnosis by repeating only one word. In a subsequent exercise, only one sentence is repeated. However, in each repetition, the participant must use variation in tone, tempo, gesture, voice locus, and so on. Clinicians who have done this exercise appreciate the experiential learning of how nonverbal methods can elicit alterations in state. Again, the focus is on developing therapist states, not competence in technique. Gaining competence in a technique stems from a state, rather than the other way around. In traditional training, however, one learns technique first, and then learns how to access a state.

Utilization

In the Psychoaerobic exercises, the exercises focusing on utilization are based in hypnosis because this method is integral to Ericksonian therapy. One exercise is conducted in triads with a hypnotist, subject, and coach. After the hypnotist elicits a trance in the subject, the coach creates interruptions at regular intervals from a list of categories that includes the names of sounds, objects in the room, and emotions. Subsequently, the hypnotist must incorporate the called-out concepts into the ongoing trance patter, utilizing them to advance trance goals, such as absorption and dissociation. And yes, you guessed it—technical mastery is not the goal. The purpose of the exercise is to offer moments in which the clinician can experientially access the utilization state. Once the state is successfully accessed, it can be accessed in future therapy sessions as needed.

Conclusion

At this stage of my evolution as a therapist and teacher, I distinguish between technical methods and clinician states. In many schools of psychotherapy, the starting point is theory and practice, which is taught didactically. I maintain, however, that offering therapy is more a matter of the therapist's state (and patient's state) than technique. Therefore, in my training, states take precedent over techniques.

There is a considerable corpus of knowledge of theory and practice in each school of therapy, and technical adequacy can be garnered through cognitive study. However, the emphasis in training didactically may inadvertently lead clinicians in counterproductive directions. The primary goals of therapy are helping people to increase self-esteem, cope, change, assume responsibility, and activate as agents on their own behalf. The patient achieves these goals through states that must be experientially realized. Therefore, if the treatment is experiential, the training of therapists should stress systematic, experiential methods.

This concept of states is like Zen. There is a distinction between what we learn didactically and what we realize experientially. Like Zen, psychotherapy training and practice can focus on experience first.

Using Erickson as a model, I have tried to separate experiential states from techniques. The Psychoaerobic exercises are part of my attempt to develop a systematic program for the experiential learning of states.

My hope is that the model has greater applicability than merely teaching Ericksonian concepts. It would be wonderful if a Psycho-aerobic program could be created to model any master clinician — Aaron Beck, Otto Kernberg, James Masterson Virginia Satir, Salvador Minuchin. Moreover, this type of model could be extended to other arenas, such as teaching and parenting. What are the experiential states of a good teacher? What are the experiential states of a good parent? What exercises could help teach these states?

The model could also be applied to patients. Using experiential exercises, clinicians could help a depressed patient develop states of being externally aware, positive in outlook, and oriented to a goal. A similar model could be used for eliciting self-esteem in patients. Divide the goal into components and devise appropriate experiential exercises for each. The goal is to promote a systematic excursion into experiential territories.

The Psychoaerobic exercises are meant to be practiced. There is the old joke about a man who is lost in the downtown area of a city. He is in new territory and cannot get his bearings. Finally, he sees a man walking toward him, carrying a violin case. He approaches the musician and says, "Sir, please excuse me. I am a bit bereft. I am in a new place. I can't find my way. Please tell me sir, how do you get to symphony hall?"

The violinist replies, "Practice, practice, practice."

CHAPTER TWELVE

Clinical Examples of an Experiential Approach

The two examples provided in this chapter were demonstration therapies, one from over 20 years ago and the other very recent. The first was conducted at the 1995 Evolution of Psychotherapy Conference. It was tabbed "Guiding Associations." (Available from ericksonfoundationstore.com) I present the transcript with some commentary. It is an early example of my experiential approach and reflects my infancy in using visual methods, such as gestures to communicate concepts. It is also an example of ordeal therapy presented in strategic steps.

The second example is from a 2017 Master Class in which I offer therapy to students. I also supervise Master Class students conducting therapy and supervision to their peers in the class. The session was conducted through a translator.

I present these transcripts as examples of different experiential orientations. They are meant to illustrate the concepts and principles in this book. Readers can recognize the Choice Points of goal-setting, tailoring, gift-wrapping and creating a strategic process. Elements of the states that I inhabited, including orienting toward and utilization, will be obvious.

Clinical Example One
The Evolution of Psychotherapy Conference
Las Vegas, Nevada, December 13-17, 1995

The following demonstration is from the 1995 Evolution of Psychotherapy Conference. There were as many as 1,000 people in the audience. Ann was a conference attendee, and she volunteered to be the subject for this demonstration. We were on the stage of the largest meeting room at the conference, which could seat more than 7,000 people. Prior to coming on stage, Ann (not her real name) indicated that she had a habit problem with biting and tearing her fingernails and she was presenting at an upcoming conference in Vienna.

Jeff: Well, Ann, you volunteered because of this problem that you have that you are kind of hiding even now. Please tell me, what is it that you need to accomplish?

Ann was sitting on her hands.

Ann: I'm not quite sure what I need to accomplish, but I am going to be presenting next year and it makes me very nervous at a conference.

Jeff: It's a conference overseas?

Ann: Yes, and that in itself makes me very anxious. I am always hiding. I am so ashamed of my nails; it's a habit. I have been attempting for years to give it up. It represents something, and I keep on working on it, and I don't know where to go with it.

Jeff: How have you worked on it? Have you had therapy?

By learning what therapy Ann had previously, I knew what not to try.

Ann: I did some EMDR on it—a little bit. I have had therapy for umpteen years. I did some gestalt work. But this is like the last thing in my life to make me totally what I would call "whole and normal."

Jeff: Then you'd be in trouble. If you cure this one, then you wouldn't have any excuse.

Ann: Right.

Jeff: You would be stuck. You'd have to live happily ever after.

I tried to use humor to lighten the tension that both of us felt, but my humor was not especially effective.

Ann: (*laughing*) Right—and be very productive and right or whatever. Help a lot of people.

Jeff: And yet your sense is that you've been hanging on to this.

Ann: It annoys the hell out of me. It's like the last thing that is preventing me from moving forward. And it's driving me crazy. And I'm thinking, 'Well it's my mother's way of really haunting me still, or my holding on to my mother's introject.'

Jeff: How do you mean that?

Ann: Like, I can torture myself. I can make myself go crazy with some fault that I have and feel really ashamed, and feel very scared. It gives me shame all the time.

Jeff: What is the longest in your adult life that you have grown your nails?

I was presupposing that Ann had been successful in growing her nails!

Ann: I can't remember—a couple of years ago. I don't remember what was happening then either.

Jeff: And you grew them well.

Ann: It was normal. I was like a lady.

Jeff: And how long did you keep them normal?

Ann: About two years or three years. At various periods of my life I did.

Jeff: Let's take it from the other side. Let's say there is some intrinsic pleasure that you get from...

Knowing the "pleasure" that someone derives from continuing a habit may generate a solution. For example, it might be possible to create the pleasure through self-hypnosis.

Ann: Not pleasurable.

Jeff: It's not pleasurable? Let's say that it is. What could be the pleasure? How do you do this? How have you bitten your nails?

*Learning the details of how someone maintains the pattern/habit could
generate a solution. For example, it might be possible to disrupt the pattern by suggesting modification in the steps of performing the habit.*

Ann: Like this (*she demonstrates*) and tearing at them.

Jeff: Tearing them, not biting them?

Ann: Sometimes, tearing at them, biting them.

Jeff: What has been the pleasure?

Ann: I think it really is my anxiety. I have enormous scare, like an
underground brook.

Jeff: And some part of you has thought that in some way perhaps it
temporarily quelled that brook.

I minimized the negative symptom and she enhanced it.

Ann: It really was a brook. It's not a low-level brook; it's like a brook
that moves fast.

I've learned to hide very well so most people don't even notice
it, but I know.

Jeff: Do you think that there has been anything pleasurable in the
mechanical act of tearing?

Ann: Not that I am aware of. Probably tearing makes me feel good. I
want to tear at a lot of people, and that's a real no-no.

Jeff: In what sense?

Ann: Well, it's not nice to be mean, and I have to be nice. Not that
I have to be nice. I want to be nice. I like being nice, and I like
liking people. In fact, I like loving people…so this part of me
that wants to tear is not good for me.

Jeff: Okay. You were talking about this presentation in Vienna (*be-*

fore she got on stage). Why is it so important? And when is the presentation?

Ann: In July.

Jeff: That gives you plenty of time. And why is it so important that you have this cured by that time?

Ann: I feel very panicky now.

Jeff: You are good at hiding that panic because I wouldn't have really known.

Ann: It represents completion of being victorious over...I discovered that I started biting my nails during the war, you know, when we left Europe. I'm a Holocaust survivor. I discovered that that's when it started—during the war when the bombs were falling. There was a lot of terror. And I relived that terror last year, and ever since then the nail-biting has really gotten out of hand.

Jeff: You relived it how?

Ann: I relived it because I went to Holland and I saw the Anne Frank Museum. And in the afternoon, I went to the Keukenhof Gardens and....

Ann loosens her scarf.

Jeff: Good for you for making yourself more comfortable.

Ann: They stole my passport and my airline tickets, and my money, and I had trouble getting it back, so I went into a real anxiety attack, and I kind of lived out what I had experienced when I was young. I relived the sobbing and the terror. I realized what my parents went through and I had a lot of forgiveness for them for the hard times they had because they had trouble getting passports and getting out. And going to Vienna is also a place where my family went to Auschwitz, so all of that is combined. By not biting my nails, it represents like conquering, conquering something, conquering comes up for me. And if I don't accomplish it, I will fail, and I will be I don't know…I might end up in Auschwitz or something like that.

Jeff: Well I have a cure for you.

Ann: Yeah. Don't go.

Jeff: No, no. I have a guaranteed cure—something that will undoubtedly put you in a situation where you will not want to tear at your nails.

Boldly offering a guaranteed cure and then withholding is a way of building drama.

Ann: That sounds great.

Jeff: I'll tell you about it shortly. First of all there are three parts, as I hear what you are saying. And because you are a very intelligent and insightful person, let's just talk about it directly for a minute. There's this underground brook, which you have been dealing with throughout your life.

Ann: Right. Always.

Jeff: And that's something we can work on. There's the tearing that you have been doing. That is something we can work on. And then there is this tendency you have to have big feelings. And that is something that we can be working on.

Ann: Sounds great.

Jeff: So somehow though, those other two pieces—the underground brook and the big feelings—those tie together in your mind with the tearing that you have been doing?

Ann: Yes, because it is so intense.

Jeff: What is so intense?

Ann: Whatever feeling I have is so intense. So one of the ways I can control my intensity is by doing this tearing.

Jeff: What are you doing right now because this an intense situation? We are in an unusual, perhaps awkward situation. How are you controlling those intense feelings now?

Here I brought therapy into the moment, reminding Ann that she had more strategies for controlling tension than what she consciously gives herself credit.

Ann: Actually, I put a bubble around us.

Jeff: Uh-huh, around us.

Ann: A little room…and nobody else is here, except you and me. That's nice. I feel good about that.

Jeff: How intelligent.

Ann: Kind of a little sanctuary that we are in.

Jeff: I just want to get more of a sense of this, which is a remnant from those early days in Europe when an intelligent little girl didn't know what to do with what could have been a tremendous intensity, so she hooked onto the idea of tearing. And, she carried that into adult life.

In this instance, I found a positive intent in the etiology of her problem.

Ann: And it's obsolete. That's the whole problem—totally obsolete. And it's bugging the hell out of me.

Jeff: It's obsolete. But, thank God for obsolete problems, because if patients didn't have obsolete problems that they brought into the present, you and I would have to do honest work for a living.

Again, I used humor to lower the tension and "normalize" the problem.

Ann: You're right. That's true. But it is still an interruption. It really is a big interruption in my life.

Jeff: And a drag that you have to sit on your hands and find awkward postures.

Ann:...and always be hiding. There's like a piece of me that always has to hide. That's what we always did.

Jeff: What is your sense of how you should get over this? Is the tearing something that you should get over slowly and gradually, or is it something that you should get over suddenly?

I put a "prop" on the stage for Ann to use. For the guaranteed cure, I need her to be able to get over the problem slowly. Also, I presuppose that she will get over the problem.

Ann: Fast. Give it all up fast—like I could dive into a new system.

Jeff: But it would be a nice sense of pride.

Ann: Oh, heaven. Like heaven on earth.

Jeff: Perhaps it would be okay though if it was something that you got over gradually. Maybe an analogy is another habit, like overeating—that if you overeat here (*gesturing with outstretched hands*), you wind up paying for it, but you pay for it here much later. You don't pay for it immediately because you have the opportunity to have the immediate reward: the satisfaction of overeating. But you have to pay for it later when you look in the mirror, or put on your clothes the next day, or weeks later. And it makes it hard to stop the habit because the payment is somewhat divorced from the problem.

Now I put another prop on the stage. For the guaranteed cure, I need her to have a different perspective on "paying" for her problem. Also, as we shall see, I am "seeding" future therapy.

Ann: I have had that too.

Jeff: I think there is something about that too, because then you might have immediate relief from a little bit of that brook. But then you wind up paying later.

Ann: That's right.

Jeff: And I would suggest that this is in line with what I was talking about before as a sort of guaranteed cure. That one of the things we could do is we could change the distance (*gesturing*) so that there could be a payment that was more approximate to the tearing. What I am thinking about is this: There are a few ways of modifying behavior. You could modify that behavior with reward, with punishment, with ignoring it, and with non-reinforcement. Somehow the problem for you has become sort of crystallized over time. It's become congealed. And like a diamond, it's become very hard. And then, if we can apply something, a little technique, on the right facet (*poking right hand at the stiffened fingers of left hand*), then it can break through and you can be free. But maybe something to change first is your impatience; that you are so impatient to have this done right now.

Ann: That would be like a dream come true.

Jeff: And what I might suggest to you is that we have something that helps you to change a little more gradually. Before we get to that, I'd like you to think in another way. Let's say that I ask you for five intelligent excuses—excuses befitting Ann—to tear one bit of one nail. And it's not only tearing your nails—That was scary, huh? I started to move forward and you were shrinking back. Five intelligent excuses to have one tear. It's not only the nail; you have been pushing at the cuticle too. Right? When I glanced at it before, it looked like you were doing something like...

Ann: Well, what I do is push them down to get them to be longer.

Jeff: Which was doing something about destroying some of the nail forming tissue, because then you had some ridges in your nail.

(*I wanted her to know that I was knowledgeable and highly observant.*)

So what would be four or five intelligent excuses befitting your intelligence to have one tear of one nail? What would you say inside your head that would give you a justification for doing that?

In working with habit problems, I have found that talking about justifications makes it more difficult to be influenced by them. It decreases the chances that the person will engage in the habit again.

Ann: Not enough.

Jeff: Not enough what?

Ann: Not enough tearing.

Jeff: Okay, what would be another excuse?

Ann: I don't understand what you mean by an excuse?

Jeff: How would you justify it? This is how I am thinking: You were free for two years; two years you were a lady. You did something about this problem. Then, after two years, somehow you lost it.

Ann: My life was getting too good.

Jeff: Okay, so would that be an excuse you would use for tearing, "My life was getting too good?"

Ann: Oh, I see what you are saying.

Jeff: I want to be sure that...

Ann: My life is getting really good.

Jeff: How would that be an excuse for tearing? Let's just take it at face value.

Ann: I shouldn't have such a good life.

Jeff: *Keinehora?*

I used a Yiddish phrase, which means, "Nothing bad should happen." It's a superstition: If someone says something positive, and then says, "keinehora" it would prevent the positive statement from being jinxed. I wanted to confront Ann's superstition. I also wanted to let her know that I was Jewish. It was another prop I placed on the therapeutic stage—one that I felt was necessary.

Ann: Keinehora—it's a good life.

Jeff: Give me another excuse.

Ann: It keeps me from moving forward. It keeps me down. God forbid that I should be totally successful—have a hundred percent.

Jeff: Keinehora. Okay, what else? Give me another excuse.

Ann: God forbid that I should be too sexy or feminine. My mom would really be mad.

Jeff: So then this is something to keep you humble; doesn't allow you to excel.

Ann: That's a good turn, to keep me humble. WOW! Keep me down, keep me humble.

Jeff: Let's do something really quick because you have some experience at doing some gestalt therapy. And would it be okay to play this out for a minute as a part? Would that be all right?

Ann: Hmmm… (*indicating assent*)

Jeff: We have this extra chair here. We'll use it. Let's say that we put Ann's nails here. We put the tearer there. This is the part of you that tears at you. What I'd like you to do is to switch. Come around; sit here. Be the tearer. Exaggerate that position. I'm going to tear at you. I am going to tear your nails; I am going to keep you humble. (*Ann moves into the persecutor chair and pulls the victim chair closer.*)

A dictum from gestalt therapy is that if someone experiences himself as the victim, then he should role-play the victimizer. It is often best to do this in an exaggerated fashion in order to access emotion. This method can generate a solution.

Jeff: Whoops, are you sure you want her that close?

Ann: Yeah, I want her to be around.

Jeff: Okay, let's move her closer. (*Moves the victim chair closer.*)

Ann: I want to tear at you. You have absolutely no right to be big in this world, to do something important. I'm going to stop you. You have no right to be that feminine. I am going to tear you down. I'm going to tear you down. I am going to tear you down!

Jeff: Okay, stop and switch. Come over here. Be Ann. Respond to her.

Ann: (*louder*) You are not going to tear me down! You are not! I'm going to fight you all the way!

Jeff: Can you straighten up as you say that. (*Ann was hunched over. I wanted her to be more "adult" and powerful in her confrontation.*)

Ann: (*to Jeff*) I want to beat this part out. (*To the chair:*) I want to fight you all the way. You are not going to get at me. You are not going to get at me.

Jeff: Once again louder.

To promote more assertive feelings.

Ann: You are not going to get at me. You are going to try and try and try and try. You are going to try to tear me down, but you are not going to get there.

Jeff: What's your original language when you were growing up? Say it in French (*to promote affect*).

Ann: (*Says some French phrase*) I do not know how to say it....

Jeff: You got the feeling. That was the important point. Come back over here. (*Ann changes chairs.*) She said, "I'm not going to let you." What is your response?

Ann: (*Says something else in French.*)

Jeff: Tell me in English. What are you saying to her?

Ann: "You can't do what you want."

Jeff: I'm going to keep tearing you down. We'll help her. Fill this in: "I'm going to keep on tearing you down until_____.

Ann: (*Says something in French.*)

Jeff: In English now please.

Ann: It's harder in English. I'm going to continue tearing you down 'till you give up.

Jeff: Try it again. I am going to keep on tearing you down until...see what else comes out.

Ann: I'm going to keep on tearing you down until you...I don't want to say the word...until you die. I'm going to keep on tearing you down until you are dead.

Jeff: Okay, please come back and be Ann. What's your response to her?

Ann: (*to the chair*) You never give up. You never give up. You are not going to win. You are not going to win. You are going to try to tear me up and tear me up, but you are not going to win. You are always on my back. You've been battling with me all the time, and you are not going to win.

Jeff: That can be said again in French. You're not going to win.

Ann: (*French*) I don't know how to say win.

Jeff: (*helping*) "Succeed."

Ann: (*Responds in French.*)

Jeff: Okay Ann, do something. Please come and stand over there for a minute. (*I asked Ann to stand in an observer's position.*) Great. Think about these two being Ann the therapist for a minute. Then, tell me how you would apportion the energy. If there was 100 percent energy, would it be 60/40 or 70/30, or 50/50? How would you apportion the energy between these two?

Scaling questions provide a benchmark.

Ann: This is not that loud; this is much louder.

Jeff: So give me a numerical rank. How would you apportion the energy?

Ann: 90/10 (*indicating that 90 percent of therapy was in the constructive chair*).

Jeff: Please, come sit back here (*gestures toward the victim chair*). Let's take her away for a minute.

Ann: But she is really getting to me now because it is 90/10. She's like Custer's last stand.

Jeff: Do you mind if I move her, or do you want to? (*Ann symbolically shoves the persecutor chair away.*) What's your sense? When I was listening, I was thinking about Shakespeare—that this part was "sound and fury."

I intended this as both an indirect suggestion and "post-hypnotic" suggestion. I was also seeding this for her future. The line from Shakespeare is "...a tale told by an idiot, full of sound and fury, signifying nothing." In the future, Ann might encounter the Shakespeare phrase and it could reactivate the therapy.

Ann: Sound and fury because it is losing a battle.

Jeff: Umm. Yes... Let's think for a second—you and I, in a creative way. Let's you and I do some thinking. Let's say that in five months, or five years, or whatever, that 10 percent evolves, and somehow she matures and grows and expands into something else. What would you imagine her evolving into? Temporarily we just turned her away....

In saying this, I am finding something positive in the negative introject.

Jeff: What could you imagine yourself? Use that creativity—you know the part of you that created the bubble. How could you imagine her—the negative introject—evolving into something useful?

There is feedback from the microphone in the auditorium.

Jeff: (*to the audience*) It is nice to get positive feedback (*laughter from the audience*).

Ann: The whistle (*referring to the feedback sound*). I have a funny fantasy in the sound and fury, that there was a parade. You know, like those Fifth Avenue parades they have, and at the parade they were all playing the drums and singing as I go to Vienna. I'll be the conductor in Vienna.

Jeff: Being a conductor. I like that.

Ann: A conductor in Vienna.

I utilized the distracting noise from the microphone and made it into something positive. Ann did the same by creating a positive image of the parade.

Jeff: Just to make things a little shorter, help me. Tell me if I understand. Could we know that 10 percent was making herself known by virtue of you tearing? Could we say that a behavioral indication was that when 10 percent came up, when you started tearing, that would be an indicator that she was there?

Ann: Oh, no question. You are right. I got you.

Jeff: And that somehow at that moment you would want to assert your 90 percent and you'd also want to be thinking that somehow she could be evolving into a sort of potent conductor. But that right now, as something temporary, we might need something to help you so there was a little artificial thermostat that prevented you from "peaking" too much, going too far with the emotion. And I'm going to come back to that, and I am going to come back to that in terms of this guaranteed cure as a little bit of a palliative measure to help you. But I had another thought in mind...

Ann: I love that sound and fury. I think that is the greatest. Wow!

Jeff: Well, I have another image.

Ann: Wow, that's so wonderful, because that's really a sound and fury. You know, I'm tearing myself with a lot of fury and sound. I love that.

Jeff: Well, I had another thought. And maybe I can ask the audience to help us on this a little bit. Because not only did I have an image of sound and fury, but I was thinking of my daughter, and I was thinking about a little children's song. And it went…it has to be done with a graphic. (*I use hand gestures that go with the song. Ann modeled me with her words; no longer hiding.*) It goes,

Little Bunny Phoo Phoo
hopping through the forest
scooping up the field mice
and bopping them on the head.
Down came the good fairy,
and she said,

"Little Bunny Phoo Phoo,
I don't want to see you
scooping up the field mice
and popping them on the head.
This is your first warning.
You have three warnings and if you don't attend,
I'm going to turn you into a goon."

The next day,
Little Bunny Phoo Phoo
hopping through the forest
scooping up the field mice
and bopping them on the head.
Down came the good fairy
and she said,

"Little Bunny Phoo Phoo,
I don't want to see you
scooping up those field mice
and bopping them on the head."

The next day, the same thing,
Little Bunny Phoo Phoo,
hopping through the forest

scooping up the field mice and
bopping them on the head.
And the good fairy comes out and says,

"Little Bunny Phoo Phoo,
I've given you three warnings:
Poof—

wrong direction (*I gestured to the floor, then changed and gestured toward the introject*)

—poof, you're a goon."

And the moral of the story: "Hare today, goon tomorrow." A pun on, "Here today, gone tomorrow."

So I had the thought that somehow we could conscript you, and you would help us a minute. (*Talking to the audience*) You've got the words. And so my thought was that when you started to know that she was coming up and that 10 percent was sneaking out and asserting herself, and she started to tear, that somehow there could be a little hallucination—like this idea of sound and fury, or maybe this little song of "Little Bunny Phoo Phoo." Could you sort of turn to them? Turn with me. They're going to help as a sort of a Greek chorus.

Ann: Like louder than that sound and fury.

Jeff: So you are going to hear them, right?

Ann: Right.

Jeff: I'd like you to just memorize it so that at that moment you could remember...

Ann: The Greek chorus—a supportive group.

Jeff: Ready? Okay. One, two, three. (*We both sing along with the audience:*)

Little Bunny Phoo Phoo,
hopping through the forest
scooping up the field mice

and bopping them on the head.
Then came the good fairy.
And she said,

"Little Bunny Phoo Phoo,
I don't want to see you
scooping up the field mice
and bopping them on the head." (*audience applauds*)

I had an audience so I utilized it. Therapists can do the same with a demonstration audience.

Ann: Oh, that's so funny.

Jeff: And to me, she was like a little Bunny Phoo Phoo. Right?

Ann: Um-hum.

Jeff: So now, to this guaranteed cure: While little Bunny Phoo Phoo is evolving into the conductor and will have a function that you and I don't know exactly what that will be like yet, I was thinking of this guaranteed cure as a palliative measure in-between. I think that you should be entitled to a severe therapy because it has been a severe and chronic problem, and it's been something that you have been ashamed of. And I think a severe problem should have a severe therapy. The therapy should be as severe as the problem.

(*This heuristic mimics the work of Jay Haley and Cloé Madanes.*)

I am going to give you a therapy that is really tough, but also a therapy that gives you a little leeway. And it will be in this line of shortening the punishment. I think you should be entitled, strange as it sounds, I think you should be entitled to tear at yourself. But it is a childish habit, and you should be entitled to pay a penalty for tearing at yourself. I don't think you would be the right person to supply the penalty, so I am going to be the person who supplies the penalty for you. Is that all right?

Now I put another prop on the stage.

Ann: It sounds good to me.

Jeff: And then you will be entitled to tear at your nails. But you will also be entitled to pay immediately. Alright?

One more prop.

Ann: Yes.

Jeff: I think there should be a little leeway because I don't know that you should just change immediately. So the little leeway...

And another prop...

Ann: I think magic would be so nice.

Jeff: You may be able to do it by virtue of some of this intrapsychic stuff that we are just doing here too. But I also want there to be something behavioral. But I am going to give you this little leeway. You'll decide; we can negotiate how to use this. But you would be entitled to three tears in any given week—and those three tears would be free. Now, if you want to negotiate that with me, I will go up to five, but then it stops. You are entitled to three discreet tears, and you'll know—not two tears. Five tears? Three tears? What should it be that you are entitled to?

Ann: How about four? Five is too many and three is too little.

Jeff: (*laughing*) Okay, I'm generous. I'll negotiate this with you. Four sounds great. You are entitled to four tears. But on the fifth tear, then you have to pay a penalty, and you have to pay that penalty immediately.

Ann: Not running 10 miles.

Jeff: No, not running 10 miles. Worse. Worse than running 10 miles.

Ann: Worse?

Jeff: You carry a purse with you wherever you are?

Ann: Yes.

Jeff: In the purse, I'd like you to put three envelopes, and these envelopes are to be addressed and stamped, and at all times, you carry with you these three envelopes addressed and stamped. And
in the first envelope, you put a dollar. It's a symbolic amount. As
you'll see, it really doesn't matter. In the second envelope you
put five dollars. Again, it's a symbolic amount; it really doesn't
matter. In the third envelope, you put ten dollars. And then for
the first infraction, you are going to send the first envelope. For
the second infraction, you send the second envelope. For the
third infraction, you send the third envelope. So you'll be entitled...

Ann: To whom?

Jeff: (*laughing*) Wait. So you will be entitled to infractions, but you
will also be entitled to pay a penalty for any of the infractions.
Again, this is just going to be a palliative measure. So you could
do 10 infractions, but then you'd have to recycle the envelopes.
You'd have to replace the dollar envelope, and that would come
fourth. You'd have to replace the five-dollar envelope; that
would come fifth. You'd have to replace the ten-dollar envelope
and that would come sixth. Got it? You would just keep three
envelopes with you at all times. As soon as one is gone, you'd
replace it with the one dollar, five dollar, or ten dollar amount.

Ann: I see.

Jeff: ...and stamped, and addressed. And it has to be sent immediately upon any infraction. There can't be any delay.

(*This was the last prop.*)

You pay the penalty immediately. Got it? Now, you are going to
have to do a bit of research about how to address the envelope.
I think you should be able to find out pretty quickly how to address it. Ready? Do you want to brace yourself?

Adding drama.

Ann: Um hum. (*Bracing herself in her chair.*)

Jeff: I want you to address the envelope to the American Nazi Party.

Ann: Are you crazy? (*Laughter from the audience.*)

Jeff: No. No. That's the penalty. It's a severe problem, and a severe problem deserves a severe therapy.

Ann: I can't do that.

Jeff: Oh yes you can!

Ann: Give money to the Nazi party? You're crazy!

Jeff: No, you will be entitled to that fifth tear. But if you tear that fifth time, you will send a dollar to the American Nazi Party.

Ann: (*smiling and reaching out to Jeff*) Let's change the negotiation to ten.

Jeff: As I said, you are the wrong person to supply the punishment. And I am supplying the guaranteed cure as a palliative measure until you evolve Little Bunny Phoo Phoo. And why? Because I had a third image of Little Bunny Phoo Phoo. And why this therapy is so appropriate. Normally, I wouldn't say, but because you are a therapist and weave in a teaching situation, I'll tell you very clearly. My image is that not only is she sound and fury, not only is she Little Bunny Phoo Phoo, but she's been a Nazi. You've had this little Nazi inside your head.

Ann: Um hum.

Jeff: So the punishment is perfectly appropriate. If you are going to honor that little Nazi inside your head, then you are going to pay the American Nazi Party for any infraction.

Ann: (*hesitantly*) I don't see why...I missed it...

Jeff: No, you think about it.

Ann: You hit something, but I am not getting it.

Jeff: That's okay. You can take a little time with that one.

Ann: I'm sure it fits somehow, but I don't know how. (*Saying more confidently:*) I feel as if I've had a Nazi inside my head, pursuing me constantly, all my life as a matter of fact. How did you realize that?

Jeff: You've been great. You've been very open in a difficult situation about something that is really personal to you, and you've shown it.

Ann: So that's why the Nazi inside of me wanted me to die all the time (*tearing up and crying softly*).

Jeff: There are some very nice kinds of tears—the kind of tears that just wash away old hurts. (*Here I redefined her tears. Firmly proceeding:*) You understand this kind of temporary assignment. And you understand that it is a severe therapy for a severe problem. And, that it's palliative because I think that you will do more growth and development work to do something about evolving that part (*Little Bunny Phoo Phoo*).

You know, we don't have very much time left, but in the bit of time, would it be all right if we just did a little hypnosis to consolidate some of the things that we have been dealing with?

Ann: Um hum. I'd like that.

Jeff: Just make yourself comfortable. And perhaps you could just, Ann, center yourself in the chair; and your hands just resting down against your sides, so that your elbows are... (*I help Ann adjust to a more open and balanced posture*)...just take any pressure off your shoulders. And then with your eyes closed, you can just search inside. And as you can, Ann...search inside. I'd like you to discover a certain sensation, and perhaps you may discover that certain sensation, and in a way it could be part of the bubble that you were talking about before.

And maybe as you search inside...search inside for that certain sensation, you can somehow realize that it begins to develop. And that certain sensation can evolve. And I am giving you a difficult task, but something you can do, and that certain sensation may evolve...in the base of your feet, and that certain sensation may evolve...in your legs. And you may understand it as a growing feeling...a growing feeling that you may even... experience in your body, that growing feeling.

And Ann, you may realize that feeling can develop in other ways, that certain sensation. Perhaps you may even recognize it as a strong feeling. And that strong feeling may be something that you can begin to now realize in your neck. And as it continues to evolve, you may, Ann, experience that growing strong feeling...in your head. And that growing strong feeling, Ann, can continue to evolve down your arms. And just like you created the bubble, you can create that growing strong feeling in your forearms, in your wrists. And perhaps there can be rhythm to that growing strong feeling, as if somehow your unconscious mind, your inner mind was a leader, a conductor, if you will, that was helping you to realize that growing strong feeling in ways that are convenient, in ways that are handy, that you can have at the tip (*pointing toward and almost touching her fingertips*) of your tongue.

And I don't know how your unconscious mind can evolve, Ann, that growing strong feeling. But it is something that I'd like you to be willing to explore, and to learn about how you can evolve, Ann, that growing strong feeling, here and now...there and then...again and again, and again and again, as you find yourself more yourself absorbed in the evolution of that growing strong feeling, recognizing that as I've been talking with you, certain present, pleasant, pleasant changes occur.

(*I purposefully stumbled on the words to emphasize both possibilities.*)

There's an alteration in the rhythm of your breathing. There's that very nice fluttery feeling around your eyelids; a change in the muscle tone; motor movements change; perhaps the sensation that you're moving your best foot forward (*Ann moved her foot*); perhaps the sensation that somehow your feet are farther away from your head—a sensation that somehow perhaps your left shoulder is more distant from the right shoulder; perhaps a sensation as if somehow your head is a bit larger, not too large.

I mention this because the theory goes that if you are tall, broad shouldered, and have a big head, you will then have good self-esteem.

And all along, making those adjustments that maximize your own sense of Ann, comfort…and the evolution of Ann, that growing strong, Ann, feeling. And the sense of a weight…that you may realize in your hands, in your arms, can be so interesting. And all along, you are learning about some of your own capacity to help yourself enjoy the flow…enjoy the flow deep inside, that underground flow of those evolving, growing strong sensations.

And I'd like you to take some time to really remember in your own way, in your own language, that growing strong, Ann, feeling, evolving as you can. And then I'd like you, Ann, to begin to reorient yourself, reorient yourself comfortably and easily, reorient yourself freely and completely. And bring yourself back fully here, now here fully, completely, Ann, take one or two or three easy breaths. Take one or two or three easy breaths, and then bring yourself back fully alert and wide awake, Ann.

Ann: Fine.

Jeff: Pleasant?

Ann: Yes, very.

Jeff: They will give you a copy of the tape should you want it. That's complimentary so that you have it to review and remember.

Ann: How nice.

Jeff: And you're set on the therapy—the three envelopes?

Ann: That really is mind-boggling how the Nazis are pursuing me to this day. It is just mind-boggling…and it really works. Thank you so much. Can I get a hug to drive away those Nazis?

Jeff and Ann hug.

Commentary and Follow-Up

Using a restaurant menu metaphor, this induction was the dessert, not the main course. It was designed to reinforce the therapy. The induction was essentially a metaphor for the solution, which entailed the evolution of the introject. The "certain" sensation would evolve into a growing sensation, into a strong sensation, etc. Although my focus was on Ann's symptom, the expectation was that there would be a snowball effect and that Ann's anxiety would lessen, too.

The hypnotic induction was composed to include steps of absorption and ratification. Ann could become absorbed in the details and possibilities of the proposed sensations. Subsequently, I "ratified" the changes by describing the physical changes that happened as she became absorbed, for example, changes in her breathing pattern. The technique of using the metaphor of the solution as an absorption device is an advanced induction method. Traditionally, induction is a means of achieving trance. In advanced methods, induction can be a method of providing therapy.

At a six-month follow-up by mail, Ann indicated she had maintained therapy gains for both the symptom and anxiety. She was calm on a stressful occasion and surprised her family with her positive attitude.

A few years later, I saw Ann at a professional meeting. She showed me her nails and I gently kissed her fingers in the same way a parent would kiss a child's wound to make it better.

At another professional meeting, I saw Ann again and noticed that she had relapsed in tearing at her nails, but later she reported that she had corrected things immediately after we met.

Clinical Example Two
2017 Master Class

This session was recently conducted through a translator because English was not Mario's native language. I offer it as an example because it illustrates principles of utilization, which in this case involved a tissue box and the client's wife, who also was a student at the seminar. It also is an example of using giftwrapping methods such as anecdotes.

Jeff Zeig (*smiling*): So help me to understand a little bit about you.

Mario: What would you like to know?

Jeff Zeig: Interests, hobbies.

Mario: I like the movies. I like literature.

Jeff Zeig: What kind?

Mario: Good literature.

Jeff Zeig: Good literature.

Mario: Any kind that is good. I like to travel.

Jeff Zeig: Super. And any particular kind of cinema that you enjoy?

Mario: Older films—the ones that are noncommercial. That's my preference. Before I used to watch a little of everything, now I want to watch that from which I can learn.

Jeff Zeig: So learning is really important and things that are deep, not superficial?

Mario: As time has gone along, it has become increasingly important to me to have a good conversation in a quiet environment with a cup of wine. I like that.

Jeff Zeig: You want the conversation to go this way (*pointer finger spiraling down*), to be deeper, to be more interesting, intellectual?

Mario: It could be, but whichever way it goes it's okay for me.

Jeff Zeig: Super.

> (*Talking to the class*) Now just as a reference for people here, stop for moment. Okay, so Mario tilts his head to his right and I tilt my head to the left and Mario sits in an open posture and I sit in open posture. And Mario has his hands clasped and I have my hands clasped. Now I don't think about this intentionally,

but I do it. I automatically attune not just to the body, but to the timing; not just to the rhythm, but to the meaning. So, attunement is the social basis of empathy and we can increase our attunement, and in psychological research this is called social mimicry. And put the words 'social mimicry' into Google you will find 50 research studies that demonstrate the effectiveness and the value of social mimicry. That research is from social psychologists who have little interest in application; they're only interested in understanding how human systems work. So, we have to find our own application, but the good thing is that there's research. Okay, so now back to you, what can I be helpful with?

Mario: I would say this, in some part of me there is a little Buddhist and I would like to wake him up.

Jeff Zeig: Uh-huh.

Mario: Because I feel like there is a great Taliban.

Jeff Zeig: Great Taliban?

Mario: Yes.

Jeff Zeig: Help me to understand, the Taliban is a terrorist.

Mario: More than terrorist, I mean like radical.

Jeff Zeig: Uh-huh. So, a radical wanting to change a social system?

Mario: Yeah.

Jeff Zeig: So Buddhist, my understanding is: accepting (*arms out in open position; Zen-like*). Radicals (*putting hand forcefully forward*)—change.

Mario: Yeah. To be intolerant, I have very little tolerance. My tolerance is very low; my tolerance range is very little.

Jeff Zeig: I'm so surprised because your presentation seemed Buddhist.

Mario: Maybe because of the context in which I am now.

Jeff Zeig: Uh-huh. Okay. So how...teach me about being intolerant.

If you were going to be my professor and you were going to explain the techniques and the joy of intolerance, please teach me how to do it.

Mario: I guess you would have to not focus on peoples' mistakes (*Jeff points dramatically at floor*), but on peoples' faults.

Jeff Zeig: Okay. So, I wait, when I get there. Okay, so I'm an art critic—oops, bad art, (*points dramatically at floor*)—oops, terrible art (*again, points dramatically at floor*).

Mario: (*laughs*)

Jeff Zeig: Okay, I can do it. You make them notice. You tell them. You let them know. (*Pointing dramatically*) You just did terrible art. Okay, well I'm a critic and I see the bad art and I confront it but I wouldn't call myself intolerant.

Mario: Of course, because the part that is missing is anger.

Jeff Zeig: Okay, how do I do that?

Mario: You make an angry face.

Jeff Zeig: Okay. (*Makes an angry face and points dramatically*) So to do disgust (*making a face of disgust and pointing dramatically*) you have to...

Mario: (*laughing*) And you also raise your tone of voice.

Jeff Zeig: Well, now you're enjoying this. I don't know how you enjoy it. So teach me how to enjoy this. Well, you know to me, as you explain it to me, there's no art to this. It's shooting fish in a barrel. This is so easy to do because I can always find something that's bad art. I can always confront it and I can always be angry with it and this is too easy. It doesn't represent any art. It's like (*crosses one leg over the other and hits knee; knee jerks up*) just a reflex.

Mario: A conditioned reflex.

Jeff Zeig: Yeah. When you look at a garden you have a choice: you can look at the flowers or you can look at the weeds. So, I suppose that the Buddhist would look at the flowers.

Mario: The Buddhist just looks at everything the way it is, not as the way they want it to be.

Jeff Zeig: Not attached. So, there's no judgment, there's just perception. I don't know. Could that be fun? And why would you want to bother to change at this point in your life? (*Turns around and looks at Mario's wife.*) You still love him even though he is a critic? That's something that you love about him?

Mary (*Mario's wife*): Yes.

Jeff Zeig: Yeah? Have you tried to change him?

Mary: Once I did.

Jeff Zeig: And did it work?

Mary: No.

Jeff Zeig: No? So, it probably won't work for me either. But you are seemingly Buddhist because this is Mario. Right? So how does this come out in your perception—what Mario's talking about?

Mary: The fact that he's intolerant?

Jeff Zeig: Yeah. Is that how you would say it? Of course, we know he's not intolerant of you. So if he's intolerant of you, how do you deal with it?

Mary: I understand it has to do with him. It's not mine. I thought I had to correct something and I understood I don't.

Jeff Zeig: Okay. So when he's intolerant of you, you allow this critical wind to just have its own life and it doesn't have to affect your state.

Mary: I am in that process.

Jeff Zeig: Very good. So, it's just (*quickly throwing arms up in the air twice*) a neural discharge? And it's just Mario (*cross one leg over the other and hitting knee again; knee jerks up*) with his conditioned reflex. So, are you changing this for Mary because you love her so much that you want to? You know, the most loving thing that a man can do is to allow his wife to influence him.

Mario: It's one of the reasons.

Jeff Zeig: Yeah. And if you are intolerant of your daughter then you're not (*makes one hand spiral upward*)—that's another reason.

Mario: I'm much, much, much less intolerant with her than with than with others—it doesn't mean I am not intolerant at all just...

Jeff Zeig: Yes. Are you sure?

Mary: It's not zero, but he is less intolerant.

Jeff Zeig: Uh-huh. What does she do that makes her so special?

Interpreter: What does he do with her?

Jeff Zeig: What does she do that makes her so special?

Mary: She's his daughter. She is like him and he takes care of her.

Jeff Zeig: Okay could you please be intolerant of me? I want to feel what it's like to be on this side of the equation. Really be intolerant. Okay, wait one second. (*Curls tightly up with feet on chair, head lowered.*)

Mario: No, this is not going to work. I'm not going to do it right.

Jeff Zeig: Uh-huh. You're not going to do it right? So now you're being intolerant of yourself? That's an idea. So let's have a symbolic Mario, (*reaches for a tissue box and puts it up on table*) right? And now, please be intolerant of yourself.

Mario: (*Reaches over; slams the tissue box a few times and then sets it upright.*)

Jeff Zeig: What was that like?

Mario: It was ugly. It was ugly. It was also unnecessary.

Jeff Zeig: Well, it would seem intelligent that we would ...it would be best to start with you being Buddhist to yourself rather than you being Buddhist to the world or to your family, because I would imagine as it's normally true that people treat other people the way that they treat themselves. So if you're ugly to yourself then you'd be ugly to others. Could you go into the black hole and really practice intentionally being intolerant of yourself?

Mario: I don't have it very clear. I don't understand.

Jeff Zeig: Well, you could get up in the morning and after you brush your teeth, you could spend 15 minutes being intolerant of yourself; being your own critic, criticizing yourself. Bad art! (*dramatically pointing; making a disgusted face*)

Mario: Yeah.

Jeff Zeig: And then by doing that for 15 long minutes, and you could do it in the bathroom after you brush your teeth because if you're going to be involved with shit you might as well do it in the bathroom. (*Laughter*). You have a wonderful laugh. And then you get it out of your system. So you do it for 15 minutes, exaggerate it and now you have honored that part of yourself; get it out of your system and then you go about your day. So, help me to understand, if you are being Buddhist and you're involved in perception and you're not involved with judgment, this seems like a more mature state, right? How old are you?

Mario: 52.

Jeff Zeig: Yeah. So now that I'm 70 this year, right, and suddenly I just give things away and I'm entering a stage of being generative—just give it. I have an unbelievable archive of the history of psychotherapy for the latter half of the 20th century and beginning of the 21st century and I'm going to give it away. And I'm doing a project now, five-minute therapy tips for therapists, and if you go on YouTube you find it, and I'm giving it away. And I think that—I didn't study Erik Erikson but one of his developmental stages was being generative and so I'm doing it. I don't know what the stage is for being 50. I don't remember, but being Buddhist, perception (*opens arms widely*) rather than judgment (*pointing harshly*) seems like it could be that you're at the right time, in the right place, in the right stage. So if you're being Buddhist with me, help me to feel what that would be like. But to start, am I being Buddhist with you?

Mario: I think so.

Jeff Zeig: Because I'm not judging you or playing or teasing. So this is a model. How does it feel when I'm being Buddhist with you?

Mario: It feels good. This feels really—it makes me feel shame. I feel embarrassed.

Jeff Zeig: You're being honest with yourself and I understand feeling ashamed but you don't want to continue mindlessly (*crosses one leg over the other and does the automatic reflex with knee*). It's not a good movie. It's not an interesting novel. It doesn't have much depth. So, shame can be a good step, anxiety, shame, guilt is the motor that makes people work. When people don't have anxiety, they don't change. Addicts, narcissists, they don't change because they don't have anxiety, they don't feel shame. And so they don't change. Anxiety is the motor that makes change possible, as long as you don't get stuck in it. I'm glad for you to acknowledge that.

So now what we're talking about is that you get to be the man who you design and this is a moment of destiny. Borges, which I can't quote, (*speaks in Spanish*): 'Destiny is the moment in a man's life when he takes account of who he will be for the rest of his life.'

Okay, so I'm standing (*stands up*) and I am the evolved Mario, Buddhist. And help me to feel what that would be like. You sit, you don't have to do anything, just tell me what to do. I want to create a representation that you can see of who you want to be for the rest of your life. So was that, you know, like this?

Mario: No.

Jeff Zeig: No? So, what is it like? Tell me what do I do? Could do something like...something like this, something like this. You tell me how to stand and to play with it.

Mario: Just the way you are.

Jeff Zeig: Just the way I am? Uh-huh. Super. Well okay, so just the way I am. I'm easy, I'm flexible, I'm grounded, I am seeing things, I am breathing easily, I am aware, I am perceptive, and this is what there is.

Mario: More or less like that.

Jeff Zeig: Okay, well what would be more? Do you want to come here and you do it?

Mario: It's more of that inner attitude.

Jeff Zeig: So, help me to get it because artists take inner attitudes and they make them come alive in their art. And Beethoven makes walking in the country come alive, in a symphony. So, I want to create this image for you of the art that represents that inner attitude.

Mario: A compassionate gaze.

Jeff Zeig: Compassionate gaze? Okay. A compassionate look. I can feel that. I have a statue of the compassionate Buddha. Do you know that one?

Mario: No.

Jeff Zeig: It's really like this. (*Crouches down and lowers head; places tips of fingers on forehead.*) It's called the compassionate Buddha. Throughout Asia you find that statue.

Mario: Something that could represent a little bit what I would like to achieve is what is expressed in the San Francisco prayer.

Jeff Zeig: Say it. Tell me. It's an induction. Tell me the prayer in Spanish.

Mario: I don't remember it well.

Mary: The one of serenity; is that the one you want?

Mario: Yes.

Mary: Lord, make me the instrument of your peace. So that where there is hate, I would sow love. So that I don't ask to be understood but that I understand, so that I don't ask to receive but to give, because giving you receive, forgetting one finds, and forgiving, one is forgiven, and dying, one is reborn to life.

Jeff Zeig: Yes, I can feel it. (*Crosses hands over heart.*) Beautiful. So that can be your destiny when this could be an orientation, compassion, giving and being reborn. And when you have a perspective point, (*points hand off forehead*) you create depth. An artist has a painting; the perspective point is invisible—that's what creates depth.

Mario: Just one thing I'd like to add. I don't want to be indulgent in the face of injustice, but also I don't want to take it personally.

Jeff Zeig: Well, you don't want to be Don Quixote but you want to confront social injustice.

Mario: Yes, but without creating further injustice.

Jeff Zeig: Right. In a nonviolent way. It's a representation of Gandhi, Mahatma Gandhi, Satyagraha. Satyagraha means truth force, force of truth, speaking truth to power, speaking truth to injustice, and how that is done is an art and it does not have to be done in rap music. So, yes, that's super. And so what's a model for... other than Gandhi?

Mario: Mandela.

Jeff Zeig: There's a beautiful story about Mandela when he was in jail and the prisoners hated him and one of the reasons that they hated him was because he was learning Afrikaans—the language of the oppressors—and they couldn't stand that he was doing that. But his perspective when he got out of prison was that to solve the social injustice he had to speak Afrikaans. He was looking more deeply into the situation and he said that if you speak to somebody in a language that he understands, it goes to his head, but if you speak to someone in his language, it goes to his heart. Okay, that's a great model.

Yeah. Okay, so now your perspective point is clear. So if you amalgamate Mandela and Saint Francis, you have an orientation. Now, then the job is (*walking across the room lowering body and bending knees*) to create the art that you have designed for yourself and that represents being 50 and that's a matter of discipline. But I don't think that that's in short supply. My sense of you is that when you put your mind to something you accomplish it. And I hope that it can be fun too, but I would certainly try to do it this way (*makes stepping motions with hands*) rather than try to just jump (*opens arms and throws them out*) into it. If you've been in a cast for a long time (*stiffens arm*) you can imagine having free range of motions (*releases the stiffened arm and moves it in wide circles*) but you really need to get it back slowly until you have a full range. Do you think that you could have a game with Mary and that you could demonstrate Mandela and Saint Francis and that she would try to catch you when you were doing these things, and if she was right, you could give her a kiss?

Mario: Yes. That would be good.

Jeff Zeig: But you would have to try to be subtle and we would see if she could catch you. And then if you wanted to we could involve your daughter in the game of you reinventing Mario, being reborn. The Dalai Lama was being interviewed on CNN and the reporter is a little kooky, crazy, and he's known for his craziness. So the reporter looked at the Dalai Lama and in a provocative way says, "Do you ever get angry?" And the Dalai Lama says, "Only when people ask me silly questions." So I suppose that there is still a space for being intolerant and ways of being intolerant that represent art.

Mario: Artistically intolerant.

Jeff Zeig: Absolutely. That's a very mature and sophisticated way to be because there have been people in my life who spoke truth, and elegantly, and they would say things that you wouldn't even dare to think because you'd be embarrassed, but they would say it. And Carl Whitaker was one of those people and he supervised my family therapy and he would just say the truth. And it was an elegant intolerance because the anesthetic was that he really cared, and so he would say his truth, but he would say it with anesthetic, and I admired that so much. It was the anesthetic that allows the surgery. And when you said artistic intolerance, he was the first person that I thought of.

Okay, well I like what you're doing and I think that it's well within your capability and I think that you would be proud of yourself for continuing into being the kind of 50-year-old man who you want to be. And a saying in Gestalt therapy is that to die and be reborn again is not easy. You know that. So I hope that our conversation gives you a clearer picture. And I don't think that you need any more tools than what you already have. Just be like the moth—the insect, the moth. Once the moth sees the light, the moth is just drawn forward. I don't have anything else to add right now. Is there a request or a question?

Mario: When we started I was really nervous.

Jeff Zeig: I didn't know.

Mario: Because I think these themes have bad PR, or don't have good PR at least. I never thought I could laugh at this.

Jeff Zeig: What has good PR is what's real. When you're being real, it's good PR. Bad PR is being insincere. I felt like you were being real, saying something that's really important in your development and I just hope to be a little bit of a catalyst that makes the reaction happen a little quicker. And who knows, maybe Saint Francis and Mandela had ways of laughing at themselves too. It made me feel closer to you that you take this opportunity to be real.

Mario: I might say something little weird, a little strange, but we have been able to talk about shit without it smelling and I am really thankful to you for that.

Jeff Zeig: Exactly.

Mario: You made it easy.

Jeff Zeig: Okay, well I like that emotion, so (*to the class*) let's take a break.

Psychotherapy is an absurd lifetime adventure, so said Carl Whitaker. It continues to be my adventure because it has taught me so much about life. It is my hope that the concepts and principles in this book add to your adventure.

REFERENCES

Bandler, R., Grinder, J., & Andreas, S. (1979). Frogs into princes: Neuro linguistic programming. Moab, UT: Real People Press.

Bandler, R., Grinder, J., & Andreas, S. (1982). Reframing: neuro-linguistic programming and the transformation of meaning. Moab, UT: Real People Press.

Bateson, G., & Ruesch, J. (1951). Communication: The social matrix of psychiatry. New York, NY: Norton.

Berne, E. (1964). Games people play. New York, NY: Grove Press.

Combs, G., & Freedman, J. (1990). Symbol, story, and ceremony: Using metaphor in individual and family therapy. New York, NY: W.W. Norton.

Erickson, M. H. (1954). Pseudo-orientation in time as an hypnotherapeutic procedure. Journal of Clinical and Experimental Hypnosis, 261-283.

Erickson, M. H. (1958). Naturalistic Techniques of Hypnosis. American Journal of Clinical Hypnosis, 3-8.

Erickson, M. H. (1964). The Confusion Technique in Hypnosis. American Journal of Clinical Hypnosis, 183-207.

Erickson, M. H. (1966). The interspersal hypnotic technique for symptom correction and pain control. The American journal of clinical hypnosis, 198-209.

Erickson, M. H. (1980). Hypnotic alteration of sensory, perceptual and psychophysical processes. New York, NY: Irvington.

Erickson, M. H., & Rosen, S. (1982). My voice will go with you: the teaching tales of Milton H. Erickson, M.D. New York, NY: W.W. Norton.

Erickson, M. H., & Rossi, E. L. (1979). Hypnotherapy: An exploratory casebook. New York, NY: Irvington.

Erickson, M. H., & Rossi, E. L. (1981). Experiencing hypnosis: Therapeutic approaches to altered states. New York, NY: Irvington.

Erickson, M. H., & Rossi, E. L. (1989). The February man: evolving consciousness and identity in hypnotherapy. New York, NY: Bunner/Mazel Publishers.

Erickson, M. H., Rossi, E. L., & Rossi, S. I. (1976). Hypnotic realities: The induction of clinical hypnosis and forms of indirect suggestion. New York, NY: Irvington.

Fisch, R., Weakland, H. J., & Segal, L. (1983). The tactics of change: Doing therapy briefly. San Francisco, CA: Jossey-Bass.

Frankl, V. E. (1946). Man's search for meaning: An introduction to logotherapy. London: Hodder & Stoughton.

Fogarty, T.F. The Distancer and the Pursuer. J.L. Framo. Ed. The Family: Compendium II. The Best of the Family 1978-1983. Rye Brook, NY: The Center for Family Learning.

Gilligan, S. G. (1987). Therapeutic trances: The cooperation principle in Ericksonian hypnotherapy. New York, NY: Brunner/ Mazel.

Gordon, D. (1978). Therapeutic metaphors: Helping others through the looking glass. Cupertino, CA: Meta Publications.

Gordon, D. C., & Meyers-Anderson, M. (1981). Phoenix: therapeutic patterns of Milton H. Erickson. Cupertino, CA: Meta Publications.

Haley, J. (1963). Strategies of psychotherapy. New York, NY: Grune and Stratton.

Haley, J. (1973). Uncommon therapy: The psychiatric techniques of Milton H. Erickson, M.D. New York, NY: Norton.

Haley, J. (1984). Ordeal therapy: Unusual ways to change behavior. San Francisco, CA: Jossey-Bass.

Hart, O. V. (1983). Rituals in psychotherapy: Transition and continuity. New York, NY: Irvington Publishers.

Kroger, W. J. (1977). Clinical and Experimental Hypnosis in Medicine, Dentistry, and Psychology. New York, NY: J.B. Lippincott

Lankton, S. R., & Lankton, C. H. (1983). The answer within: A clinical framework of Ericksonian hypnotherapy. New York, NY: Brunner/Mazel.

Madanes, C. (1981). Strategic Family Therapy. San Francisco, CA: Jossey-Bass.

Madanes, C. (1984). Behind the one-way mirror : advances in the practice of strategic therapy. San Francisco, CA: Jossey-Bass.

Mead, M. (1977). The originality of Milton Erickson. The American Journal of Clinical Hypnosis, 20, 4-5.

Palazzoli, M. S., Boscolo, S., Cecchin, G., & Prata, G. (1978). Paradox and counterparadox: A new model in the therapy of the family in schizophrenic transaction. New York, NY: Jason Aronson.

Rohrbaugh, M., Tennen, H., Press, S., & White, L. (1981). Compliance, defiance, and therapeutic paradox: Guidelines for strategic use of paradoxical interventions. American Journal of Orthopsychiatry, 51(3), 454-467

Sulloway, F. J. (1997). Born to rebel: Birth order, family dynamics, and creative lives. New York, NY: Vintage Books.

Szasz, T. (1961). The myth of mental illness. New York, NY: Harper & Row.

Watzlawick, P., Bavelas, J. B., & Jackson, D. D. (1967). Pragmatics of human communication. New York, NY: Norton.

Watzlawick, P., Weakland, J. H., & Fisch, R. (2011). Change: Principles of problem formulation and problem resolution. New York; London: W.W. Norton.

Weeks, G. R., & L'Abate, L. (1982). Paradoxical psychotherapy: Theory and practice with individuals, couples, and families. New York, NY: Brunner/Mazel.

Zeig, J. K. (1974). Hypnotherapy Techniques with Psychotic In-Patients. American Journal of Clinical Hypnosis, 17, 56-59.

Zeig, J. K. (1980). Symptom Prescription and Ericksonian Principles of Hypnosis and Psychotherapy. American Journal of Clinical Hypnosis, 23, 16-22.

Zeig, J. K. (1980). Symptom Prescription Techniques: Clinical Applications Using Elements of Communication. American Journal of Clinical Hypnosis, 23, 22-33.

Zeig, J. K. (1982). Ericksonian approaches to hypnosis and psychotherapy. New York, NY: Brunner/Mazel.

Zeig, J. K., (1985). Therapeutic patterns of Ericksonian influence communication. In J. K. Zeig (Ed.), The evolution of psychotherapy: The second conference (pp. 392-405). New York, NY: Brunzer/Mazel.

Zeig, J. K., (1992). The virtues of our faults: A key concept of Ericksonian therapy. In J. K. Zeig (Ed.), The evolution of psychotherapy: The second conference (pp. 252-266). New York, NY: Brunzer/Mazel.

Zeig, J. K., (2002). Clinical heuristics. In J. K. Zeig (Ed.), Brief therapy: Lasting impressions (pp. 41-62).Phoenix, AZ: The Milton H. Erickson Foundation Press.

Zeig, J. K. (2015). Psychoaerobics: An experiential method to empower therapist excellence. Phoenix, AZ: Milton H. Erickson Press.

Zeig, J. K., & Erickson, M. H. (1980). Teaching seminar with Milton H. Erickson, M.D. New York, NY: Brunner, Mazel.

Zeig, J. K., & Erickson, M. H. (1985). Experiencing Erickson: An introduction to the man and his work. New York, NY: Brunner/Mazel.

Zeig, J. K., & Foundation, M. H. (2014). The induction of hypnosis: An Ericksonian elicitation approach. Phoenix, AZ: The Milton H. Erickson Foundation Press.

Zeig, J. K., & Munion, M. W. (1990). What is psychotherapy?: Contemporary perspectives. San Fancisco, CA: Jossey-Bass Publishers.

Zimbardo, P. G., & Boyd, J. (2009). The time paradox: the new psychology of time that will change your life. New York, NY (Original work published in 2008): Free Press.

ABOUT THE AUTHOR
Jeffrey K. Zeig, Ph.D.

Jeffrey K. Zeig, Ph.D. is the Founder and Director of The Milton H. Erickson Foundation. He is the architect of The Evolution of Psychotherapy Conference (www.evolutionofpsychotherapy.com), which is considered the most important conference in the history of psychotherapy. He is also the organizer of the Brief Therapy Conference (www.brieftherapyconference.com), the Couples Conference (www.couplesconference.com), and the International Congress on Ericksonian Approaches to Hypnosis and Psychotherapy (www.ericksoncongress.com).

Dr. Zeig is on the Editorial Board of numerous journals; is a Fellow of the American Psychological Association (Division 29, Psychotherapy. Division 30 Hypnosis); and a Fellow of the American Society of Clinical Hypnosis. He is a Distinguished Practitioner in the National Academy of Practice in Psychology of the National Academies of Practice and an Approved Supervisor of the American Association for Marriage and Family Therapy. Dr. Zeig was also a Clinical Member of the International Transactional Analysis Association (1974-1985).

A psychologist and marriage and family therapist, Dr. Zeig has a private practice and conducts workshops internationally (40 countries). He has been an invited speaker at major universities and teaching hospitals, including the Mayo Clinic, Menningers, and the MD Anderson Cancer Center. He is president of Zeig, Tucker & Theisen (behavioral sciences publisher,www.zeigtucker.com) and is also the founder of the Erickson Foundation Press (www.erickson-foundation.org/press).

Dr. Zeig has edited or co-edited and authored or coauthored more than 20 books and monographs on psychotherapy and human development, which are printed in 14 foreign languages.